lo

MADAGASCAR

Northern
Madagascar
p136

Western
Madagascar
p112

Eastern
Madagascar
p174

Antananarivo
p44

Central
Madagascar
p62

Southern
Madagascar
p86

Nandih Andrianarisoa, Joe Bindloss, Keith Drew,
Mark Eveleigh, Anthony Ham

CONTENTS

Plan Your Trip

The Guide

Nosy Be (p142)

Hook-billed vanga

Tsaranoro Valley (p83)

Toolkit

Storybook

TOP: ESHOOT/SHUTTERSTOCK ©

Veiled chameleon

MADAGASCAR
THE JOURNEY BEGINS HERE

In this age of globalisation and the world becoming much the same, Madagascar is a special place: no matter where you are in the country, you couldn't mistake it for anywhere else on Earth. And what there is to see and experience can be quite incredible.

This is a land of lemurs and other wildlife that exist only in a Madagascan rainforest. There's the *tsingy*, those great forests of limestone that take on the most otherworldly shapes. Then there's Tana (Antananarivo), the capital city, with its mix of deeply rooted Malagasy culture coexisting with cutting-edge culinary journeys. In between, expect world-class beaches and first-rate activities, from spectacular hiking to diving and snorkelling or whale watching. Planning is quite the challenge: it can be difficult to fit it all in.

But above all, Madagascar is an adventure where, very often, the journey itself is a thing of great wonder.

Anthony Ham

anthonyham.com

Anthony writes about wildlife and the wild places of the planet for publications around the world. He is the author of The Last Lions of Africa.

My favourite experience among many is wandering the limestone pinnacles of the tsingy in Parc National Bemaraha. No other experience for me quite speaks to Madagascar's uniqueness.

WHO GOES WHERE

Our writers and experts choose the places which, for them, define Madagascar

In many ways, **Parc National Isalo** (p92) is a microcosm of everything that makes Madagascar such a fascinating place to visit. The landscapes are extraordinary: a canvas of deep canyons, eroded escarpments and palm-fringed pools. The plant life is unique, and there's a good chance of spotting ring-tailed lemurs and giant Oustalet's chameleons on many of the hiking trails. And then there's the local Bara tribe, whose cave tombs lie high up in the cliffs and whose customs are proudly portrayed by the excellent park guides.

Keith Drew

@keithdrewtravel

Keith writes about Africa for a variety of publications, including National Geographic Traveller UK, BBC Travel and AFAR.

Visiting **Nosy Be** (p142) and the north of Madagascar is a proper tropical adventure. Travelling by boat means getting your feet (and probably trousers) wet. Travelling by road means hours of spine-crunching rattling and shaking on even the shortest journey. And walking means stifling heat and a good chance of mosquitoes. But the amazing and prolific wildlife, the tropical air, the friendly people and the fascinating sights make these things feel like just minor inconveniences.

Joe Bindloss

bindloss.co.uk

Joe has been writing guidebooks for Lonely Planet for more than 25 years, and he also contributes widely to newspapers, magazines and travel websites.

While **Parc National Andringitra** (p83) seems to become more difficult to access with each cyclone season that passes, it is worth all the hassles many times over. The Betsileo and Bara homesteads around the park boundaries make for wonderfully hospitable overnight spots and the highland landscapes around Pic Boby (Madagascar's second highest mountain) must rank among the most spectacular in all Africa.

Mark Eveleigh

markeveleigh.com

Mark Eveleigh once trekked across northern Madagascar with a zebu 'pack-bull', collecting material for his Maverick in Madagascar *book.*

Nosy Be
Go diving in tropical paradise (p142)

Baie d'Antongil
See humpback whales in Madagascar's east (p201)

Île Sainte Marie
Watch whales off the east coast (p196)

Île aux Nattes (Nosy Nato)
Chill on white-sand beaches (p200)

Antananarivo
Explore Madagascar's historical and cultural capital (p44)

Parc National Bemaraha
Marvel at Madagascar-only limestone pinnacles (p129)

COMOROS

Mayotte (France)

Mozambique Channel

Parc National de Montagne d'Ambre

Diego Suarez (Antsiranana)

Parc National de l'Ankarana

Ambodibonara
Ambilobe
Nosy Be
Hell-
Ville
Ankify
Ambanja

Parc National Marojejy
Maroijy Massif

Maromokotro

Tsaratanana Massif

Béalanana
Antsohihy

Sambava
Antalaha

Cap Est

Musrvala Peninsula

Baie d'Antongil
Mananara
Maroantsetra
Mandritsara
Île Sainte Marie

Parc National Mananara-Nord
Soanierana-Ivongo

Sofia River

Boriziny (Port Bergé)
Ambondromany

Parc National Ankarafantsika

Mahajamba River

Marovoay
Ambatondrazaka
Parc National Zahamena

Katsepy
Betsiboka River

Vohipeno
Lac Alaotra
Vohiojala

Maevatanana

Lac Kinkony

Soalala

Besalampy

Tamatave (Toamasina)
Mahambo
Mahambo

Tamboharano

Maintirano

Parc National Bemaraha

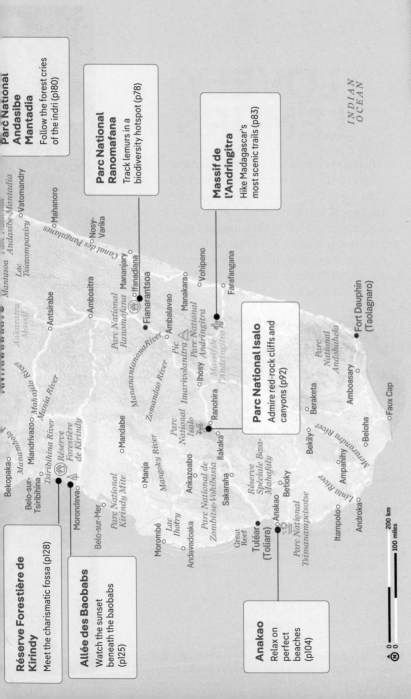

Réserve Forestière de Kirindy

Meet the charismatic fossa (p128)

Allée des Baobabs

Watch the sunset beneath the baobabs (p125)

Anakao

Relax on perfect beaches (p104)

Parc National Andasibe Mantadia

Follow the forest cries of the indri (p180)

Parc National Ranomafana

Track lemurs in a biodiversity hotspot (p78)

Massif de l'Andringitra

Hike Madagascar's most scenic trails (p83)

Parc National Isalo

Admire red-rock cliffs and canyons (p92)

INDIAN OCEAN

7

LOVELY LEMURS

There are many ways in which Madagascar is utterly unlike anywhere else on Earth, and its lemurs are at the heart of this unique appeal. From the largest lemur species to the mouse lemurs, among which are the world's smallest primates, the variety is astonishing. Some are seen by day, others are nocturnal, and there are new species being discovered all the time. Wherever you go, there'll be a guide who knows where to find them.

Only in Madagascar

Lemurs are prosimians (primate ancestors) found only in Madagascar. They have been on a different evolutionary path since Madagascar broke away from Africa 160 million years ago.

Largest & Smallest

The largest lemur is the *indri* (up to 77cm long; weighs nearly 10kg; pictured above). The smallest is Madame Berthe's mouse lemur (around 9cm long; barely 30g; pictured left).

Night Vision

Several national parks do not permit walking forest trails after dark. To see many nocturnal lemur species, you'll need to visit nearby private reserves.

BEST LEMUR EXPERIENCES

Follow the haunting cries of indri through the forest in **❶ Parc National Andasibe Mantadia**, and take a nearby night walk to see the aye-aye. (p180)

Track down the 12 (and soon-to-be 13) different kinds of lemurs in the biodiversity hotspot of **❷ Parc National Ranomafana**. (p78)

Increase your chances of seeing the gremlin-like aye-aye, by visiting **❸ Aye-Aye Island** in Mananara in Madagascar's east. (p203)

Enjoy the eight different lemur species, including the cute-as-a-button Coquerel's sifaka, in **❹ Parc National Ankarafantsika**. (p121)

Tick off the charismatic ring-tailed lemur, the handsome Verreaux's *sifaka* and other species in **❺ Parc National Isalo** down in the country's south. (p92)

LEFT: MICHAIL_VOROBYEV/SHUTTERSTOCK ©; RIGHT: MIROSLAV HALAMA/SHUTTERSTOCK ©, JEAN-PHILIPPE NAVARRO/SHUTTERSTOCK ©

Allée des Baobabs

MORE THAN JUST LEMURS

Madagascar's forests are places of quite extraordinary biodiversity. Look for lemurs, by all means, but there's so much more to see. You can also see varied birdlife, chameleons, boa constrictors, tomato (and other) frogs and even the fossa, Madagascar's top predator. And then there's the baobab, that iconic giant of the Madagascan wild.

The Upside-Down Tree

Legend has it that God made the baobab the most beautiful tree on Earth. The devil was jealous and decided to plant baobabs upside down so he could see them from hell!

The Baobab

Madagascar has seven of the world's eight baobab species. They can stand 30m high, have a circumference of 21m and live for centuries.

BEST NON-LEMUR WILDLIFE EXPERIENCES

Meet the fossa, a carnivore with a charismatic presence at ❶ **Réserve Forestière de Kirindy**. (p128)

Wander through an honour guard of baobabs at sunrise or sunset along the ❷ **Allée des Baobabs**. (p125)

Stare intently at every branch in ❸ **Parc National Andasibe Mantadia** for the photogenic Parson's chameleon. (p180)

Scan the Madagascan coast for turtles as you dive or snorkel, but don't miss the turtle sanctuary of ❹ **Nosy Sakatia**. (p148)

Take a tour de ville and spot the bulbous tomato frog in the lush tropical gardens and backyards of ❺ **Maroantsetra**. (p208)

WATCH WHALES

Every year from July to September, hundreds of whales make the long journey from Antarctica to mate and give birth in the warmer waters further north. Conveniently, they swim up both sides of the island, including into lovely Baie d'Antongil. Whether you head out in a wooden fishing canoe or a proper sea-going ship, it's a brilliant experience.

Humpbacks

The humpback is the sixth-largest whale species in the world's oceans: it can reach 15m in length and weigh 35 tonnes.

Whale Sharks

Not to be confused with whales, this large, endangered shark species feeds exclusively on plankton and each has a unique spot pattern.

Responsible Whale Watching

Only go on a whale-watching safari with an operator accredited by Cétamada (cetamada.org), a local conservation organisation that promotes responsible whale watching.

❹
❶
❷

❺
❸

BEST WHALE WATCHING EXPERIENCES

Watch humpback mothers swim with their newborn calves in ❶ **Baie d'Antongil**, in Madagascar's east. (p205)

Head out beyond the beaches and brave big ocean swells to look for humpbacks off the east coast of ❷ **Île Sainte Marie**. (p197)

Let a fisherman who knows the sea take you out beyond the reef in a simple wooden fishing boat off the coast of ❸ **Anakao**. (p104)

Head out to sea from ❹ **Nosy Be** to watch these giants of the sea breaching in the Mozambique Channel. (p149)

Ignore the crowds at other whale-watching spots and join an excursion from ❺ **Ifaty**, on Madagascar's southwestern coastline. (p103)

BEAUTIFUL BEACHES

They may not receive the attention of other Indian Ocean beach destinations, but that's fine with us and all the better for you: you may just have Madagascar's beaches all to yourself. With two oceans and 5000km of coastline, they're among the country's top attractions. But it's not just about the scale: these are pristine arcs of white sand, backed by palm trees and bathed in seas of the most intense cerulean blue.

Warning: Rough Seas Ahead

Save for the occasional private resort, most Madagascan beaches are not patrolled by lifeguards. Currents can be strong and waves even stronger.

Islands of Madagascar

Discounting Australia, Madagascar is the world's fourth-largest island. The Madagascan coastline is shadowed by around 250 islands; Nosy Be and Île Sainte Marie are the largest.

When Not to Go

If you're planning a beach holiday, avoid January to March, which corresponds to both the cyclone and rainy seasons.

LEFT: ARTUSH/SHUTTERSTOCK ©; PIERRE-YVES BABELON/SHUTTERSTOCK ©; RIGHT: SGARBO/GETTY IMAGES ©

BEST BEACH EXPERIENCES

Kick back on a perfect arc of white sand and turquoise water at ❶ **Anakao**, the pearl of the Great Reef. (p104)

Take to the sheltered waters around ❷ **Vohémar**, one of the loveliest stretches along the northern Madagascar coast. (p171)

Wish you could stay a lifetime on ❸ **Île aux Nattes (Nosy Nato)**, with white-sand beaches, reclining palms and an inviting sea. (p200)

Feel like Robinson Crusoe at ❹ **Salary**, along the southwestern coast, where there's just one resort for 7km of beach. (p101)

Watch two islands become one at ❺ **Nosy Iranja**, as this postcard-perfect duo becomes one at low tide. (p150)

LEFT: PIERRE-YVES BABELON/SHUTTERSTOCK ©. RIGHT: BLUE-SEA.CZ/SHUTTERSTOCK ©. ©: BLUE-SEA.CZ/SHUTTERSTOCK ©

Vanilla manufacturing, Sambava

URBAN MADAGASCAR

Madagascar is not known for its urban charms, but you just need to know where to look and you'll find some real gems. Most are scattered along the coastline, but don't forget the capital, Antananarivo (Tana). If you learn to enjoy the traffic and noise, many travellers end up loving the city.

Ditch the Car

If you can't beat the traffic, join it: take a cycle rickshaw tour of Antsirabe for a whole new perspective on life.

Largest Cities

Madagascar's five largest cities (by population) are Antananarivo (1.4 million), Tamatave (350,000), Antsirabe (275,000), Majunga (250,000) and Fianarantsoa (200,000).

BEST URBAN EXPERIENCES

Join the locals in the late afternoon in ❶ **Majunga** to promenade along the Corniche. (p116)

Enjoy the colonial-era buildings and irresistible tropical atmosphere of ❷ **Diego Suarez (Antsiranana)**. (p154)

Inhale deeply as you wander the fragrant town of ❸ **Sambava**, which is scented with vanilla, coffee and cloves, and has a gorgeous beach. (p165)

Dive into the country's urban heartbeat in ❹ **Antananarivo**, with its many historical sites, and fantastic places to eat. (p44)

Dine on fresh seafood at ❺ **Morondava**, visit a mangrove ecotourism project, and sunset at magnificent Allée des Baobabs. (p124)

DIVE & SNORKEL THE REEFS

Madagascar is home to the world's fifth-largest coral reef, and the diving and snorkelling can be exceptional, with fish, corals, sharks, turtles, whales and rays. There are three main diving/snorkelling areas in Madagascar: Nosy Be and the surrounding islands; Île Sainte Marie in the east; and the Great Reef, from Anakao to Andavadoaka, in the southwest.

When to Dive & Snorkel

Although diving takes place year-round, the best time everywhere is October to January when seas are calm and underwater visibility is best.

Protect the Coral

Don't touch living marine organisms or drag equipment across the reef. If you must hold onto the reef, only touch exposed rock or dead coral.

Fins & Fish-Feeding

Even without contact, the surge from fin strokes near the reef can damage delicate organisms. Do not feed fish, even if operators offer it.

BEST DIVING & SNORKELLING EXPERIENCES

Take your pick of dozens of dive sites off **❶ Nosy Be**, with a huge variety of seascapes, shipwrecks, reefs and spectacular drops. (p147)

You're almost guaranteed to see turtles off **❷ Nosy Tanikely**, one of the best and most accessible snorkelling spots in Madagascar. (p147)

Choose from a great range of dives, including the famous 'Cathedral', a network of stunning rocky arches from **❸ Ifaty and Mangily**. (p103)

Explore the waters off **❹ Anakao**, the best spot on Madagascar's southern reef, with good snorkelling and even better diving. (p104)

Sample the amazing underwater variety of marine life and discover shipwrecks off the coast of **❺ Île Sainte Marie**. (p196)

HIKING THE HIGH COUNTRY

You'll often trek along short forest trails in search of lemurs and other wildlife. But for serious trekkers there's so much more to look forward to all across the rugged interior of the island: with such an alluring shoreline, it's easy to forget that about 70% of Madagascar's land surface sits at a lofty 1000m to 1500m above sea level. Cue superb mountains, extinct volcanoes, dramatic peaks and, of course, fabulous hiking.

Camping Equipment

Operators usually provide all equipment for camping, cooking etc; bring your own sleeping bag or a sleeping liner, to avoid bed bugs.

Health & Safety

For remote treks, carry a decent first-aid kit, water-purifying equipment (such as LifeStraw or chlorine tablets), battery pack and a good torch.

Degree of Difficulty

Check the trails' difficulty with your operator: some treks are notoriously hard (Maroantsetra to Cap Est, Marojejy etc) and require good physical condition.

BEST HIKING EXPERIENCES

Hike the nearly deserted forest and high-altitude trails of the world-class ❶ **Massif de l'Andringitra**. (p83)

Trek through primordial rainforest on everything from a scenic walk to full-on climbing expedition in ❷ **Parc National Marojejy**. (p167)

Scale the weird and wonderful *tsingy* (limestone pinnacle formations) along numerous trails and *via ferrata* (mountain route) in ❸ **Parc National Bemaraha**. (p129)

Explore ❹ **Parc National Isalo**, southern Madagascar's trekking destination par excellence, with stunning canyons and gorges. (p92)

There are short and long-distance trails through the pristine primary rainforest of ❺ **Parc National Masoala-Nosy Mangabe**; few travellers make it out this way. (p205)

WILD LANDSCAPES

It can be easy in Madagascar to become too focused on the up-close – on the lemur resting in the fork of the tree, or the perfectly camouflaged gecko or chameleon. Sometimes, it pays to step back and take in the bigger picture. And what a picture that can be. Madagascar must surely be one of the most beautiful countries on the planet, from wild and beautiful coastline to the *tsingy* (limestone pinnacles), which you only find here.

Tsingy

Northern and western Madagascar host impressive limestone karst (*tsingy*; pictured) formations – jagged, eroded rocks that contain caves, potholes, underground rivers and forested canyons.

Natural Unesco Sites

Of Madagascar's five Unesco World Heritage-listed sites, two are natural landscapes: Parc National Bemaraha and the Rainforests of the Atsinanana.

Wild Inhabitants

When humans first arrived, Madagascar's wild landscapes supported hippopotamuses, aardvarks, gorilla-sized lemurs and the world's largest bird (the 3m-high elephant bird, Aepyornis).

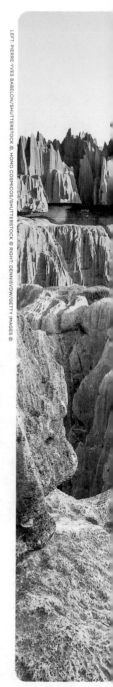

⑤

❶
❸

❷ ❹

BEST BEAUTIFUL LANDSCAPE EXPERIENCES

Admire the *tsingy* (limestone pinnacles) that look like forests of otherworldly formations in ❶ **Parc National Bemaraha**. (p129)

Watch as the setting sun sets fire to the red-rock escarpments of ❷ **Parc National Isalo**, a landscape unlike any other in the country. (p92)

Drift down the ❸ **Tsiribihina River** in a pirogue (traditional dugout canoe) through valleys and gorges between Miandrivazo and Belo-sur-Tsiribihina. (p132)

Discover the drama of the ❹ **Parc National Andringitra**, a glorious mountain massif in the country's heart. (p83)

Experience the magical world of weirdly wonderful landscapes around ❺ **Majunga**, including the Grottes d'Anjohibe and Cirque Rouge. (p116)

REGIONS & CITIES

Find the places that tick all your boxes.

Western Madagascar

UNFORGETTABLE ADVENTURES OUT WEST

Drift down the Tsiribihina River. Hike the quintessentially Madagascan limestone pinnacles of Parc National Bemaraha. Look for fossa in Réserve Forestière de Kirindy. Kick back by an isolated beach in Belo-sur-Mer. Dine in rickety splendour at Mad Zebu. And watch the sunset in the Allée des Baobabs. What more could you want?

p112

Western Madagascar
p112

Southern Madagascar

CANYONS, CORAL AND WILDLIFE-RICH SPINY FORESTS

Southern Madagascar might just have it all. Parc National Isalo is a glorious land of red-rock escarpments and is utterly superb. The coral-rich Great Reef runs along the southwestern coast with whales passing just offshore. And the deep south is remote and vast, and custom-made for adventurers.

p86

Southern Madagascar
p86

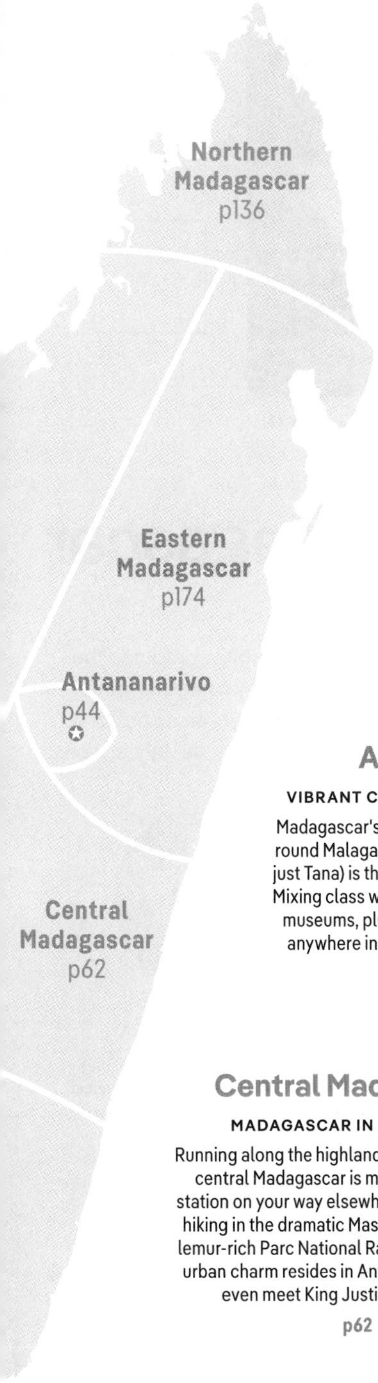

Northern Madagascar

PLANTATIONS, BEACHES AND WILDLIFE

Madagascar's tropical north is everything that's good about the country. Beach resorts and coral reefs are major calling cards, and historic towns, often bathed in the scent of vanilla, add cultural depth. But the region has its adventurous side with wild national parks and challenging but rewarding back roads.

p136

Eastern Madagascar

WELCOME TO THE WILD EAST

Two of Madagascar's biggest attractions – the indri-filled parks around Andasibe and Île Sainte Marie – reside out east. In between, the Pangales Lakes, the diabolical RN5, and the magical far north around Baie d'Antongil, Nosy Mangabe and the Masoala Peninsula are custom-built for explorers.

p174

Antananarivo

VIBRANT CAPITAL OF HIGHS AND LOWS

Madagascar's capital and largest city – and all-round Malagasy cultural star – Antananarivo (or just Tana) is the human heartbeat of the country. Mixing class with traffic chaos, historic sites and museums, plus some of the best places to eat anywhere in the Indian Ocean, Tana can be a whole lot of fun.

p44

Central Madagascar

MADAGASCAR IN A NUTSHELL

Running along the highland spine of the country, central Madagascar is more than just a way station on your way elsewhere. There's first-rate hiking in the dramatic Massif d'Andringitra and lemur-rich Parc National Ranomafana. Plenty of urban charm resides in Antsirabe. And you can even meet King Justin of the Tanala.

p62

Northern
Madagascar
p136

Eastern
Madagascar
p174

Antananarivo
p44

Central
Madagascar
p62

DAVIDE GANDOLFI/SH-SHUTTERSTOCK ©

La Fenêtre de l'Isalo (p94)

ITINERARIES

Highlights of Madagascar

Allow: 10 days **Distance:** 1250km

Visit the best that Madagascar has to offer. Begin in the capital, detour to the east to see the *indri,* then journey down through the country's heartland into the deep south, with its extraordinary rock formations and glorious coastline. Along the way, you'll see whales and lemurs, and get a taste of the landscapes that this remarkable country has to offer.

1

ANTANANARIVO ⏱ 2 DAYS

Immerse yourself in the captivating city of **Antananarivo** (p44) with its fine restaurants, excellent museums, and intriguing historical sites. Ignore its traffic and dive into its markets and crowded streets, enjoy its day spas and bakeries, and walk the steep streets of the Haute Ville. It's the kind of city that can grow on you, thanks to strong fusion of Malagasy culture with a French colonial past.

🚗 *5 hours*

2

PARC NATIONAL ANDASIBE MANTADIA ⏱ 2 DAYS

Head east of the capital to **Parc National Andasibe Mantadia** (p180), gateway to some of Madagascar's best parks. Of the 12 lemur species on show, it's the *indri* that everyone comes to see. But the dense forests also shelter all manner of birdlife, chameleons, reptiles and other wildlife. Take a night walk or a village tour, and don't miss the private reserves nearby. 🚗 *8 hours*

3

ANTSIRABE ⏱ 1 DAY

One of the more interesting towns of central Madagascar, **Antsirabe** (p71) is littered with historical buildings and monuments; there's no better way than to explore in a rickshaw. The city is known for its craft shops and renowned countrywide for its thermal baths. But it's also just a fun and slightly chaotic place to take the urban pulse of the nation.

🚗 *5 hours*

🚗 *5 hours*

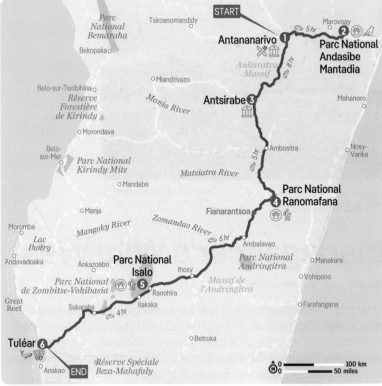

START

Antananarivo ①

Parc National
Andasibe
Mantadia ②

Antsirabe ③

Parc National
Ranomafana ④

Fianarantsoa

Parc National
Isalo ⑤

Tuléar ⑥

END

0   100 km
0   50 miles

④
PARC NATIONAL RANOMAFANA ⏱ 2 DAYS

One of the best places anywhere in Madagascar to see lemurs, **Parc National Ranomafana** (p78) is criss-crossed with forest hiking trails that are among the best (and most rewarding) in the country. Not far from the park itself, in Tanambao, you'll enjoy the rare opportunity to rub shoulders with royalty when you meet the local king. 🚗 *6 hours*

⑤
PARC NATIONAL ISALO ⏱ 2 DAYS

There is no more beautiful park in Madagascar than **Parc National Isalo** (p92), an astonishing landscape of red-rock escarpments cut through with oasis-like valleys and waterfalls. The scenery here is superb, with loads of opportunities to encounter lemurs. Accommodation in the area is excellent; the town of Ranohira is the main base. 🚗 *4 hours*

⑥
TULÉAR ⏱ 1 DAY

The end of the long road from Antananarivo is the start of so many more. Beyond the town of **Tuléar** itself – which has good places to stay and eat and the rewarding Arboretum d'Antsokay – stretches mile upon mile of unspoiled coastline, shadowed by the **Great Reef** (p98), with its quiet seaside villages, whale-watching excursions, and fine diving and snorkelling.

Parc National Bemaraha (p129)

ITINERARIES

Madagascar's Wild West

Allow: 9 days   **Distance:** 805km

Exploring Madagascar's west means experiencing an astonishing mix of wildlife and wild landscapes. Begin in Antananarivo, and head for Parc National Bemaraha, stopping along the way for one of the country's best meals, the iconic Allée des Baobabs, time with the elusive fossa, and a fab ecotourism project in the mangroves.

1
ANTANANARIVO ⏱ 1 DAY

Madagascar's capital **Antananarivo** (p44) is the place to experience urban charms and comforts before taking to the long and dusty road. In particular, enjoy a good bed, a high-class meal, and a smattering of cultural and historical sites. Where you're going, most of the attractions are likely to be of the wild and natural kind, so enjoy Tana while you can. 🚗 *8 hours*

2
MIANDRIVAZO ⏱ 1 DAY

At the end of the long, scenic drive from Tana, the road drops down off the high plateau to **Miandrivazo** (p132). This low-key provincial town is a gateway to the Tsiribihina River, but is otherwise all about the views – it's the perfect place to relax overnight for the final leg into Morondava. 🚗 *4 hours*

🚣 *Detour:* Take a boat trip down the Tsiribihina River to Belo-sur-Tsiribihina. 3 days (boat)

3
MORONDAVA ⏱ 2 DAYS

Where the road meets the sea, **Morondava** (p124) feels every bit the end-of-the-road tropical beach town. Enjoy seafood overlooking the Indian Ocean, and dedicate a day to exploring the mangroves and nearby village life at the Kivalo Soa Honko (p126), a fantastic ecotourism project. Don't miss sunrise or sunset (or both) at the superb Allée des Baobabs (p125). 🚗 *4 hours*

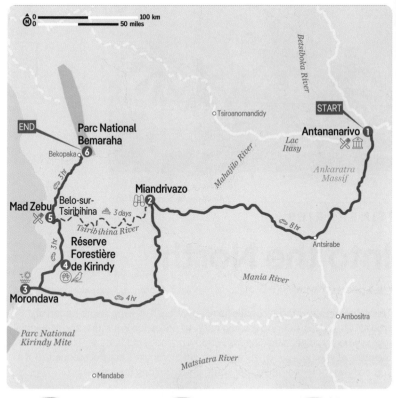

Map labels:
- 100 km / 50 miles
- Betsiboka River
- Tsiroanomandidy
- START
- Antananarivo 1
- Lac Itasy
- END
- Parc National Bemaraha 6
- Bekopaka
- Ankaratra Massif
- Mahajilo River
- 3 hr
- Miandrivazo 2
- Belo-sur-Tsiribihina
- Mad Zebu 5
- 3 days
- Tsiribihina River
- 8 hr
- Antsirabe
- 3 hr
- Réserve Forestière de Kirindy 4
- Mania River
- Morondava 3
- 4 hr
- Ambositra
- Parc National Kirindy Mite
- Matsiatra River
- Mandabe

4 RÉSERVE FORESTIÈRE DE KIRINDY ⏱1 DAY

An island of dense forest of incredible biodiversity, the **Réserve Forestière de Kirindy** (p128) is worth visiting for its lemurs and birds alone. But this is also the best place in Madagascar to see the fossa, the country's charismatic puma-like carnivore. Hang around the Ecolodge long enough and one is sure to appear. 🚗 *3 hours*

5 MAD ZEBU ⏱1 DAY

The food at **Mad Zebu** (p129), in the backwoods village of Belo-sur-Tsiribihina, is some of the best and most creative you'll find anywhere in Madagascar: expect fresh local ingredients, innovative combinations, and refreshingly casual service. The roadside setting is similarly relaxed, but don't be fooled: tables fill up fast. 🚗 *3 hours*

6 PARC NATIONAL BEMARAHA ⏱3 DAYS

One of the most beautiful parks in the country, **Parc National Bemaraha** (p129) is home to forests of uniquely Madagascan landforms known as *tsingy*: limestone pinnacles in the most wonderful shapes and sizes that are ripe for exploration. Hiking trails through two main areas, canyon pirogue trips, and scrambling across fixed *via ferrata* are all a part of this memorable experience.

BY VALET/SHUTTERSTOCK ©

Ampasipohy, Nosy Be (p150)

ITINERARIES

Into the North

Allow: 5 days (7 including Parc National Marojejy) **Distance:** Approximately 400km

This route through Madagascar's far north offers a winning combination of beautiful beaches, deeply forested national parks rich in lemurs, and provincial towns where you get a fascinating window on modern Malagasy life. To make the most of your time, you'll fly each leg, which requires careful planning. But if you do have more time, consider some detours along the way.

❶
SAMBAVA ⏱ 1 DAY

One of Madagascar's more pleasant towns, **Sambava** (p165) has a wild and beautiful beach, which is as perfect for long walks as it is for swimming the waves; strong swimmers only and please take care in the rough seas. The town's sensory overload comes mostly from the scent of vanilla, cocoa, cloves, coconuts and coffee: there are plantations around the town at every turn.

🛫 *Sambava to Diego Suarez: 45 minutes*

Stop 2 detour: Sambava to Parc National Marojejy:
🚗 *3 hours by 4x4*

❷ DETOUR
PARC NATIONAL MAROJEJY ⏱ 2 DAYS

On a detour from the main route, **Parc National Marojejy** (p167) has exciting forest trails, spectacular mountain views and 11 lemur species. You'll need a couple of days to explore from Sambava and back again. With a couple more, you could extend the detour to **Réserve Spéciale Anjanaharibe-Sud** (p172), which is home to black *indri*, silky *sifaka* and hot springs. If you plan to travel on to Diego Suarez from Réserve Spéciale Anjanaharibe-Sud, you'll need to head back to Sambava and catch a flight.

🚗 *Parc National Marojejy to Réserve Spéciale Anjanaharibe-Sud: [car icon] 2 hours by 4x4*
Réserve Spéciale Anjanaharibe-Sud to Sambava:
🚗 *4-5 hours by 4x4*

PIERRE-YVES BABELON/SHUTTERSTOCK ©, MBRAND85/SHUTTERSTOCK ©

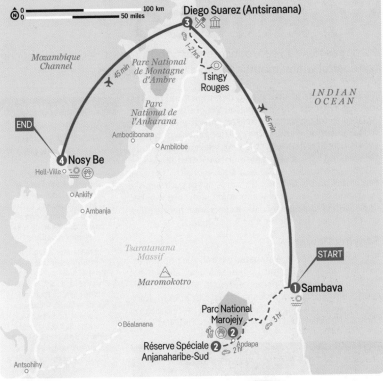

Diego Suarez (Antsiranana)

Mozambique Channel

Parc National de Montagne d'Ambre

Parc National de l'Ankarana

Tsingy Rouges

INDIAN OCEAN

Ambodibonara

Ambilobe

END

Nosy Be

Hell-Ville

Ankify

Ambanja

Tsaratanana Massif

Maromokotro

START

Sambava

Parc National Marojejy

Béalanana

Réserve Spéciale Anjanaharibe-Sud

Andapa

Antsohihy

0 100 km
0 50 miles

❸ DIEGO SUAREZ (ANTSIRANANA)
⏱ 2 DAYS

With its wide streets and old colonial-era buildings, especially along Rue Colbert, **Diego Suarez** (p154) is a tranquil place that rouses to life with good restaurants, vibrant local markets, and interesting streetlife in the evenings. What Diego lacks in beaches (although there are plenty nearby), it makes up for with amazing bay views. ✈ *45 minutes by plane*

🚶 *Detour: The terracotta-coloured Tsingy Rouges are true natural wonders. 1–2 hours.* 🚗 *1 hour*

❹ NOSY BE ⏱ 2 DAYS

Madagascar's number-one beach destination, **Nosy Be** (p142) has powder-white sand, turquoise waters and it's ideal for water-based activities, including whale watching and swimming with whale sharks. Taking up a large chunk of the island, **Parc National Lokobe** (p150) has black lemurs, boa constrictors, owls, chameleons and much more. Nosy Be has a fabulous culture of culinary fusion, blending Chinese, European and Malagasy influences with the freshest local seafood.

WHEN **TO GO**

Madagascar is a year-round destination, but most people visit during the austral winter months to avoid the rainy season.

Madagascar sits mostly within the tropics and has two distinct seasons. The dry season generally lasts from April to October; the rainy season runs from November to March, although the only real time you might want to avoid is the first quarter of the year, when cyclones buffet the east and west coasts and some roads are impassable. All things considered, the best time to visit is between September and November. It's warm but not stifling, the jacaranda trees are in bloom, market stalls are weighed down with plump mangoes and lychees, and there are fewer visitors, yet the wildlife viewing is great.

Staying Power

Few hotels outside of Antananarivo and the popular areas of Isalo, Nosy Be and Île Sainte Marie have official high- and low-season prices, although many offer discounts during the low season (January to March). Book ahead if you're visiting at Easter or during the high season (July and August, and around Christmas and New Year).

Hira gasy (p53), Antananarivo

LEFT: PIERRE-YVES BABELON/SHUTTERSTOCK © RIGHT: NATANDCAU/SHUTTERSTOCK ©

<aside>

⊛ **I LIVE HERE**

WINTER IN THE HIGHLANDS

Sitraka Batsola Randrianjakanavalona is a local tour guide in Antananarivo and a singer with the *hira gasy* group Akon'ny rova Manjakamiadana.

In the winter, our group attends events in the central highlands to sing *vakisova*, a song about patriotism, justice and tradition that is the special song at circumcision ceremonies. It's a lovely time to be up in the Hauts Plateaux – the fields are busy with people planting rice and the air is crisp and fresh.

</aside>

<aside>

LAND OF CONTRASTS

The change in climate in Madagascar is extreme, with the tropical east coast pounded by up to 3700mm of rain each year, while the arid south, the driest place in the country, has a semi-desert environment that receives less than 800mm of rainfall annually.

</aside>

Weather Through the Year (Antananarivo)

JANUARY	**FEBRUARY**	**MARCH**	**APRIL**	**MAY**	**JUNE**
Avg daytime max: **29°C** Days of rainfall: **15**	Avg daytime max: **29°C** Days of rainfall: **13**	Avg daytime max: **29°C** Days of rainfall: **10**	Avg daytime max: **28°C** Days of rainfall: **4**	Avg daytime max: **27°C** Days of rainfall: **2**	Avg daytime max: **25°C** Days of rainfall: **1**

THE REALLY WILD SHOW

The hot and humid summer months of January and February are prime time for spotting reptiles and amphibians. Birdwatching is best in September, when it's easier to observe the country's 280 species among the bare dry deciduous forests. For the oh-so-cute sight of baby lemurs clinging to their mother's fur, come in November.

The Big Tickets

Easter is fervently celebrated in Madagascar, with extended families – dressed in their finest – gathering to attend Mass together at churches across the country. Antananarivo's Haute-Ville (p48) is particularly busy. ☀ **April**

The official celebrations for Madagascar's **Fête de l'Indépendance** feature military parades in the capital, Antananarivo (p44). Elsewhere, there are street celebrations, themed parties and a profusion of red, green and white decorations.
☀ **26 June**

Visitors are often welcome at traditional *famadihana* (turning of the bones) ceremonies (p250) – ritual exhumations to commemorate the ancestors of Betsileo and Merina people. These joyous events take place in the highlands region between Tana to Ambalavao. ☀ **July to September**

Antananarivo is the best place to catch *hira gasy* (p53), a colourful performance of traditional storytelling, narrated through dancing, singing and oratory jousting. ☀ **August and September**

Other Festivals & Events

For a shot of artistic zing, head to **Zegny'Zo** (p140), an international street-arts festival with a carnival-like atmosphere in Diego Suarez. ☀ **May**

Nosy Be's week-long **Donia** (p140) is Madagascar's most high-profile arts festival. It's primarily a music event, although the fringe also involves a carnival and various sporting events. ☀ **End May/ Early June**

Welcome in the start of the whale-watching season at the **Whale Festival** (p198), a medley of costumed parades, concerts and competitions on Île Sainte Marie. ☀ **July**

Going strong for more than 30 years, the annual **Madajazzcar** festival in Antananarivo taps into the country's rich musical tradition and brings together local and foreign jazz performers. ☀ **October**

⊙ I LIVE HERE

HEADING

Joe Kennedy lives in Fort Dauphin (Taolagnaro), Southern Madagascar. He is Madagascar's National Surf Champion and runs Lenda Surf School at Ampotatra beach. @joe_kennedy_surf

Fort Dauphin is a year-round destination, but for those of us with an eye on the surf, the conditions May through July are undoubtedly bigger, cleaner and better. Empty back lines, deserted coco-backed beaches and deep-orange sunsets are what we call home.

Fort Dauphin (p106)

BLOWIN' IN THE WIND

Madagascar's climate is dictated by the *varatraza* (southeast trade winds), and the northwest monsoon winds. The southwest is also subject to the *tsiokatimo*, a powerful southern wind that can whip up sandstorms. January to March is cyclone season; three or four make landfall each year.

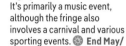

JULY	AUGUST	SEPTEMBER	OCTOBER	NOVEMBER	DECEMBER
Avg daytime max: **24°C**	Avg daytime max: **25°C**	Avg daytime max: **27°C**	Avg daytime max: **28°C**	Avg daytime max: **29°C**	Avg daytime max: **29°C**
Days of rainfall: **2**	Days of rainfall: **1**	Days of rainfall: **2**	Days of rainfall: **4**	Days of rainfall: **10**	Days of rainfall: **11**

PLAN YOUR TRIP WHEN TO GO

LEFT: KATJA TSVETKOVA/SHUTTERSTOCK © RIGHT: LUBO IVANKO/SHUTTERSTOCK ©

Parc National Andringitra (p83)

GET PREPARED
FOR MADAGASCAR

Useful things to load in your bag, your ears and your brain.

Clothes

Play the long game Pack plenty of long-sleeve tops and long trousers, both for rainforest walks and to wear in the evenings, and a long-sleeved waterproof jacket. Long socks (to cover ankles) are also a good idea.

An extra layer A lightweight sweater or fleece is handy at any time of year – as it can get quite chilly in the highlands (and Antananarivo) in the early mornings and evenings – and essential in the austral winter months of May to August.

Head to toe Take a hat for the sun and the rain – and the insects. You'll need

Manners

Take it easy Adopt the Malagasy mantra of *mora mora* ('slow, slow') and you won't be fazed when things (inevitably) take time or don't quite go to plan.

Respect your elders It's polite to add the word *tompoko* (equivalent to sir or madam) to the end of a sentence when talking to an older person.

It's rude to point It is *fady* (taboo) to point at tombs with an outstretched finger.

sturdy shoes for hiking; light walking boots are ideal, although trainers are also good.

📖 READ

Beyond the Rice Fields (Naivo; 2016) Dual narrators portray the changing face of Madagascar in the early 19th century.

Hainteny: The Traditional Poetry of Madagascar (Leonard Fox; 1990) Translations of beautiful Merina poems charting love, revenge and sexuality.

Lords and Lemurs (Alison Jolly; 2004) A history of Berenty, weaving together stories of its French plantation owners and the local Antandroy.

The Natural History of Madagascar (Steven Goodman and Jonathan Benstead; 2003) The most comprehensive overview of the island's natural heritage.

Words

Madagascar has two official languages: Malagasy and French. Malagasy is the everyday spoken language, while French is often used for business and administrative purposes, and in the more upmarket sectors of the tourism industry. In some rural areas, you will find that only Malagasy is spoken.

Malagasy belongs to the Malayo-Polynesian branch of the Austronesian language family – its closest relative is a language from southern Borneo. The modern Latin-based alphabet was developed in the early 19th century; Malagasy was originally written using a form of Arabic script.

Saying **hello** varies between regions: use *'manao ahoana'* (maa·now aa·hon) in the highlands, *'mbola tsara'* (em·bool·a tsaar) in the north and east, and *'akory'* (a·koor·y) in the south and west. *'Salama'*, another form, is understood everywhere – and is an example of the Arabic influence in Malagasy vocabulary.

Inona no vaovao? *(i·noon vow·vow)* 'How's it going?' (more precisely, 'What's new?')

Azafady *(aa·zaa·faad)* 'Please' or 'excuse me' (literally, 'may it not be taboo to me')

Misaotra *(mi·sotr)* 'Thank you'; add 'be' afterwards (ie *'misaotra be'*) for 'thank you very much'.

Iza no anaranao? *(i·zaa nu aa·naa·raa·now)* 'What's your name?'

Ohatrinona? *(o·trin·naa)* 'How much is it?' is an essential phrase to use in the markets.

Vonjeo! *(vun·dze·u)* is the key phrase if you need to call for help.

📹 WATCH

When the Stars Meet the Sea (Raymond Rajaonarivelo; 1996) Drama tracing the story of a mythological boy born during a solar eclipse.

Madagascar, a Journey Diary (Bastien Dubois; 2009) This French animated film, about *famadihana* (p250), was nominated for an Oscar.

Nofinofy (Michael Andrianaly; 2019) Documentary following the hopes and frustrations of a barber in Tamatave (Toamasina).

Madagascar (Michael Gunton; 2011) This seminal BBC series, narrated by Sir David Attenborough, is an inspirational introduction to the Red Island.

Forests (Jeff Wilson; 2019) Sobering episode of Netflix's *Our Planet* series, which shows the destruction of the dry Menabe forests in the southwest.

🎧 LISTEN

E tiako (Jaojoby; 1997) Breakout album from 'The King of Salegy'; an electrified update of northern Madagascar's choral antsa music.

Valiha (Justin Vali; 2005). An hour and a half of ethereal sounds from a master of the bamboo-tube valiha, Madagascar's national instrument.

Live à l'Olympia (Mahaleo; 2008) Live recording in Paris celebrating the 35th anniversary of the immensely popular poetic folk-pop band.

Valimbilo (Damily; 2018) Latest release from the veteran *tsapiky* performer; a fast, guitar-driven blend of Township pop and southwest Malagasy music.

ANDRZEJ LISOWSKI TRAVEL/SHUTTERSTOCK ©

Malagasy breakfast

THE FOOD SCENE

Madagascar offers wonderfully varied local and international cuisine, along with enough unexpected culinary specialities to challenge intrepid gourmands.

'*Manasa Hihinam-bary*!' (Let's eat rice!) – is the typical way in which a Malagasy will issue an invitation to get together for a meal. By some estimates, the average Malagasy eats almost 0.5kg of rice each day over the course of three meals. Needless to say, in one of the world's poorest countries, there are many who are lucky to be able to flavour their rice with vegetables, beans or with a condiment like *sakay* (made with chilli, ginger and garlic) or with *lasary* (a side dish made with carrots, onions, green mangoes and vinaigrette).

For the more privileged, chicken features heavily on restaurant menus, along with duck (often baked in orange sauce or with honey and ginger). Zebu, the commonest meat, is prepared in hearty stews, succu-

lent steaks or sizzling kebabs, but look out for the traditional slow-cooked, crispy zebu dish known as *varenga*.

Malagasy cuisine is richly influenced by European (specifically French and Italian) styles, and Chinese fusion is immensely popular among wealthier locals.

Malagasy Fare

Unless rice is the order of the day, breakfast in a rural village will often consist of boiled cassava or maize porridge, washed down with a sweet tea made with a refreshing concoction of local herbs or simply with *rano ampango* (water boiled in the rice pot).

At lunchtime, local-style Malagasy *hotely* (small roadside places that serve hot meals)

Best Malagasy Dishes	ROMAZAVA	HENAKISOA SY AMALONA	AKOHO SY SAKAMALAO	LASARY
	National dish of a rich, ginger-flavoured zebu soup or stew.	Once reserved for royalty; a combination of pork and eel.	Baked chicken legs cooked with ginger, garlic, lemon and coconut.	Rare vegetarian speciality usually featuring cabbage, onions and tangy mangoes.

normally offer a plate of rice with a choice of whatever *laoka* (accompanying side dish) is typical to the region. On the coast and islands these will frequently include fish, crab, octopus or other seafood, and in the highlands they will more likely be stews made with chicken, duck or zebu. Tilapia (freshwater perch) from the flooded rice fields is often cooked in a fish curry known as *trondro gasy*.

The national dish *romazava* – a zebu-meat stew, usually with mustard greens, peppery paracress and spinach-like *anamamy* and *ravimbomanga sy patsa mena* (boiled sweet potato leaves with dried shrimp) – is found all over the island.

Foza sy hena-kisoa (stir-fried crab, lobster and pork cooked in lime juice and ginger) is a real highlight, and if you're feeling particularly adventurous, you could try *smalona* (smoked eels that have been stuffed – often with onions, mushrooms, olives and apple).

Foreign Influence

If zebu steak and pommes frites (French fries) could be described as fusion cuisine, then it's certainly the commonest internationally influenced dish that you'll find on restaurant menus.

One of the first culinary impressions you're likely to have on arrival in Madagascar is that the ubiquitous pizza could well be the national dish. You'll find all the usual suspects in the pizza hit-

Romazava

parade, but might also come across some irresistible fusion quirks along the lines of 'goat's cheese and wild honey pizza' or 'zebu carpaccio pizza'.

Along with Italian influences, French dishes are centre stage on all western-style menus. You'll find baguettes for sale in even the remotest Malagasy markets, and in the highlands you're sure to see menus featuring foie gras and *cuisses de nymphe* (literally 'nymph thighs'...but better known as frogs' legs).

Asian favourites include *mine sao zebu* (boiled noodles), *van tan frite* (fried won ton) and *tsa tsiou porc* (sweet and sour pork).

Very Limited Vegetarian Options

In a country where few people are vegetarian by choice (rather than by economic obligation) it can often be hard to avoid meat. *Vary amin anana* (stewed greens served with rice) is often served in a vegetable-only form, although you should check when you order because meat is sometimes added. *Lasopy* is essentially a hearty vegetable soup...but beware that, in this case too, the vegetables are often simmered with bones for flavouring.

Zebu steak and pommes frites

LASOPY TONGOTRI OMBY	VARENGA	TRONDRO GASY	MOFO GASY
Surprisingly delicious vegetable stew made with slow-cooked zebu hoof.	Seasoned zebu which is first stewed then baked until crispy.	Tilapia fish curried with onions and tomatoes, served over rice.	Sweetened rice flour cooked as succulent little cakes.

MEALS OF A LIFETIME

La Varangue (hotel-restaurant-lavarangue-tananarive.com) The big name for French fusion cuisine in Antananarivo for sheer creativity, presentation and romantic setting.

Le Papillon Restaurant (facebook.com/lepapillonresto) The go-to place on Nosy Be in Hell-Ville, and justifiably famous also for its cocktails.

Litchi Tree (thelitchitree.com) In Joffreville, it's celebrated for its endeavours to use 100% local ingredients.

Le Tsara Be Vaovao Located in Diego Suarez, it's highly recommended for the best crabs and lobsters on the north coast.

Marais Restaurant (marais-restaurant.com) Over in Antananarivo, head chef Lalaina Ravelomanana is the first African chef inducted into the prestigious Culinary Academy of France.

Lychees

Culinary Taboos

While food *fady* (taboos) are most frequently handed down along tribal lines or within villages, you'll also often find complex taboos within families or even on a personal level. Some headmen and traditional healers among the Tanala tribe, for example, believe that they'd lose all their powers if they, even inadvertently, eat chicken. Most Malagasy believe that it is bad luck to hurt a snake.

THE YEAR IN FOOD

SPRING

September and October are the months when the markets seem to explode with a kaleidoscope of fresh fruit and vegetables. It's a period of celebration: a time of (relative) plenty in the rural areas.

SUMMER

Summer sees the start of the 'cricket season' (insects, not the sport!). *Akoho sy voanio* (chicken cooked with tomatoes, onions and ginger in coconut milk) is the typical Christmas dinner in Madagascar.

AUTUMN

Harvest season is a time of celebration, with markets at their busiest. Many Catholics refrain from eating meat during Lent (Easter). In the Muslim areas there are the usual daytime prohibitions associated with Ramadan.

WINTER

The *famadihana* (exhumation) ceremonies and accompanying feasts take place throughout winter. Merina royal festivals (timing varies each year) are the time for eating *voanjobory sy henakisoa*, a traditional pork dish cooked with Bambara nuts.

LEFT: PIERRE-YVES BABELON/SHUTTERSTOCK © RIGHT: GORAN_SAFAREK/SHUTTERSTOCK ©

Fruit market, Andringitra

A traditional *fady indrazana* (tribal *fady*) that is prominent among the Antandroy people has it that sea turtles and cows without horns cannot be eaten, and most Sakalava avoid eating eel or pork. Pig meat is, in fact, probably the most widespread culinary taboo. Even westerners should avoid including ham sandwiches, for example, in picnics at many waterfalls and rivers, since these spots are often associated with ancient kings (for whom pork was almost always a powerful *fady*).

Many Malagasy will tell you too that singing while eating can make your teeth grow uncomfortably long.

Tropical Fruit

Malagasy markets are an explosion of colour most of the year, as various fruits come into season. Stalls are stacked high with coconuts, oranges, pineapples, bananas, apples and lychees. Depending on the time of year, you'll see a vast array of different types of mangoes and *goyava* (guavas). Look out for creamy custard apples, tangy soursop and the little scarlet fluff balls of rambutan (known locally as Chinese lychee).

Juice stalls sell everything from refreshing baobab juice to potently nutritious *moringa* juice. Herbal remedies are common too, such as guava leaf tea for upset stomachs – a timely boost to many a traveller.

FLAVOURED RUM

The astounding assortment of *rhum arrangé* (homemade rum with fruit inside, also known as 'punch') is undoubtedly the island's alcoholic highlight. Madagascar produces most of the world's vanilla and it's easy to believe when you see the 5L glass jars of vanilla and honey rum that take pride of place on every bar top in the country. Other common flavours include pineapple, mango, lychee, coffee and local fruits, such as *pok pok* (similar to gooseberry) and Uapaca bojeri (endemic tapia) .

Look out for or the sweat-inducing, lip-tingling, super-spicy clove-, cinnamon- and ginger-flavoured version known as *rhum arrangé aux épices*.

DENNIS VAN DE WATER/SHUTTERSTOCK ©

Parc National Masoala (p205)

THE OUTDOORS

From the rainforest to the reef, Madagascar provides the perfect canvas for a smorgasbord of activities, whether you want to hike through canyons or surf barrelling waves.

With 5000km of coastline, dozens of islands and a fringing coral reef, Madagascar is a tropical playground for diving, snorkelling and a whole host of other water sports, particularly surfing and kitesurfing. Many of the beaches here rival traditional sun-and-sand destinations, with the added bonus of fewer visitors. Inland, a network of over 40 national parks and special reserves, along with dozens of privately protected areas, offers great opportunities for hiking and some incredible wildlife watching, much of it found nowhere else on Earth.

Hiking

Nearly three-quarters of Madagascar's land surface sits at a lofty 1000m to 1500m above sea level. Cue dramatic mountains, rambling highlands, sandstone canyons – and some fabulous hiking. Trails traverse the country's slew of national parks and reserves, and the standard of guiding is excellent; unlike on the Africa mainland, there are no dangerous animals to worry about, either.

There's some truly world-class trekking in the hardly visited Massif de l'Andringitra. Parc National Bemaraha is home to the weird and wonderful limestone *tsingy*, while the trails in Parc National Isalo,

---

Other Activities

CYCLING
Hit the mountain-bike trails in **Parc National Isalo** (p92) and whizz past bizarre rock formations and eroded canyons.

CLIMBING
Tackle the via ferrata in **Parc National Bemeraha** (p129) or scale the experts-only vertical rock face of **Tsaranoro** (p83).

PIROGUE TRIPS
Ride in a traditional dugout canoe to **Île Sainte Marie** (p196) or the tropic-bird reserve of **Nosy Ve** (p105).

FAMILY ADVENTURES

Hit the beach at tranquil **Anakao** (p104) or around fun-filled **Nosy Be** (p142).

Enjoy the wacky landscapes at **Parc Natural Isalo** (p92), the alien plant life at the **Arboretum d'Antsokay** (p99) and the bizarre tsingy

pinnacles of the **Réserve Spéciale Ankarana** (p163).

Learn to cook classic Malagasy dishes (after buying the ingredients in the local market first) at **Tana Kitchen** (p57) in Antananarivo.

Visit a village at Kivalo (p126), near Morondava, to learn about

local life while crab fishing and tree planting in the mangroves.

Soak in natural hot springs in the thermal towns of **Antsirabe** (p71) and **Ranomafana** (p78).

Snorkel in the waters off at **Nosy Sakatia** (p148), a sanctuary for green turtles.

southern Madagascar's trekking destination par excellence, lead through stunning canyons to natural swimming pools. Jungle trekking is best in the primordial Massif de Marojejy, where the trail progresses from a scenic walk to a full-on climbing expedition, and the thickly forested Parc National Masoala-Nosy Mangabe, whose difficult trails are worth it for the exceptional wildlife.

Longer, multi-day treks, such as Maroantsetra to Cap Est and between the Zafimaniry villages, require more preparation; check what equipment your operator provides and how hard the hikes are, as they can vary greatly in difficulty.

Tsingy, Parc National Bemaraha (p129)

GTW/SHUTTERSTOCK ©

Wildlife Watching

Famed for its wildlife, Madagascar is to nature lovers what France is to foodies. You'll have to be patient, time your visit right and have Lady Luck on your side to see the best the country has to offer, but at the very least you're likely to spot a variety of lemurs, several of the country's rich portfolio of chameleon species and a number of different birds.

Wherever there's a national park, you're likely to find lemurs (of both the daytime and nocturnal persuasion) and guides adept at tracking them down. Each species has their own landscape niche, all across the island: emblematic ring-tailed lemurs, for example, are easily seen at Réserve d'Anja, Parc National Isalo and Berenty; Parc Nacional Marojejy harbours the beautiful (and endangered) silky *sifaka*, the so-called Angel of the Forest; while the reserves around Andasibe are the best places to see – and hear – the *indri*, Madagascar's largest lemur. Night walks normally turn up a dinky mouse lemur or two, zipping along the upper branches, their saucer-like eyes reflecting torchlight through the treetops. They can be found across most of Madagascar, in a variety of different species, although the rare Madame Berthe's mouse lemur, the smallest primate in the

QUAD BIKING	HORSE RIDING	FISHING	OFF-ROADING
Explore the crater lakes surrounding **Mont Passot** (p148) on a quad bike (or ATV).	Trot through the grassy plains and around the sandstone canyons of **Parc National Isalo** (p92), visiting Bara villages along the way.	Wrestle with a giant trevally in the seas around Nosy Be; **Tropical Fishing** (p153) and **Sakatia Lodge** (p149) can organise trips.	You'll need a sturdy 4WD to tackle the legendary RN5, which runs from **Soaniera-Ivongo to Maroantsetra** (p192).

NATIONAL PARKS

Parc National Analamazaotra (p181) Pristine forest; great for lemur-watching (especially the *indri*).

Parc National Andohahela (p110) Humid, transition and spiny forest, with flora and fauna to match.

Parc National Andringitra (p83) Trek among rugged granite peaks and superb scenery.

Parc National Ankarafantsika (p121) Diverse landscapes, from dry forest to canyon and lakes.

Parc National Bemaraha (p129) Spectacular limestone pinnacles, navigated by rope bridges and *via ferrata*.

Parc National Isalo (p92) Sandstone escarpments and gorges with natural pools.

Parc National Marojejy (p167) Remote peaks, lush rainforest and treks in search of silky sifakas.

Parc National Masoala-Nosy Mangabe (p205) Primary rainforest, mangroves and protected marine areas.

Parc National Montagne d'Ambre (p162) Humid forest (home to tiny Brookesia chameleons) and waterfalls.

Parc National Ranomafana (p78) Forested slopes harbouring a variety of lemur species.

---

world, is restricted to the dry forests of Menabe Antimena in western Madagascar.

Other wildlife prizes include the strange-looking fossa, Madagascar's only large carnivore, which is a rare sight everywhere except the Réserve Forestière de Kirindy, and humpback whales, which migrate to the waters off Anakao and Île Sainte Marie to mate and give birth between July and September.

Snorkelling & Diving

Madagascar is home to the world's fifth-largest coral reef, which partly explains why snorkelling and diving here is so good. The fauna is exceptional, with sharks, turtles, whales and rays, and plenty of multicoloured reef fish. Although diving takes place year-round, the best time is usually between October and January.

There are three main snorkelling and diving areas. Nosy Be, and its surrounding islands, is generally considered the best all-around, with a huge variety of seascapes and phenomenal marine biodiversity, including manta rays and hammerhead sharks. Parc National Marin de

Nosy Tanikely is especially good, while you can dive with green turtles in the turtle sanctuary at Nosy Sakatia. Île Sainte Marie is the best spot on the east coast, with a wide range of sites and the chance to dive shipwrecks colonised by soft corals.

The Great Reef, which runs for 450km along the southwest coast, has dozens of dive sites but is best accessed from Ifaty/Mangily and Anakao. The former is home

Sea turtle, Nosy Be (p142)

Best Beaches

ANAKAO
A perfect arc of white sand, turquoise water and a laid-back atmosphere; the pearl of the Great Reef. (p104)

ÎLE AUX NATTES (NOSY NATO)
A classic tropical island, with curving white-sand beaches, reclining palms and the most inviting sea. (p200)

SALARY
This is what exclusivity feels like: one resort for 7km of beach, off the coastal track north of Túlear (Toliara). (p101)

to the famous 'Cathedral', a network of stunning rocky arches, while the latter has good snorkelling in its lagoon and some interesting dives both along the reef and around the island of Nosy Ve. Salary, further north, is the best place along this stretch for wreck diving.

Surfing

As the biggest landmass in this part of the Indian Ocean, Madagascar catches the brunt of the Roaring Forties, powerful westerly winds that come barrelling around the Cape of Good Hope to hit the country's southern coastlines. The result is consistently good swell and some sizeable waves.

Most of the best waves in southwest Madagascar break on the fringing reef a few kilometres offshore or on the long sand spit in Sarodrano Bay. The 60km stretch north of Anakao features around 20 surf breaks that are suitable for all levels of surfers, although most of them are only accessible by boat. April to September is best, with waves averaging up to 2.5m. Surfing in southeast Madagascar is centred around Fort Dauphin (Taolagnaro), either along Anakoba, the main town beach, on Monseigneur Bay's reef break or at the powerful beach break at Vinanibe. The waves are best between April and July. There's also a much smaller scene at Mahambo, in the northeast, which has a few shallow reef breaks within easy reach of the village.

Kitesurfing

A combination of reliable wind and near-perfect sea conditions has turned Les Trois Baies in northeast Madagascar into the Malagasy capital of kitesurfing. The trade winds blow from April to November, peaking between July and September with speeds of up to 40 knots.

Kitesurfing, Sakalava (p161)

The Baie de Sakalava is the prime spot, with a sheltered lagoon, reef breaks for more advanced riders, and access to the windblown Mer d'Émeraude. A number of hotels and kitesurfing schools in the bay offer equipment rental and courses.

On the southwest coast, there's great kitesurfing in the lagoon and along the inner reef breaks at Anakao. Local operators provide equipment and tuition and can organise day-trips to Nosy Ve that end with a downwind kitesurf back. There are also some good spots along the Northern Reef, around Ambolimailaka and Tsiandamba.

ACTION AREAS

Where to find Madagascar's best outdoor activities.

National Parks

❶ Parc National Andringitra (p83)
❷ Parc National Isalo (p92)
❸ Parc National Masoala-Nosy Mang (p205)
❹ Parc National Ranomafana (p78)
❺ Parc National Montagne d'Ambre (p162)

Surfing/Kitesurfing

❶ Anakao (p104)
❷ Fort Dauphin (p106)
❸ Baie de Sakalava (p161)
❹ Mahambo (p92)
❺ Northern Reef (p133)

COMOROS

Mayotte (France)

Mozambique Channel

Sofia River

Mahajamba River

Betsiboka River

Lac Kinkony

Soalala

Besalampy

Tamboharano

Maintirano

Parc National Bemaraha

Katsepy

Marovoay

Parc National Ankarafantsika

Ambondromany

Maevatanana

Soalala

Boriziny (Port Bergé)

Antsohihy

Bealanana

Ambanja

Ankify

Hell-Ville

Nosy Be

Ambodibonara

Ambilobe

Diego Suarez (Antsiranana)

Parc National de Montagne d'Ambre

Parc National de l'Ankarana

Sambava

Tsaratanana Massif

Maromokotro

Andapa

Parc National Marojejy

Antalaha

Cap Est

Marojejy Massif

Maroantsetra

Parc National Masoala-Nosy Mangabe

Masoala Peninsula

Baie d'Antongil

Mananara

Île Sainte Marie

Mandritsara

Parc National Mananara-Nord

Soanierana-Ivongo

Vohipeno

Lac Alaotra

Ambatondrazaka

Vohiojala

Parc National Zahamena

Mahambo

Tamatave (Toamasina)

INDIAN OCEAN

Walking/Hiking

1. Parc National Andringitra (p83)
2. Parc National Marojejy (p167)
3. Parc National Bemaraha (p129)
4. Parc National Isalo (p68)
5. Zafimaniry villages (p68)

Beaches

1. Anakao (p104)
2. Île aux Nattes (Nosy Nato) (p200)
3. Salary (p101)
4. Nosy Iranja (p150)
5. Libanona (p107)

Snorkelling/Diving

1. Nosy Be (p142)
2. Ifaty/Mangily (p103)
3. Anakao (p104)
4. Île Sainte Marie (p196)
5. Parc National Marin de Nosy Tanikely (p147)

MADAGASCAR

THE GUIDE

Chapters in this section are organised by hubs and their surrounding areas. We see the hub as your base in the destination, where you'll find unique experiences, local insights, insider tips and expert recommendations. It's also your gateway to the surrounding area, where you'll see what and how much you can do from there.

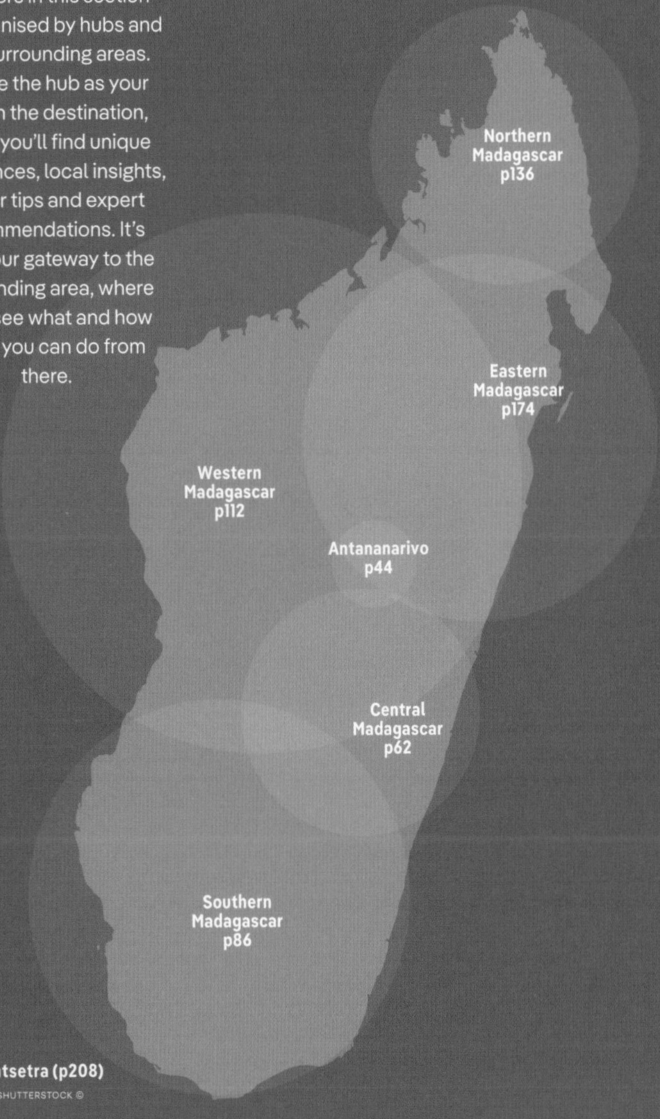

Northern Madagascar p136
Eastern Madagascar p174
Western Madagascar p112
Antananarivo p44
Central Madagascar p62
Southern Madagascar p86

Maroantsetra (p208)

ENGEL.AC/SHUTTERSTOCK ©

ANTANANARIVO

VIBRANT CAPITAL OF HIGHS AND LOWS

Love it or hate it, historic, manic, absorbing Antananarivo never fails to leave a lasting impression.

Antananarivo is an enigma. In the right light, Tana, as the capital is universally known, can be quite beautiful, with its hotchpotch of colourful terraced houses, glittering lakes, purple clouds of blossoming jacaranda trees, and a patchwork of rice fields that intermingles with the city limits.

And yet Tana is often given short shrift by travellers. Many are put off from staying here entirely by the polluted, overcrowded city centre, with its dreadful traffic and well-earned reputation as a dangerous place to wander after dark – on most itineraries, Tana is relegated to the role of necessary stop-off en route to more enticing parts of the country.

But bypassing the capital would be a mistake. Madagascar's political and economic centre, Tana has been the home of Malagasy power for 300 years – nowhere else in the country can you gain such an insight into the kings and queens who unified the island's tribes.

The city is best explored in the same way that it developed: from top to bottom. The ridgetop Haute-Ville, home to the Rova (fortified palace) of Antananarivo, is an aesthetic blend of Malagasy houses, British churches and French colonial architecture. Unesco believes the area 'has no equivalent in sub-Saharan Africa' and is currently considering it for World Heritage status. There are more echoes of the country's colonial past in the Basse-Ville, once little more than marshland but now a city-centre sprawl of wide boulevards and jam-packed markets – the area's problems are indicative of a population that is growing 60 percent faster than the rest of the country.

At the other end of the spectrum, Tana is by far the best place in the country to experience contemporary Malagasy culture, with an emergent arts scene and several thriving cultural centres. The capital is also *the* place in Madagascar to treat yourself to a fine meal, with the French-Malagasy fusion cuisine at some establishments rivalling Europe's Michelin-starred restaurants, but without the price tag.

Welcome to Tana, a city that – in the words of an old Malagasy proverb – is very much 'like the chameleon; one eye on the future, one eye on the past'.

DENNIS VAN DE WATER/SHUTTERSTOCK ®

THE MAIN AREAS

HAUTE-VILLE	BASSE-VILLE	AROUND ANTANANARIVO
Tana's historic quarter. p48	Buzzy core of the colonial capital. p56	Sacred heartland of the Merina. p59

ERIC VALENNE GEOSTORY/SHUTTERSTOCK ©

Find Your Way

Tana is a city of levels: the flat, sprawling Basse-Ville and then the ridges rising up from this reclaimed marshland. The Moyen-Ville that spreads across the lower slopes is a stepping stone to the historic hilltop Haute-Ville.

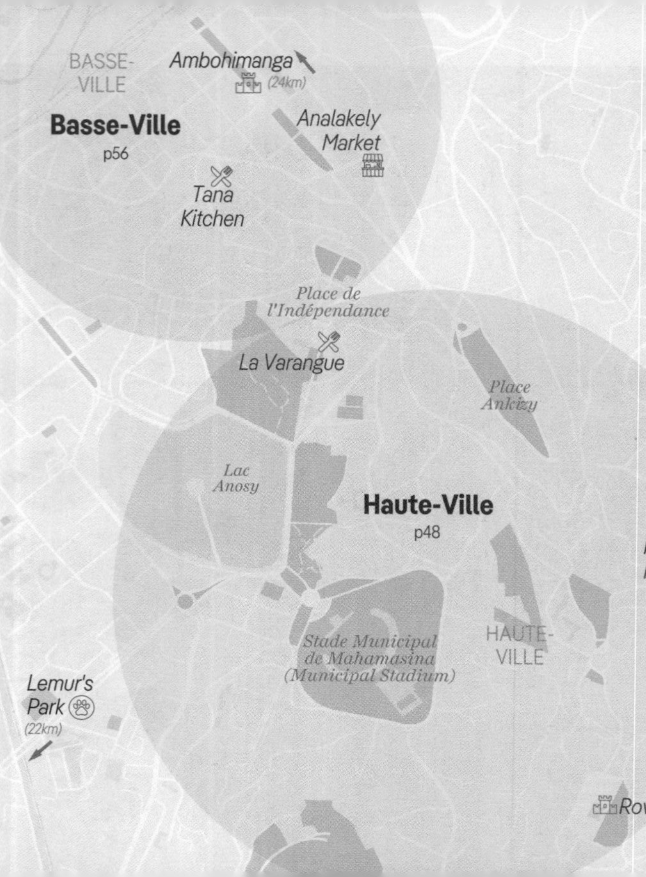

BASSE-VILLE

Basse-Ville
p56

Ambohimanga 🏛 (24km)

Analakely Market 🏬

🍴 Tana Kitchen

Place de l'Indépendance

🍴 La Varangue

Place Ankey

Haute-Ville
p48

Lac Anosy

Stade Municipal de Mahamasina (Municipal Stadium)

HAUTE-VILLE

Musée de la Photo Madagascar 🏛

🏛 Rova

Lemur's Park ⊛ (22km)

N ⌖ 0
0

500 m
0.25 miles

FROM THE AIRPORT

Ivato Airport is 13km northwest of the city centre. You can pick up an official metered taxi outside arrivals or arrange a transfer with your hotel.

TAXIS & TAXI-BES

Tana's cream-coloured taxis are plentiful and cheap. It is not safe to walk after dark; always travel by taxi at night. The most useful *taxi-be* (large minivan) route is the 134, served by silver minivans with a black stripe, which runs between the Rova and Analakely.

Analakely Market (p57)

Plan Your Days

Split your time between the pastel-painted tumbledown houses of the Haut-Ville and the Basse-Ville's thrumming markets. It's worth venturing beyond the city limits to visit Ambohimanga, the cradle of modern Merina society.

Overnight Stopover

Head straight for the hilltop **Haute-Ville** (p48) to immerse yourself in Tana's most historic quarter, taking in the **Rova** (p49), the **Cathédrale de l'Immaculée Conception** (p55) and the **Musée de la Photo Madagascar** (p50). Or, to avoid spending too much of your time stuck in Tana's notorious traffic, stay at one of the hotels out near the airport and visit **Ambohimanga** (p60), a Unesco World Heritage site.

Two Days to Explore

Enjoy a **walking tour** (p55) of the Haute-Ville, then soak up some culture at the city's **art galleries** (p51) or the **Institut Français Madagascar** (p58). You can't go wrong with dinner at one of the capital's excellent French-Malagasy restaurants. Browse the Moyenne-Ville's **boutiques** (p52) and the piled-high stalls at **Analakely Market** (p57); for a unique souvenir, visit the incredible community workshop of **Atelier de Violette & Dieudonné** (p60).

You'll Also Want to...

POP INTO A PATISSERIE

Tana is in a league of its own when it comes to cakes and pastries – those with a sweet tooth swear by **Bread Mafan'** (p53).

CATCH A SHOW

Visit **Fondation H** (p51) or **Hakanto Contemporary** (p51) for thought-provoking art, or catch a **hira gasy performance** (p53).

LEARN TO COOK

Whip up a three-course Malagasy meal at **Tana Kitchen** (p49); you can even help them shop for the ingredients.

HAUTE-VILLE

TANA'S HISTORIC QUARTER

Spreading down the slopes of Tana's highest hill, the Haute-Ville, or Upper Town, is the capital's historic heart. King Adrianjaka founded the city here in 1610, stationing a garrison of troops on the hill and renaming it Antananarivo, 'Place of 1000 Warriors'. It's still home to some of the most impressive historic sights in the country, most notably the Rova, visible from miles around. Extending along the ridge to Andohalo and Faravohitra, the area is a colourful mishmash of Asian influences, European designs and Malagasy beliefs. Look out for the tiled-roofed buildings, known as *trano gasy*, which became the style of choice for Tana's noble classes in the late 1800s. During the early French colonial period, a Moyenne-Ville, or Middle Town, developed across the lower slopes; this is now a great place to base yourself in Tana, with a glut of hotels and trendy restaurants.

TOP TIP

At 1460m above sea level, the Haute-Ville is noticeably cooler than downtown Tana. It's very hilly, with *plenty* of stairs, but the views from the top are superb – try the lookouts below the Rova and behind the Cathédrale de l'Immaculée Conception in Andohalo.

HIGHLIGHTS
1 La Varangue
2 Musée de la Photo Madagascar
3 Rova

SIGHTS
4 Fondation H
5 Is'art Gallerie

6 Jardin d'Ambohijatovo
7 Jardin d'Antananarenina

ACTIVITIES & TOURS
8 Akany Avoko Faravohitra (AAF)
9 Balnéoforme Spa
10 Centre Fihavanana

11 Le Royal Palissandre Spa
12 Spa du Louvre
13 'Wednesday Children' Centre

ENTERTAINMENT
14 Ivon-toeran'ny Kolontsaina Malagasy (IKM)

15 Kianjan'ny Kanto

SHOPPING
16 Kawaii Mode
17 La Ferme de Morarano d'Ambatolampy
18 La Tee-shirterie
19 Lisy Art Gallery
20 Roses & Baobab

Explore the Rova of Antananarivo

HISTORIC HQ OF MALAGASY KINGS AND QUEENS

Visible throughout the city, the Rova (fortified palace) of Antananarivo was the seat of power of Merina kings and queens for nearly 300 years, its authority only fading when the French abolished the monarchy in 1896.

The complex is dominated by the Queen's Palace, the Manjakamiadana (A Fine Place to Rule), which was built for Ranavalona I by the French engineer Jean Laborde in 1841. The outer stone structure – the first of its kind in Tana – was added in 1867 by the Scottish missionary James Cameron, although the roof and interior remained wooden. Gutted by a fire in 1995, it has been under endless restoration for years but is finally rescheduled to reopen as a museum in 2024.

Succeeding rulers built (and destroyed) a number of other palaces on the premises, including the traditional wooden Besakana, where sovereigns were enthroned, and Mahitsielafanjaka, the residence of King Andrianampoinimerina after he moved his capital here from Ambohimanga; both buildings have been fully restored following the fire. North of this, to the left of the main gate, lie the tombs of the country's greatest monarchs; the plain grey ones are those of kings, while the queens' are painted red (the colour of nobility).

Remember that it is *fady* (taboo) to point your finger directly at the royal tombs or the palace itself; photography is also forbidden on the site.

THE GUIDE

ANTANANARIVO

THE 'CRUEL QUEEN'

The first female sovereign of the Merina Kingdom, **Ranavalona I**'s reign (1828–61) was marked by war, disease, forced labour and religious persecution. Her brutal rule – during which the country's population was reduced by half – earned her the nicknames the Cruel Queen and the Mad Monarch of Madagascar.

Ranavalona was already pursuing a policy of isolationism when, in 1835, she outlawed Christianity; any Malagasy caught practising the religion was fined, jailed, poisoned or executed.

Memorial churches now mark the spots where the queen had her victims burned (at Ambatonakanga) or thrown from cliffs (at nearby Tsimihatsaka).

Rova of Antananarivo

FRAMALICIOUS/SHUTTERSTOCK ©

FROM ONE ROVA TO ANOTHER

The first capital of the unified Merina Kingdom, **Ambohimanga** (p60) tops a hill 21km north of Antananarivo. Its *rova* is home to the King's Palace, from where Andrianampoinimerina ruled before moving his capital to Tana.

Fine-Dining at La Varangue

ATMOSPHERIC SETTING FOR FUSION FOOD

One of the best addresses in Tana for a real gourmet dining experience, La Varangue elaborately fuses French gastronomy and Malagasy flavours. Exquisitely presented meals are served either in the beautiful dining room, with its low lighting and fabulous antique collection, or on the veranda *(varangue)*, which overlooks a charming garden. Highlights from the menu include duck aiguillette with *cromesquis* curry and green mango or seafood en papillote with lemongrass scent. Look out for the vintage cars in the courtyard on your way in.

Tenderloin with Madagascar sauce

Photo Synthesis

SNAPSHOTS OF MALAGASY LIFE

Set across the former Mayor of Antananarivo's house, in the upper reaches of the Haute-Ville, the contemporary **Musée de la Photo Madagascar** is Antananarivo's best museum. Whitewashed walls provide a canvas for temporary exhibitions that focus on Malagasy themes or moments in history, while several small rooms showing films (in English) offer a fascinating window on the country's past.

Previous exhibitions have included the chic black-and-white portraiture work of Malagasy photographer Ramilijaona, whose family left the museum 50,000 of his glass negatives, and the *lamba*, the ubiquitous Malagasy silk shawl. Exhibitions usually spill over into the museum's pretty garden and excellent cafe.

Antananarivo

WHY I LOVE TANA

Keith Drew, writer

Tana is dismissed by some visitors as being too noisy, too gritty, too intense. But this is exactly what draws me back to the capital each time. I love squeezing through ramshackle Analakely Market, joining locals haggling over unidentifiable cuts of zebu meat, and catching exotic aromas from the stalls selling dried fish and herbal medicines. Then hopping on a crowded *taxi-be* up to the historic monuments in the Haute-Ville, or out to Ambohimanga to soak up the sense of powers past in the palace of King Andrianampoinimerina. There's nowhere better to work up an appetite, either – Tana's Malagasy-French dining scene is by far the best in the country.

MORE IN HAUTE-VILLE

Culture in the Capital

GALLERIES AND CULTURAL CENTRES

Tana has the best cultural scene in the country, with a number of art galleries spread across the capital and several institutes that host changing exhibitions and Malagasy events.

Its newest hub, **Fondation H** (closed Mon), opened in April 2023 in the city's former post office on Rue Refotana. Owned by art collector Hassanein Hiridjee, the foundation's inaugural annual show was dedicated to the late Madame Zo (Zoarinivo Razakaratrimo) and her creative takes on traditional weaving.

There are more thought-provoking works at **Hakanto Contemporary**, an arts centre in Ankadimbahoaka, 4.5km south of the Haute-Ville (see map on p59). The exhibitions and artists' residencies here tend to explore the idea of Malagasy identity, the creative fixation of its founder Joël Andrianomearisoa, who became the first artist from Madagascar to exhibit at the prestigious Venice Biennale in 2019.

Is'art Gallerie, in Ampasanimalo, a kilometre or so east of the Haute-Ville, showcases the work of local

MORE ART AND CULTURAL EVENTS

See work by Joël Andrianomearisoa outside the **Town Hall** (p58) or pick up a wrought-iron sculpture at the **Atelier de Violette & Dieudonné** (p60). Cultural events are hosted by the **Institut Français Madagascar** (p58).

 WHERE TO STAY IN THE HAUTE-VILLE

Sakamanga
Perennial favourite offering a range of accommodation. Artefact-stuffed corridors lead to a pool with terrace. **$$**

Madagascar Underground
A hostel buzz unlike anywhere else in Madagascar. Excellent rooms, and male and female dorms. Dorms **$**, rooms **$$**

La Résidence Lapasoa
Beautifully restored 19th-century building with a modern twist on colonial decor. Top-floor rooms are loveliest. **$$$**

ARIADNE VAN ZANDBERGEN/ALAMY STOCK PHOTO ©

Lemon and mango chutneys

FANORONA

Throughout Antananarivo, you'll see groups of men gathered together, absorbed in *fanorona*, a game of strategy that dates back to the seventeenth century. Often compared to chess, *fanorona* is played on a wooden board, engraved with markings that are likened to a spider's web – although in Tana the 'board' is often scratched into the pavement, with players using anything handy (seeds, stones, broken bits of ceramic) for pieces.

Games can last for hours, as an important part of play is *manalavela*, the concept of giving your opponent a chance: if you have nine pieces left and your opponent has two, for example, you are obliged to give them some of yours. Only if you are victorious for a second consecutive time are you declared the winner.

contemporary artists, with monthly exhibitions as well as workshops. Regulars include visual artist Andre Anjoanina, Taka Andrianavalona and graffiti artist Clipse Teean. The gallery also hosts live music on Friday nights.

You'll get the best introduction to contemporary Malagasy culture at **Ivon-toeran'ny Kolontsaina Malagasy** (**IKM**), the Malagasy Cultural Centre, in Antsahavola, which hosts screenings and discussions (in French) from Malagasy filmmakers, slam sessions, poetry, and musical showcases. Similar events, from emerging artists, are scheduled by the **Centre de Resources des Arts Actuels de Madagascar** (**CRAAM**) (see map on p59), at the University of Antananarivo in Ankatso, every Wednesday and Friday afternoon.

Shop Till You Drop

BROWSE BOUTIQUES AND STOCK UP ON SOUVENIRS

Antananarivo has, unsurprisingly, the widest range of shops in the country, with plenty of excellent places to snag a souvenir before your flight home.

You can pick up one of Madagascar's funky T-shirts at **La Tee-shirterie** on Rue Adrianary Ratianarivo, which stocks all the main brands (Baobab Company, Carambolé, Maki) and has a large selection of styles. Further up the hill, the boutiques in

 WHERE TO STAY IN THE HAUTE-VILLE

Hotel Niaouly
Punching well above its weight for the price, the pretty rooms feature polished wooden floors and Malagasy crafts. **$**

Le Cocooning
Eager-to-please hotel on a busy street, with airy rooms and a Reunionese restaurant. **$$**

Citizen Guest House
Quiet sophistication: three gorgeous rooms, sprinkled with antiques, with balconies overlooking Lac Anosy. **$$$**

Isoraka are worth a browse; look for the capital's latest fashion trends at **Kawaii Mode**, on Rue Dok Villette. The super cheery staff at **La Ferme de Morarano d'Ambatolampy**, on Rue de Russie (the next street along to the west), will gladly guide you through their colourful collection of essential oils, jams, chutneys and the like, which are all handmade on their farm in the central highlands village of Ambatolampy. Back down the hill, **Roses & Baobab**, on Rue 77 Parlementaires Français in Antsahavola, is a collective of local artists showcasing sculptures, woodcarvings, paintings, metalwork and more. The quality varies, but it's worth poking your way around the warren of rooms in search of treasure.

If you're looking for a one-stop-shop, head out to **Lisy Art Gallery**, on Rue VVS in Antanimora, about 1.5km east of the Moyen-Ville. This huge shop stocks just about anything you could possibly want to bring back from Madagascar, from paintings and leather goods to raffia baskets and *fanorona* boards. It's also a good place to buy a bottle of *rhum arrangé* (rum with macerated fruit), with at least a dozen flavours on offer.

Spa-ing Partners

FACIALS, EXFOLIANTS AND COCONUT MASSAGES

Spas, massages and treatments are good value in Tana – and the perfect remedy if you've just arrived back in the capital after some hard hiking. For a truly indulgent experience, try the **Balnéoforme Spa** at Hôtel Colbert, on Rue Prince Ratsimamanga, with its mosaic swimming pool, Finnish sauna and Turkish hammam; treatments here use essential oils infused with herbs and spices from across the country. The gorgeous **Le Royal Palissandre Spa**, on Rue Andriandahifotsy, has a similar set-up, with a heated outdoor pool and hammam, and is a good place to come for a facial or a seaweed body scrub. In a 1930s building designed by the Gustave Eiffel group (of Eiffel Tower fame), the **Spa du Louvre** offers a range of relaxing massages (hot stones, bamboo and coconut) and hosts aquagym sessions in its atmospheric indoor pool.

Hira Gasy: Performance Art

STORYTELLING SHOWS OF SONG AND DANCE

Hira gasy ('Malagasy song') are popular music, dancing and storytelling spectacles that originated in the central highlands. Brightly clad troupes – the men in red tunics (a nod to French colonial dress), the women in colourful *lambas* (scarves) –

IN THE MARKET

There are several **markets** in the Basse-Ville and out towards the airport – including **Analakely Market** (p57), the largest of its kind in the country – where you can buy clothes, herbs and a variety of souvenir goods.

WALKING TOURS

The friendly folk at Tana's ORTANA regional tourist offices run guided tours of the capital twice a day on Mondays, Wednesdays and Saturdays (mornings only in the rainy season). Book at their kiosk in the Jardin d'Antananarena for a one-hour circuit around the Moyen-Ville, taking in Antananarenina and Ambatonakanga, or a two-hour tour that also ventures further up the hill to Amparibe and Faravohitra. Tours from their kiosk on Place Andohalo explore the historic monuments of the Haute-Ville, including the Palais Andafivaratra, the Cathédrale de l'Immaculée Conception and the Rova (entry fees are not included).

WHERE TO EAT IN THE HAUTE-VILLE

Bread Mafan'	**Le Saka**	**Nerone Ristorane Italiano**
Part patisserie, part cafe, with seriously good breads and a finger-licking range of pastries and cakes. **$**	This Tana institution, chockful of artwork, strikes the perfect balance between gastro French and local cooking. **$$**	Cosy, rustic Italian trattoria with a good selection of *primeri* and *segundi* courses, plus proper pizzas. **$$$**

THE BEST BARS IN TANA

Jeannie Claudia Randrianasolo is a guide specialising in tours of Antananarivo and Ambohimanga.

Irish Pub Tana
A good location in Ambohijatovo, with great views of the city centre, especially from the veranda. There are regular happy hours, and every week they suggest new tasting sessions for drinks or food from all over the world.

Outcool Web Bar
This place in Ampasamadinika is really cosy and has a nice ambiance: the staff are welcoming and there's always good music being played. It's my favourite place to hang out with friends after work.

no comment bar
This bar in Isoraka has a large choice of drinks and cocktails – I like coming here for a sundowner. They also have live music shows, with different artists and styles of music.

perform social themes to a backdrop of violins, trumpets and drums. An important part of *hira gasy* is *kabary*, in which a performer delivers an oratory using allegory, double entendre, metaphor and simile.

Despite the performances being solely in Malagasy, this is a cultural event well worth seeing. Shows are held every Sunday at the **Kianjan'ny Kanto**, next to the Municipal Stadium in Mahamasina. From July to October, Tana's ORTANA regional tourist office also organises a free *hira gasy* on Sunday afternoons; check for the latest venue, as shows have previously been held at the Rova and in the Jardin d'Ambohijatovo.

Green Spaces
THE LUNGS OF THE CITY

Tana doesn't have many proper public green spaces, so leafy **Jardin d'Antananarenina** (Place de l'Indépendance) comes (literally) as a breath of fresh air after the dust of downtown, particularly when its jacaranda trees are in full purple bloom. You can often see people gathered under the trees here playing games of *fanorona* (p52). The gardens are reached via the Stairs of Ranovana, built by Queen Ranovana I in 1861 to provide access to the market at Analakely. The larger **Jardin d'Ambohijatovo**, on the border between the Moyen-Ville and the Basse-Ville, to the southeast, is also a pleasant place to wander. Its name means 'Corner of the Young Ones', although it's now more popular with families, especially at weekends.

Giving Something Back
LEND VITAL SUPPORT TO CHILDREN'S CENTRES

The impact of Madagascar's crushing poverty is unfortunately all too evident on the capital's streets, but there are several initiatives where you can help make a difference. **Akany Avoko Faravohitra** (**AAF**), on Rue Joël Rakotomala, provides refuge for destitute girls, offering them food, shelter, healthcare and education. At the **Centre Fihavanana**, a day centre run by nuns in Mahamasina, vulnerable children are given catch-up lessons to help get them back into mainstream schools, while the **'Wednesday Children' Centre**, held at the church in Isotry, feeds around 400 street kids and assists their parents with finding work and accommodation.

You can learn about the centres' inspiring efforts on a short visit (arrange in advance with Money for Madagascar) and lend your support by buying some of the items the children produce, such as basketry and embroidered linen. Gifts of stationery, sewing materials, first-aid kits or leftover ariary are greatly appreciated.

 WHERE TO EAT IN THE HAUTE-VILLE

Toko Telo
Expert Malagasy dishes such as zebu *romazava*; and, for the adventurous, *zanadandy* (fried caterpillars). **$$**

La Petite Brasserie
Expect hearty, wholesome cooking at this dark-wood bistro. Worth visiting for its charcuterie and wine list. **$$**

Le Citizen
Fine French-Malagasy dining overlooking Lac Anosy, with attentive service and some superb French wines. **$$$**

This walk starts at the **1 viewpoint below the Rova**, from where it's easy to understand why the city's rulers decided to build their palace on this lofty hilltop: the Malagasy landscape unfolds in every direction. Slightly downhill, on your right-hand side, is the striking **2 Palais de Justice d'Ambatondrafandrana**, an Ionic-style courthouse that would look more at home in Ancient Athens than Antananarivo. Built by James Parret for Queen Ranavalona II in 1881, it was designed so the rulings of the court could be heard by all.

Keep heading downhill to the magnificent baroque **3 Palais d'Andafivaratra**, which served as the grand home of Prime Minister Rainilaiarivony, the power behind the throne of the three queens he married in succession (Rasoherina, Ranavalona II and Ranavalona III) between 1864 and 1895; the **4 Church of Ambonin' Ampamarinana**, directly below you

to the southwest, was built in 1819 on the spot where Ranavalona I ordered Christian martyrs to be hurled from the cliffs at Tsmihatsaka. Wend your way down to the **5 Cathédrale de l'Immaculée Conception**, which contains relics of the Twelve Apostles and is back-ended by an enormous statue of the Virgin Mary, gazing out across some of the best views in Tana (ask the *gardien* to unlock the gate).

Turn left onto Rue Ramilijaona and then follow the steps down past the **6 Association Fanambinantsoa**, the district's water station, usually busy with washerwomen – only a third or so of Tana's residents have access to running water. From here, amble down to **7 Rue Ratsimilaho**, famous for its jewellers, then turn left on to Lalana Printsy Ratsimamanga to finish your walk at the former **8 Presidential Palace**, with its white, green and red sentry boxes that match the Malagasy flag colours.

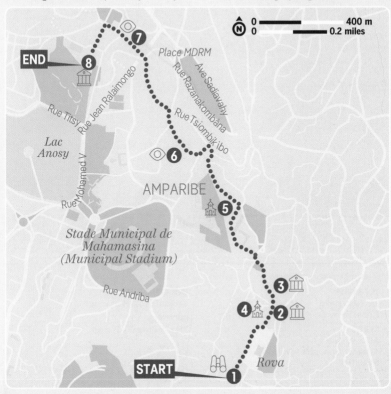

BASSE-VILLE

BUZZY CORE OF THE COLONIAL CAPITAL

Just over a century ago, what now constitutes Tana's downtown area – the Basse-Ville, or Lower Town – was little more than a patchwork of rice fields and marshland. In the early 1900s, the French drained twenty hectares to create present-day Analakely and the gridded district of Tsaralalana to its west. A monumental boulevard was built, the Ave Fallières (present-day Ave de l'Indépendance) along with a grand train station, and the city's population boomed.

Ave de l'Indépendance is still the area's hub today, connecting the cultural enclaves of Tsaralana, a predominantly Indian neighbourhood, and Behoririka, a Chinese quarter that is on the verge of becoming the capital's official Chinatown. The Basse-Ville is hot, dirty and traffic-clogged, but it thrums with the chaotic energy of everyday life – Analakely Market, at the other end of Ave de l'Indépendance, is the Basse-Ville's beating heart and its one unmissable sight.

TOP TIP

The markets in the Basse-Ville are popular with pickpockets – don't bring any valuables with you, and if you do bring a bag, wear it on your front, placing anything that you might need to carry (wallet, mobile phone, etc) securely inside.

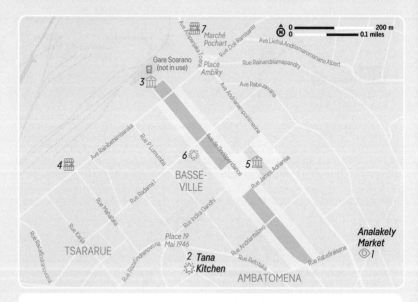

TOP SIGHTS
1 Analakely Market
2 Tana Kitchen

SIGHTS
3 Gare Soarano
4 Marché Communal de Petit Vitesse
5 Town Hall

ENTERTAINMENT
6 Institut Français Madagascar

SHOPPING
7 Marché Communal Pochard

Browse the Stalls at Analakely Market

PAVILIONS PACKED WITH PRODUCE

Teeming, aromatic Analakely Market is a fascinating insight into everyday local life. The oldest and biggest open-air market in the country, it was founded by King Andrianampoinimerina, who moved the Friday (*zoma*) market down here from Andohalo, where it had been the preserve of the Royal Family and the noble classes. What was once a 'little forest' (*ala kely*) is now home to a swathe of tiled-roof pavilions and surrounding stalls, each one operating beneath a brightly coloured parasol.

There are around 250 stores here, selling clothes, household items and just about every food product you could imagine – plus a few you probably couldn't. Wander among the fruit and vegetable sellers, with their stacks of lychees and bunches of medicinal herbs, and the stalls specialising in beans and spices; look out for the *kapoakas* (old cans of condensed milk and pureed tomatoes that are used as measuring devices). In the fish market, you'll see tilapia from the lakes around Tana and fat eels from Morondava; in the rows of butcher stalls, you'll find every conceivable part of the zebu on display.

Spices, Analakey Market

SWEETHOUR/SHUTTERSTOCK ©

WHAT'S COOKING?

If all the fresh produce on display at Analakely Market has stirred your creative culinary juices, then you can sign up for a cookery class at **Tana Kitchen** and learn how to prepare and cook a traditional three-course Malagasy lunch. It's run by local chef Landi, an engaging and knowledgeable teacher. If you arrange it in advance, you can also visit a local market for the necessary ingredients beforehand. Tana Kitchen is on Rue Jean Jaurès, a couple of streets back from Ave de l'Independance.

Scan this QR code to find out more about Tana Kitchen.

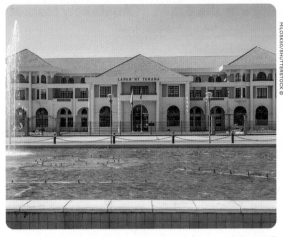

Town Hall

MORE MARKETS IN THE BASSE-VILLE

Marché Communal Pochard
Two markets for the price of one: clothes (Palm Angels tees and football shirts) in the main entrance on Place Ambiky and, further down Rue Ampanjaka Toera, crafts from across the country.

Marché Communal de Petit Vitesse
A mix of traditional healers' stalls and electronic goods, along Arabe Rainibertsimisaraka. A bit rough around the edges – if your phone's been stolen in Tana, this is where you'll find it.

Marché Artisanal de la Digue
Bargain hard for souvenirs (raffia bags, woodcarvings, leatherwork and the like) at this popular stop on the way to the airport.

MORE IN BASSE-VILLE

French Tana

LEGACIES OF THE COLONIAL ERA

Built in 1912 by the French colonial administration, the wide, Parisian-style boulevard of Ave de l'Independance is a quirk among the narrow, tangled streets of Tana. The commercial arcades on either side were added in 1935 and still bear the faded French names of their original occupants. You'll find the **Institut Français Madagascar**, Antananarivo's foremost cultural venue, under one of the arches on the western side.

The avenue became the traditional place to protest during the political crises that engulfed the country between 1972 and 2009. The **Town Hall**, or Lapan'ny Tanana, halfway along, was burnt down by university students in 1972 and only rebuilt (in its original style) in 2019. The geometric sculpture installed outside, titled *Eto Isika*, is a poetic piece by Joël Andrianomearisoa that points to a brighter future. It reads: 'From Here We Convey the Dreams of the World'.

At the avenue's north-western end, beautiful **Gare Soarano**, completed in 1910, is reminiscent of the old railway stations of small-town France. The last passenger trains rolled out in the mid-1990s, and its more recent lease of life, as an upmarket shopping centre, seems all but over, too. The marker outside the front of the station, KM 0, is from where all distances on Madagascar's roads are measured.

 WHERE TO STAY IN THE BASSE-VILLE

Chez Aina
Inhabiting a traditional Malagasy home, with five beautifully decorated rooms and a gorgeous garden. **$$**

Mandrosoa
Colourful *maison d'hôtes* just up the Tavao staircase. Stylish rooms, plus a lovely pool in the pretty garden. **$$**

Les Trois Metis
Old Tana residence that once housed the US embassy. Good-sized rooms (with balconies) and a great restaurant. **$$$**

AROUND
ANTANANARI

SACRED HEARTLAND OF THE MERINA

The highlands around Antananarivo are often ignored by tr
ellers pushing on to other parts of Madagascar, but the who
area is perfect day-trip country.

The region is known as Imerina (Land of the Merina Tribe) and
is a rural patchwork of rice fields and undulating ridges. The most
prominent of these have been dubbed the Twelve Sacred Hills of
Imerina, summit states (which also included Analamanga in Tana's Haute-Ville) that waged war on one another until King Andrianampoinimerina unified them in 1887.

Two of the sacred hills are easily accessible from the city: Ambohimanga, listed as a Unesco World Heritage Site in 2001, and
the hilltop hunting lodge of Radama II at Ilafy.

st a night or two
between flights, it can
be a good idea (given
Tana's terrible traffic)
to stay in the village-
suburb of Ivato, around
13km north-west of the
city centre. There are
some excellent hotels
here and you're just a
few kilometres from the
airport.

TOP SIGHTS
1 Ambohimanga
2 Lemurs' Park

SIGHTS
3 Hakanto Contemporary
4 Ilafy

5 Le Village

ACTIVITIES
6 Atelier de Violette
& Dieudonné

ENTERTAINMENT
7 Centre de Resources des
Arts Actuels de Madagascar
(CRAAM)

SHOPPING
8 Marché Artisanal de la Digue

were
...shed around the
...th century, and by the
late 19th century they
were the dominant tribe
in Madagascar.

Merina hierarchy was
based on a three-tier
caste system: the
andriana (fairer-
skinned and with
pronounced Asiatic
rather than African
features) comprised
the nobility, while the
hova (commoners)
made up the middle
class. The remainder –
descendants of former
slaves – were known as
the *andevo* (workers).

The Merina's position
was enhanced by the
choice of Antananarivo
as the seat of the French
colonial government,
and today many
remain at the forefront
of public life: recent
former presidents
Hery Rajaonarimam-
pianina and Marc
Ravalomanana, and
the current president
Andry Rajoelina, are all
Merina.

Explore the Royal Hill of Ambohimanga

PALACES OF KINGS AND QUEENS

Ambohimanga ('Blue Hill'), 21km north of Tana, was the original capital of the Merina royal family. Even after the seat of government was shifted to Antananarivo, it remained a sacred site and was off-limits to foreigners for many years.

The entrance to the Rova is marked by a traditional gateway, which was sealed off (by up to 40 slaves) with a *vavahady*, the 30-tonne granite disc 'door' to its side. Inside the compound is the very simple but striking palace of King Andrianampoin-imerina (r. 1787–1810), a dirt-floored wooden building of black palisander wood. Among the king's belongings on display are his tiny throne and his bed, positioned in the northeast corner (the north is considered sacred) and elevated to indicate his superior status. It is tradition to enter the palace with your right foot and exit, backwards, with your left, so as not to turn your back on the king.

Next door are the elegant summer palaces, beautifully restored and with original European furniture. They were built in 1871 for Queen Ranovana II, but were also used by Ranovana III – the dining room was lined with mirrors to allegedly allow Ranovana II to check that no one was poisoning her food .

Ambohimanga is still revered by many Malagasy as a sacred site. You will see offerings (zebu skulls, candles, honey) at various shrines around the compound, as well as fish, left as 'lucky' gifts, in the open-air baths behind the palace, where the king performed his annual royal ablutions.

MILOSK50/SHUTTERSTOCK ©

Ambohimanga

Art with Heart

WORTHY COMMUNITY WORKSHOP

Part weird and wonderful souvenir showroom, part groundbreaking social enterprise, the **Atelier de Violette & Dieudonné**, in Ankazobe Alasora, 6km southeast of the Haute-Ville, is unlike anything else in Antananarivo. Dieudonné Razafinjatovo trained as an iron worker in Paris and, together with

his wife Violette Ralalaseheno, founded this highly worthy workshop in 1996, which provides employment to some of the most disadvantaged people in the neighbourhood.

You can watch the metalworkers – many of them vision impaired or with other disabilities – fashion

recycled oil drums into baobab sculptures, giant cacti and other unique objects, which are then displayed for sale in the main building. The workshop also provides its employees with housing, schooling for their children, and daily meals using produce grown on their organic farm.

Sacred Hill of Ilafy

HUNTING LODGE TURNED MUSEUM

Another of the Twelve Sacred Hills of Imerina, **Ilafy** was founded around the turn of the 17th century on a peak 12km northeast of Tana. It was used as a hunting lodge by Radama II, whose body was initially buried in a modest tomb on the grounds before being transferred to the Rova of Antananarivo. Reconstructed in 1957 after the original had fallen into disrepair, the lodge now houses an interesting ethnographic museum (closed Mon).

A Model Village

BOAT-BUILDERS' BOUTIQUE

The highly skilled artisans at **Le Village**, a boat-making workshop in Talatamaty, 6km south of the airport, craft intricate scale models of historic ships, fishing boats and famous vessels. You can watch the artists at work (weekdays only) and visit the showroom to see remarkably accurate replicas, including *HMS Bounty* and *HMS Endeavour*, the ship in which Captain James Cook first travelled to Australia.

Wildlife Within Easy Reach

RESERVE FOR RESCUED LEMURS

Nestled on a bend of the River Katsaoka, 22km west of the capital, **Lemurs' Park** is a beautiful private wildlife reserve that provides refuge to seven species of lemurs from across Madagascar, most of whom were either pets or had their habitat threatened. The reserve has a breeding program with an eye on reintroducing young lemurs back into the wild. Catch a taxi or book a transfer directly with the park; *taxis-brousses* run here from Anosibe.

TAXI

MOVING ON FROM TANA

The easiest way of moving around Madagascar is with a driver-guide (p214). If you're heading on from Antananarivo by public transport, the best bus service is Cotisse, opposite the Ambodivona bus station, whose smart Mercedes minivans run between Tana and Fianarantsoa, Majunga, Morondava and Toamasina.

MalagasyCar's comfortable, air-con vehicles depart from Hôtel Le Grand Mellis (for Majunga and Ankify) or from Motel Anosy (for Morondava).

The most useful *taxi-brousse* station is modern MAKI, in Andohatapenaka, with services to Andasibe, Diego Suarez, Majunga, Sambava and Toamasina.

The regional stations are in Ambodivona, 2km northeast of the centre (for the north); Ampasampito, 3.5km northeast of the centre (the east); and Fasan'ny Karana (the south), in Anosibe, 4km southwest of Lac Anosy.

THE GUIDE

ANTANANARIVO

 WHERE TO STAY NEAR THE AIRPORT —

Meva Guest House
Gorgeous guesthouse adjoining rice fields, with spacious rooms, kitchen access and a lovely garden. **$$**

San Cristobal
Good choice for an airport bolthole: swish modern rooms (most with great views) and a decent restaurant. **$$$**

Relais des Plateaux
Has enough add-ons – restaurant, pool, gym and spa – that you could easily not step foot outside its gates. **$$$**

CENTRAL MADAGASCAR

MADAGASCAR IN A NUTSHELL

Central Madagascar is the most easily accessible – and perhaps most diverse – part of the Great Red Island.

Many of Central Madagascar's most popular sights are condensed in a relatively small area either side of the tarmac ribbon of the Route Nationale 7 (RN7).

Wildlife buffs will be charmed by lemurs and chameleons in Réserve d'Anja and Parc National Ranomafana, and trekkers will find challenging multiday hikes through the isolated mountains of Parc National Andringitra or traditional communities in the Zafimaniry region. Take the FCE railways down to the eastern coast to experience humid rainforests, cascading jungle rivers and the meandering waterways of Canal des Pangalanes. The RN7 running from Antananarivo all the way southward beyond Ambalavao (500km) offers a chance to witness the steady transformation of tribal cultures, from the clustered red-brick hamlets of the Merina through the fortress-like houses of the Betsileo to the simple baked-mud bungalows of the Bara.

On market day the towns are rainbow-hued with Betsileo traders and shoppers dressed in their favoured Day-Glo outfits. Pretty pastel-coloured cottages and homesteads are decked with bougainvillea, roses and poinsettia (known locally as *madagascars* for the green leaves, red blooms and white sap that are said to represent the national flag). If Central Madagascar is your first taste of this wonderfully intriguing island, then it will be the ideal introduction. If it's the last stop...well, then it's sure to make you want to slow down and savour it.

HAJAKELY/SHUTTERSTOCK ©

THE MAIN AREAS

Above: Ranomafana (p78); left: Canal des Pangalanes (p85) 63

Find Your Way

We've uncovered the natural and cultural riches that are the highlights of Central Madagascar and defined the ideal hubs to make it easy to experience the very best the region has to offer.

TAXIS-BROUSSES

The commonest form of long-distance public transport is the ubiquitous *taxi-brousse* (bush taxis). They're invariably overcrowded but in the interests of safety try to pick one with only minimal overloading on the straining roof-racks.

CAR

Given the rough state of roads, car hire can be expensive. It's often more cost-effective to hire a car and driver (around Ar200,000 per day), since a good driver will function too as a guide/translator/fixer.

Ambositra, p66

The Betsileo art-and-craft capital, and access point to the mountain communities of Zafimaniry and the Merina city of Antsirabe.

Fianarantsoa, p74

Madagascar's most charming old town is the ideal base for Parc National Andringitra, and to visit Parc National Ranomafana's lemurs.

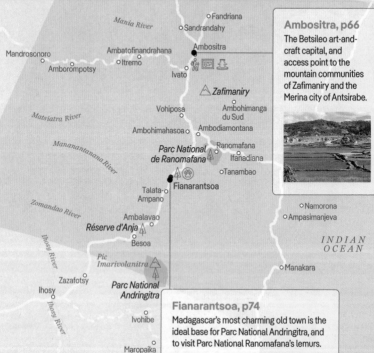

Map labels (geographic features and towns):

Tsiafahy
Lac Itasy
Ankaratra Massif
Ambatolampy
Ambohimandroso
Ampitatafika
Antanifotsy
Antsirabe
Vinanikarena
Mania River
Fandriana
Sandrandahy
Ambositra
Mandrosonoro
Ambatofinandrahana
Itremo
Amborompotsy
Ivato
Zafimaniry
Vohiposa
Ambohimanga du Sud
Matsiatra River
Ambohimahasoa
Ambodiamontana
Mananantanana River
Parc National de Ranomafana
Ranomafana
Ifanadiana
Tanambao
Talata-Ampano
Fianarantsoa
Zomandao River
Namorona
Ampasimanjeva
Ambalavao
Réserve d'Anja
Besoa
INDIAN OCEAN
Pic Imarivolanitra
Ihosy River
Zazafotsy
Manakara
Ihosy
Parc National Andringitra
Ihosy River
Ivohibe
Maropaika

0   50 km
N 0   25 miles

STEVE BARZE/SHUTTERSTOCK ©

Tsaranoro Valley (p83)

Plan Your Time

Central Madagascar has a lot to offer. Maximise your time so that you can experience the diversity of culture and nature that is the essence of this region.

Pressed for Time

Base yourself at **Ambalavao** (p80) to take in the **zebu market** (p81) and visit the acrobatic ring-tailed lemurs of **Réserve d'Anja** (p81). Make a day trip to **Fianarantsoa** (p74) to explore the old town or – if you're feeling more energetic/intrepid – head for a hike among the mixed **Betsileo and Bara communities of Tsaranoro Valley** (p83) or in the spectacular **Parc National Andringitra** (p83).

A Week to Explore

Ideally time your arrival in **Ambositra** (p66) for market day (Saturday) before a few days of hill-walking among the artistic **Zafimaniry communities** (p68). Continue south to **Fianarantsoa** (p74) for **the slow train to Manakara** (p84). Spend a day paddling a pirogue on **Canal des Pangalanes** (p85). Stop for some jungle-trekking and lemur-spotting at **Parc National Ranomafana** (p78) on your way back to the highlands.

Seasonal Highlights

SPRING

September and October are great months in which to travel in Central Madagascar. Weather is cool and dry, and lemurs are nursing their babies.

SUMMER

January to April is cyclone season and the weather – especially on the humid east coast – can be unpredictable (or downright soggy), but it's pleasantly uncrowded.

AUTUMN

The landscape is at its greenest. Harvest season sees the colourful markets at their busiest. Savika (Betsileo zebu-wrestling festivals) are a regular occurrence around Easter.

WINTER

The *famadihana* (exhumation) ceremonies of Betsileo and Merina tradition take place throughout Winter. June is the height of 'cricket season' (the gastronomic speciality, not the sport).

AMBOSITRA

Most travellers tend to overlook Ambositra in their single-minded dash along the RN7 between the capital and Fianarantsoa. Am-boo-str (as locals pronounce it) has traditionally been seen as Antsirabe's poorer sister and when tourists do stop it's usually to explore the spectacular landscapes and surrounding villages. Yet there's a laid-back atmosphere in Ambositra that's highly appealing. The town's relatively diminutive size (population 38,000) makes it a delightfully manageable place to stroll and its reputation as Madagascar's arts-and-crafts capital is reason enough to spend a few days exploring.

Due to the hilly terrain, finding a *cyclo-pousse* is rare, but there are arguably more hand-drawn pousse-pousse per head in Ambositra than in any other town of comparative size. There's a good selection of accommodation too and, when you want to explore farther afield, a reliable network of experienced guides can advise on your ongoing adventures into the region's hills and craft communities.

ANTANANARIVO

Ambositra

TOP TIP

Unfortunately, poverty is rife in this area. The urge to try to help is irresistible, but giving in to the requests for bonbons (sweets) or cadeaux (gifts) from children on the street is only likely to exacerbate problems. It's better to give books/pens directly to a school.

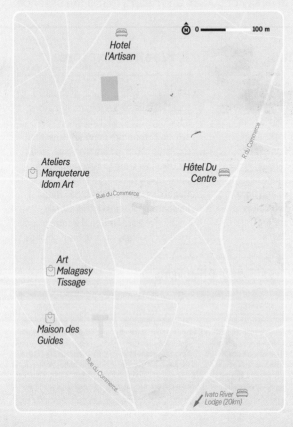

Hotel l'Artisan

Ateliers Marqueterue Idom Art

Hôtel Du Centre

R du Commerce

Rue du Commerce

Art Malagasy Tissage

Maison des Guides

Rue du Commerce

Ivato River Lodge (20km)

0   100 m

N

Ambositra Arts

WANDER THROUGH MADAGASCAR'S ART CAPITAL

The southwestern end of Rue de Commerce is the epicentre of Ambositra's art industry. At the row of shops, stalls and workshops that stretches for 300m you will see finely woven baskets, Betsileo-style raffia hats, ornate carvings and some of the finest marquetry you're ever likely to see. Much of the merchandise is certainly aimed at the tourist market (marquetry images from *The Adventures of Tintin*, raffia chameleons, etc) but some of the finest pieces are destined for the local market.

Look out for the small stall marked **Maison des Guides** where Honorine Razananivosoa spends her days weaving beautiful raffia bags that have been commissioned by locals. Honorine occasionally offers weaving classes for foreign visitors. Just opposite the big souvenir shop called L'artisan, there's a tiny hole-in-the-wall silk-weaving workshop (closed on Sunday) with a sign reading **Art Malagasy Tissage**. Madame Josianne, a 3rd-generation silk-weaver, produces fine scarves from wild cocoons, and colours them with natural dyes. The most sought-after fabrics woven here are never sold to tourists; they are the undyed 2m × 2m burial *lambas* that fetch prices of more than Ar400,000.

Directly opposite the silk workshop, a cobbled alley descends (about 600m) to the suburb of Vohiday. Ask anyone for **Ateliers Marqueterie Idom Art** (idom-art.com) where Mirijamanana Rasolofoniaina creates astoundingly detailed marquetry with sheets of naturally coloured wood. Works of art are created from simple photographs using a hand-operated jigsaw that uses wire from car tyres as blades. The work is invariably commissioned and a 1m-wide picture, taking 2 months to make, typically costs around Ar1.2 million.

Handmade baskets

TAMARIN60/SHUTTERSTOCK ©

PLACES TO STAY IN AMBOSITRA

Hôtel du Centre
Cheap, cheerful, with a slightly bedraggled appeal, recommendable for its location near Ambositra's craft centre. $

Hotel l'Artisan
Spacious ensuite rooms, or (much smaller) Zafimaniry-style timber bungalows, and access to Ambositra's best restaurant. $$

Ivato River Lodge
On the dirt track to Zafimaniry, this riverside property is set to become a regional favourite. $$$

GETTING AROUND

Ambositra is easily small enough to explore on foot. If you want to roam a little farther afield (or simply take a tour for the novelty) there are plenty of pousse-pousse. These vehicles are an everyday mode of transport for the majority of local shoppers, and during school-run rush hours you might be lucky to find an unoccupied one.

If you're northbound from here, the *taxi-brousse* terminal is a 10-minute walk from city centre along the RN7. If you're heading south, it's a 15-minute walk in the opposite direction.

A Three-Day Hike through the Zafimaniry Villages

A 4WD is not strictly necessary to get to Antoetra but the drive from Ambositra (a mere 42km) is rough, even by Malagasy standards and demands a confident and determined driver. The Zafimaniry communities (a subgroup of the Betsileo) are typically very isolated, and a hike here requires dedication, a reasonable level of fitness and a healthy dose of intrepidity. Travelers of Madagascar (travelersofmadagascar.com) can arrange hikes through Zafimaniry and even to Ranomafana.

1 Antoetra

Ideally, start your trek on a Wednesday, when Antoetra comes alive with Zafimaniry's most vibrant market. Everything from farm tools to livestock to secondhand clothes to home-brewed rum is sold here.

The Hike: The 11km trail to Faliarivo is an unexpectedly sociable hike, broken by breathtaking mountain views and a rest-break at the little coffee stall on the peak that is a real convivial occasion for homeward-bound villagers.

2 Faliarivo

At Faliarivo village (1530m), nestled in the crook of a mountain pass, you sleep in carved timber houses, distinctive of Zafimaniry. Apart from enjoying the deeply symbolic woodcarving, meet the people who weave colourful satroka bory hats and make traditional fire-starter boxes.

The Hike: The hilltops here are clustered with standing stones, commemorating villagers whose bodies never made it home. You will pass many of these during the 4km hike to Tetezandrotra.

Sakaivo

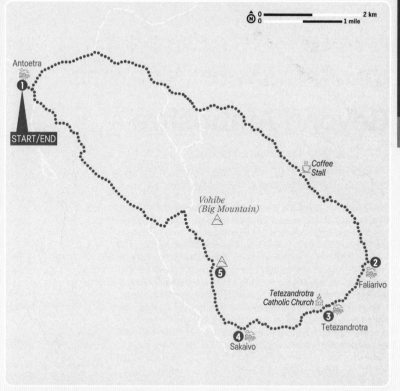

3 Tetezandrotra

Circled by green fields and dominated by a monumental Catholic church, Tetezandrotra could have been teleported here from the Loire Valley. Notice the absence of dogs; they've been *fady* (taboo) here since, it's said, a honey-collecting ancestor was eaten by dogs.

The Hike: A steep climb out of Tetezandrotra is followed by a steady descent into Sakaivo Valley. You could walk all the way to Ranomafana (p78) in about seven days, but if you simply cross the paddy fields, and climb the opposite side, you will reach Sakaivo 6km after leaving Tetezandrotra.

4 Sakaivo

Picturesque Sakaivo (1350m) is popular with visitors so, while accommodation tends to be (slightly) more sumptuous, there are also more beggars. Life is hard here but the children entertain themselves with a wild as-

sortment of traditional games, such as *kisa baka* (complex version of hopscotch) and *topy* (extreme spinning tops).

The Hike: The steep climb to the Alaibory ridge (while less than 3km) can be brutal in full sunshine. There's a more gradual (longer) path, but it misses out on the unforgettable views.

5 Alaibory Mountain

Resting on the summit of Alaibory (Round Mountain) you have the – apparently inaccessible – peak of Vohibe (Big Mountain) at your back as you gaze across mountains and valleys, with villages and rice paddies clustered among them.

The Hike: About halfway through the 12km hike back to Antoetra you'll pass an ancient stone monolith – be careful because it is *fady* in this area to step on the shadow of such a stone. The trail to Antoetra is mostly downhill through secondary forest. Look out for colourful chameleon and rare endemic palms.

Beyond Ambositra

The Ambositra area retains the fascination and cultural appeal of the traditional border country between the Betsileo and the ruling Merina.

The Talaviana River (an hour's drive north of predominantly Betsileo Ambositra) marks the frontier of what was traditionally the Merina homelands. You'll note changes in architecture throughout this area: the red-brick homes of the Merina; the carved balconies of Betsileo houses. Few tourists take time to stop in Tsarasaotra (40 minutes north of Ambositra) but, with its pastel-painted houses and exploding clusters of poinsettia blossoms this might be the most photogenic village in Madagascar.

The town of Antsirabe, famous for the thermal springs that once attracted royalty, is worth exploring for a day or two. However, the real highlights of this area are in the countryside, with its rolling hills, crater lakes and rural hamlets.

TOP TIP

It's considered taboo to point at a tomb with the index finger. Gesture with all fingers lest bad luck befall you.

Antsirabe Railway Station

PIERRE-YVES BABELON/SHUTTERSTOCK ©

MILOSK50/SHUTTERSTOCK ©

Fahaleovantena Monument

Touring Antsirabe in a Rickshaw

CRUISE ANTSIRABE IN A POUSSE-POUSSE

Hundreds of pousse-pousse ply the streets of Antsirabe (a pleasant two-hour drive from Ambositra along the RN7). You might not feel comfortable riding in a hand-drawn rickshaw – but either a *cyclo-pousse* (cycle-trishaw) or the hand-drawn variety can be hired for around Ar20–30,000 per hour.

An ideal tour starts at **Antsirabe Railway Station** (abandoned) and heads westwards, passing grand old mansions from the colonial era. On the cobbled streets of the **old town**, the rider will wait while you explore fascinating craft shops (featuring work in raffia, batik and handmade paper). This part of town is quite hilly and you might hear your rider calling 'pousse-pousse' to friends to give the rickshaw a helping shove. (You're welcome to jump out and push too.)

From here you pass the **Fahaleovantena Monument** – depicting the island's main tribes – and continue to the Hotel des Termes where (if it's quiet) staff will show you the royal suite where the King of Morocco stayed in the 1960s.

After passing **Notre Dame de la Salette Church**, stop to explore Antsenakely Market. From here, follow the shoreline of **Lac Rano-Maimbo** to the old **Thermal Baths**. The

LAC TRITRIVA

Most people arrive by car but those who cycle the dusty 17km from Antsirabe to the forested summit of Tritriva Volcano (about 1600m above sea level) invariably appreciate a cool swim in the crystal water of the crater-lake. There's no taboo against this but there are numerous strange stories about the lake; the two ducks you might see here are said to be the spirits of the local Romeo and Juliet who took their own lives rather than be separated.

If you want to imitate their leap of death there's a 20m-high 'jumping rock' from which reckless souls occasionally hurl themselves just for fun/bravado.

 WHERE TO STAY IN ANTSIRABE

Green Park Hotel
Best of the cheaper options in Antsirabe town, it's next to excellent Chez Jenny restaurant. **$**

Hotel des Thermes
Seen better days since the king of Morocco stayed here, but still has faded charm. **$$$**

Souimanga Hotel
Comfortable suites, set in a tropical food-garden. Restaurant ingredients come from within a 5km radius. **$$$**

Heading out of Antsirabe on the RN34 turn left (after 6km) where you see a sign pointing towards **1 Lac Andraikiba**. The lake (300m farther up the road) is peaceful and a pleasant place for a picnic. Cycle around the southeastern shore to the **2 Gemstone Shops** (which also sell snacks and cool drinks). Antsirabe locals come here at weekends to swim or jump from the 5m-high diving board. If you fancy a break from pedal power, stop at the **3 Boat Jetty** and charter one of the small motorboats (maximum about Ar35,000) to explore the lake. This lake, the larger of the two you'll see on this tour, is a little over a kilometre in diameter, but you can see pretty much everything in about 30 minutes while puttering around.

Moving on from here, the dirt track deteriorates steadily over the next 10km, but it's impossible to get lost as long as you stick to the main route. After 6km you'll see a steep, wooded hill dead ahead at the bottom of which is the pretty village of **4 Tritriva**. This traditional Merina village, with its balconied cottages clustered around the church steeple, looks like it could have been dropped here from the French Pyrenees. It's now a short, sharp 1km climb up the flank of **5 Tritriva Volcano**, where you'll find the security gate that provides access to **6 Lac Tritriva**. The one-way ride from town is only 17km but, especially in the heat, allow two hours each way.

You can rent bicycles from many places in town including Green Park Hotel (tel: +261 20 44 051 90).

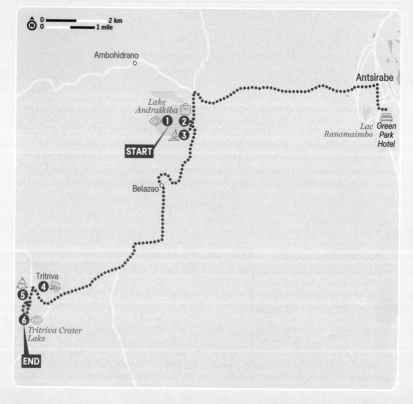

swimming pool is open to the public, but bear in mind that, as a *vazaha* (foreigner), you're sure to attract a lot of attention from excited kids.

From here it's all uphill and that cry – 'pousse-pousse!' – may well go up again before you arrive back at the railway station and your starting point.

Hiking the Betafo Highland Trail

EXPLORE THE MERINA'S SPIRITUAL HOMELANDS

It might only be an 8km stroll but you could easily spend a day or more exploring the highland trails and hamlets around **Betafo** town (50 minutes by *taxi-brousse* from Antsirabe).

Apart from the distinct probability of losing your way on the maze of paddy dykes or in the meandering valleys, a guide/translator is crucial since an in-depth insight into the region's rural lifestyle is the real highlight of this walk. (Liva Ralaifanjaniaina – livabetour@gmail.com – is well known in the area.)

The trail starts on the RN34, 22km west of Antsirabe. A cart track – heading north through fields of pumpkins, peanuts, corn, sugar cane, sisal (for rope) and unbelievably monstrous sunflowers – climbs slowly through a series of unexpectedly busy hamlets where the inhabitants will explain agricultural practices and demonstrate food preparation chores. You will be invited into a traditional double-storey Merina house. With livestock safely locked up on the ground floor, the family lives on the upper floor, with simple bedrooms on one side and a wood-fire kitchen on the other.

The path continues through Tafofo village ('Windy village') to a craggy hillside crowned with monumental tombs. At times it's a tightrope walk along the tops of narrow paddy dykes – with zebu-ploughs churning the mud – as you make your way toward the little raffia-weaving hamlet of Malaza and into Landratsay Valley.

The spectacular Tafofo Falls is an idyllic picnic spot: while there's no restriction against swimming, please refrain from bringing any pork products in your picnic since this is *fady* here.

From the falls it's a hot, dusty trek over the hills to Lac Tatamarina, with the village of Ambonavaratra on one side and Betafo town (end of your trail) on the other.

MERINA TOMBS EXPLAINED

The little town of Betafo is said to be the spiritual capital of the Merina tribe, and the surrounding hilltops are studded with huge family tombs. The Lutheran Church peers down on Betafo from across Lac Tatamarina, and the Catholic Church (Madagascar's second-oldest) dominates the centre of town. But, up on the hilltops, a glance at the crypts – each of which might house as many as 70 corpses – will show you that most of them are still periodically reopened and that the traditional Merina religion is alive and well.

The *famadihana* ('turning of the bones'), taking place after a corpse has been buried seven years, remains a regular occurrence here during the winter months.

GETTING AROUND

The RN7 is well served by public transport – from relatively comfortable and spacious buses to the cramped (often dangerously overloaded) *taxis-brousses* that reach even some of the remotest hamlets. Antsirabe-based driver Jocelyn Andriamalala (WhatsApp: +261 34 03 485 16) offers transport in a comfortable 4WD for Ar200,000 per day, including driver's food and accommodation, but not fuel. You could hire a hand-drawn pousse-pousse or *cyclo-pousse* (cycle-rickshaw) from Antsirabe's town centre. Since Bajaj tuk-tuks arrived, regular four-wheel taxis have been driven to the brink of extinction. The railway line running from Antananarivo to Antsirabe was knocked out of service by a cyclone, but expectations are high that it should be running again by late 2023.

FIANARANTSOA

ANTANANARIVO

Fianarantsoa

You typically arrive in Fianarantsoa (fi-a-na-rant-soo) via the clamour of Basse-Ville (Lower Town) and Nouvelle Ville (New Town), but it's in the historic Haute-Ville (Upper Town) where 'Fiana's' unique charm lies. Ambozontany Cathedral has dominated the hilltop since 1870, but the so-called Antrano Biriky ('The Brick House') remains the real jewel in Haute-Ville's crown. This elegant Protestant church (built in 1856) was the first brick building in Southern Madagascar. More than the wealth of churches (six on this hilltop alone!), it's the cobbled alleyways around Lálana Rova (Palace St), lined with historic brick houses, that make Haute-Ville so enchanting. The sedate hum of Antsinakeli (small market) – with a delightful lack of souvenir vendors – adds to the pleasure.

Things were not always so peaceful: the Rova (palace) is now a primary school, but in the playground you'll see the 'Slaughtering Stone' where some of Queen Ranavalona I's countless victims met their fate.

TOP TIP

Fianarantsoa's old town is surely one of the most attractive historic quarters in sub-Saharan Africa. But every cyclone season the precious buildings face irreparable damage. Visit the information centre opposite 'the Brick House' to find out how the *trano gasy* (traditional houses) are being preserved and protected.

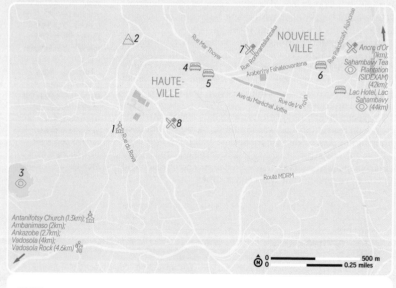

Antanifotsy Church (1.3km);
Ambanimaso (2km);
Ankazobe (2.7km);
Vadosola (4km);
Vadosola Rock (4.6km)

NOUVELLE VILLE

HAUTE-VILLE

Ancre d'Or (1km);
Sahambavy Tea Plantation (SIDEXAM) (42km);
Lac Hotel, Lac Sahambavy (44km)

Rue Mar Thoyer
Rue Rondbaratsianzaka
Araben'ny Fahaleovantena
Rue de Verdun
Ave du Maréchal Joffre
Rue du Rova
Route MDRM
Rue Rakotozafy Alphonse

0 / 0   500 m / 0.25 miles

SIGHTS	SLEEPING	EATING
1 Ambozontany Cathedral	4 Petite Bouffe	7 La Chaud'Hier
2 Kianjasoa	5 Tsara Guest House	8 La Rizière
3 Lac Anosy	6 Zomatel	

Ambozontany Cathedral

Explore Fianarantsoa On Foot

WANDER THROUGH THE HISTORIC CITY

There is a wonderful walk that takes in Fianarantsoa's old town and the Betsileo farming communities in the surrounding valleys.

Begin your walk in front of the majestic **Ambozontany Cathedral** and turn northwards along the eucalyptus-forested ridge of **Kianjasoa**. It was here, an appropriately elevated vantage point over the city, where Queen Ranavalona I originally established her fortified city. Beyond the Catholic Seminary, a steep dirt track leads westward, dropping away from the forested hilltop to the bridge over the Mandranofotsy River ('river of white water').

Crossing the valley floor through a landscape of rice paddies, you'll reach **Vadosola** village. You can now climb up **Vadosola Rock** – where it is said that a Betsileo king once lived – to hike right along the top of the ridge. If you prefer to stick to the valley floor, you'll pass through the friendly rural hamlets of **Ankazobe** ('place of many trees') and **Ambanimaso** (known as 'under the eyes', perhaps because it was easily visible from the palace on the Fianarantsoa hilltop). Finally reaching the tarmac again near **Antanifotsy Church** you emerge at **Lac Anosy** and climb the steep flight of stone steps all the way back to the cathedral and your starting point. Mad Trekking (WhatsApp: +261 341422173) can arrange excellent guides to accompany you on this trek.

WHERE TO EAT IN FIANARANTSOA

Pierrot Men, Madagascar's most celebrated photographer, has lived in Fianarantsoa all his life and the Pierrot Men Gallery (@pierrotmen) showcases his career. Here are some of his favourite restaurants.

L'Ancre d'Or
(+261 20 75 508 15)
Offers a wonderful Malagasy-fusion menu that is popular with locals and tourists. Favourites are the chicken with vanilla, foie gras and zebu fondue.

La Rizière
(lariziere.org)
At the foot of the old town is a training centre, and the menu, which features local produce and varies each week, is prepared and served by the students.

La Chaud'Hier
(+261 34 84 821 63)
One of the liveliest of the city's eateries often hosts cultural exhibitions and live music.

 WHERE TO STAY IN FIANARANTSOA

Petite Bouffe
Fianarantsoa's best budget option is located just below the Haute-Ville and has a great-value restaurant. **$**

Zomatel
Perhaps the best-equipped hotel in town, with a swimming-pool, Jacuzzi and Fiana's best cafe/boulangerie attached. **$$**

Tsara Guest House
Spacious suites in 100-year-old church and outbuildings. Owner active in local building preservation. **$$$**

A 'Cuppa' at Sahambavy Tea Estate

TOUR A VINTAGE TEA PLANTATION

Sahambavy village lies on the route of the old FCE railway line (see p84) and, back when it was founded in 1969, the tea plantation was ideally located for ease of transportation to the coast. These days **Madagascar's only tea plantation** is less conveniently situated. These rolling hills of neon-green tea bushes are well worth a 26km detour down a potholed dirt track off the RN7, especially if you stop over beside the lovely **Lac Sahambavy**.

The tea factory (officially known as **SIDEXAM**) is open Monday to Saturday morning, and if you simply walk up to the front office, the duty manager will be happy to organise a tour. There are few English-speaking staff so, unless you speak French (or Malagasy), you'll need a translator. The tour takes you from the fields (with plants that are 50 years old) through the five stages – preliminary drying, chopping, fermentation, secondary drying and sorting – in the production of Sahambavy's celebrated black tea. You'll also see how green tea is produced (a similar method but skipping the fermentation process). The plantation has received international acclaim for the way it has uplifted the local community and established social (and educational) programmes in what was traditionally an underrepresented area. The factory has a permanent workforce of about 50 people but, at the height of harvesting season (October–May), a further 100 people from Sahambavy village and surrounds are em-

HOHO COSMICOS/SHUTTERSTOCK ©

ployed. After the tour you'll be invited to sample the final product and to appreciate the difference between the more powerful black tea and the subtly fragrant green (which sells for around Ar45,000/kg).

Sahambavy tea fields

LAC SAHAMBAVY

Known in Malagasy as Farihy Sahambavy, this little **lake** (about 2km long) is a wonderful place to relax. **Lac Hotel** has become a destination in its own right with Fianarantsoa residents, who make regular pilgrimages out of the city for great food or simply to relax by the lake. The hotel has a variety of rooms, from simple A-frame bungalows to luxuriously romantic stilted suites, and a renovated railway carriage has been converted into a truly sumptuous 'Nuptial Express' suite. Nonguests can also rent pedalos or kayaks to explore the lake, and there's a lovely 6.5km circular hike or ride (cycles are available for rent) circumnavigating it.

GETTING AROUND

Fianarantsoa's Basse-Ville is a chaotic area, made more frantic by the *taxi-brousse* terminals and train station. The city is safe to walk around and it's not difficult to stroll from Basse-Ville to Nouvelle Ville, where most of the hotels are. If you want to get to Sahambavy, a private car might set you back a hefty Ar150,000 for the 45km. However, a *taxi-brousse* costs just Ar3,000 per person, making Sahambavy a worthwhile destination even for a day trip from Fiana.

Beyond Fianarantsoa

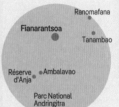

The Betsileo homelands are picturesque hamlets of tall brick houses clustered among paddy fields, under the shadow of dramatic granite ridges.

Southward from Fianarantsoa, RN7 sweeps through the dramatically rolling landscapes of the Betsileo homelands. Rural life here is hard and you'll see crops, charcoal and water cans hauled on hand-drawn *kalesa* (like go-carts) in a region where even zebu carts are a sign of opulence. The eastern seaboard is a place of lush rainforests, perhaps best experienced at Parc National Ranomafana, with wildlife sightings that include a dozen species of lemur.

The highland town of Ambalavao is famous for its huge zebu market and for the ring-tailed lemurs of Réserve d'Anja. This area is also the launching pad for trips to Parc National Andringitra and Tsaranoro Valley (with its mixed culture of Betsileo and Bara communities).

TOP TIP

Many people visit Parc National Ranomafana during the return trip from Manakara after descending from Fianarantsoa in the FCE train.

Fossa

MIROSLAV HALAMA/SHUTTERSTOCK ©

NATURAL RICHES OF RANOMAFANA ARBORETUM

Thanks to the diversity of habitats – and the incredible variety of insect-attracting fruit trees – you're almost guaranteed to come face to face with colourful belted chameleons and Parson's chameleon (measuring over 60cm from nose to tail) in Ranomafana Arboretum (2km east of town).

There are also around 250 species of plants here, including some of the world's rarest: the *Dypsis robusta*, for example, is the only known palm of this species growing in the wild on the planet. It's worth hiring a guide (optional) just for a chance to run an experiment with the seeds of the so-called miracle tree (*Synsepalum dulcificum*), which have the bizarre ability to make raw lemons taste deliciously sweet.

STEVE BARZE/SHUTTERSTOCK ©

Ranomafana

Ranomafana Hiking Trails

JUNGLE HIKE THROUGH SCIENCE/MYTHOLOGY

Madagascar is famous for unique wildlife, and **Ranomafana** (two hours from Fianarantsoa by *taxi-brousse*) has picturesque trails that make for particularly exciting jungle trekking. Most people trek in the mornings, so try to go in the afternoons when you'll have the trails to yourself, and the habituated bamboo lemurs will often approach within a few feet of you.

There are 12 lemur species in Ranomafana (with a 13th on the verge of being recognised at the time of writing). The real stars of Ranomafana are greater bamboo lemurs and the rare golden bamboo lemurs and, if you're prepared to invest a few hours in searching, you have a good chance of seeing both. These creatures leap from branch to branch on their powerful hind legs as they gnaw with deceptively powerful teeth on bamboo shoots and even trunks. Both species feed almost exclusively on bamboo and eat soil to counteract a diet that is loaded with cyanide. Brown lemurs are relatively common and, with luck, you might come across the

 WHERE TO EAT IN RANOMAFANA

Ihary Hotel
An unusually extensive menu ('pink pepper zebu fondant') complemented by a selection of flavoured rums. **$$**

Centre ValBio
Research complex near park entrance with dining room where you can lunch with resident scientist. **$$**

Grenat Hotel
The most popular lunchstop in central Ranomafana: well-filled baguettes and a selection of fresh juices. **$**

southern black-and-white ruffed lemur (the 'Malagasy panda') or the red-bellied lemur. In remoter primary forest you stand a chance of seeing the Milne-Edwards' sifaka or the grey gentle lemur.

As if this wasn't enough, Ranomafana's enthusiastic and highly trained local guides can explain unique aspects of the Malagasy jungle that you might never hear of elsewhere. There are sacred sites with funereal standing stones and burial graves – heavily protected by *fady* – from the local Tanala tribe. Word has it that supernatural creatures like the kalanoro (a kind of miniscule hairy pygmy) haunt the riverbanks. If you want to know about this, wait until you're out of the jungle before you ask, because it's considered dangerous even to mention such things when you're still in the rainforest.

Ranomafana Night Walk

SEARCHING FOR RANOMAFANA'S NOCTURNAL WILDLIFE

It might not be an intense wilderness experience, but this three-hour search along the national park boundary road is one of Ranomafana's most popular crowd-pullers. With an opportunity to see some of the region's five nocturnal lemur species – brown mouse lemur, greater dwarf lemur, sportive lemur, woolly lemur and aye-aye – it's easy to see why.

Nocturnal lemurs are very good at what they do...and what they do best is hiding (specifically from the fossa, Madagascar's apex predator). With powerful flashlights and the help of a trained wildlife guide, you have an excellent chance of seeing a brown mouse lemur or two, along with an entire spectrum of vibrantly hued chameleons, including blue-legged chameleon, big-nosed chameleon, nose-horned chameleon and side-striped chameleon. Ace wildlife guide Gaëtan Rabemiafara (gaetanflycatcher@gmail.com) claims to have seen both fossa and the fabled aye-aye from Ranomafana's trails at night. (He purposefully does his utmost not to spot the rodent-like tenrec though, since among his tribe it's considered taboo even to set eyes on one.)

The park authorities do a good job of enforcing laws; you can only visit with a registered guide and there are only two specific areas where night walking is allowed. Along with the wildlife you are likely to see dozens of other *vazaha* stumbling over potholes in the dark...but it's worth the crowded atmosphere for a once-in-a-lifetime encounter with the unbearably cute mouse lemurs.

RAVIN-KAZO (MEDICINAL PLANTS) TOUR

For generations the Tanala – 'people of the forest' – have harvested the hills around Ranomafana for *ravin-kazo* (medicinal plants). A *mpitsabo* (shaman) called Pierre Rakoto oversees the small plantation, 2km south of Ranomafana town, where more than 120 of these plants are now cultivated for medicine. For example, a bush is regularly harvested by passing *taxi-brousse* drivers for leaves that stave off drowsiness. Another bush nearby cures travel-sickness in their passengers. There is, of course, a shrub that is a local form of Viagra and another that cures hangovers. Another that counteracts depression has been pruned worryingly regularly.

English-speaking naturalist Santatranirina Razanakolona (shantraz@gmail.com) at ValBio research centre can arrange visits and acts as an interpreter.

CULTURAL EXPERIENCES IN RANOMAFANA

Ranomafana Thermal Baths
Ranomafana means 'hot water' and the springs are on the western bank of Nomorona River.

Basket-Making
ValBio research centre, working closely with the local community; excellent basket-making classes (1½ hours).

Craft Market
Rather than support ambushing street vendors, consider the craft market in the centre of town.

HIKING IN PARC NATIONAL RANOMAFANA

Parc National Ranomafana can only be visited on a walking tour. Trails are well maintained, but this is real rainforest with leeches, bugs and thorns, and there will be some scrambling to do when close to lemur groups. There are three hikes – two hours, four hours and seven hours – but the shortest offers minimal chance for lemur encounters. Only the seven-hour hike gets you into true primary forest.

Be aware that parts of the park remain sacred to the Tanala people (there are burial monoliths in secluded places). This means that there are powerful *fady* in place: your guide may not feel comfortable discussing the ancestors until you are out of 'earshot' of such places.

Tanala Tribe Village Visit

MEET THE KING OF TANAMBAO

While Ranomafana is essentially a tourist town – with 90% of its population coming from other parts of Madagascar – the village of **Tanambao** (about 10km to the south) is a traditional community of Tanala people.

It is possible to arrange a meeting with Justin Miaraka, a king of Madagascar's smallest tribe. As with any king, there are certain rules of etiquette – and in this case *fady* – so it would be unwise to visit without a guide/translator. English-speaking guide Gaëtan Rabemiafara (gaetanflycatcher@gmail.com) has contacts right up to the highest echelons of the Tanala community. Your guide will explain that it is crucial to take a small bottle of local rum that the king will share with the ancestors while explaining who the new visitors are. You'll be expected to drink a small shot too but, if you prefer to abstain, it's acceptable simply to pour a little on your hand and then rub it over your head and down your legs. The king (sitting in his mud-daubed palace and dressed in traditional bright red) is happy to answer questions on aspects of tribal life, such as the taboo that prohibits villagers from panning for gold (a common pastime in this area).

Village lifestyle and architecture is fascinating too and, if you are fortunate, you might even witness the Tanala's impressive welcoming dance known as *dumbulu*, performed with stumps of bamboo.

Ideally, try to visit on a Saturday to coincide with the vibrant market that brings traffic to a standstill on the highway at Kelilalina (just down the road from King Justin's 'palace').

Tour Ambalavao by Tuk-Tuk

ZIP AROUND THE OLD TOWN

A whistle-stop tour on a tuk-tuk (known locally as a Bajaj) is an exciting way to explore **Ambalavao** (1½ hours from Fianarantsoa by *taxi-brousse*).

First stop is Soalandy Atelier, where you can see how silk harvested from wild silkworms is converted into beautiful shawls and scarfs. From here you can head past a series of colonial-era buildings and the statuesque Saint Joseph Cathedral to the traditional market, where you'll find everything from *boucherie* selling hunks of zebu to stalls selling a bizarre array of *beauté* products (including fake eyelashes and hair extensions). Moving onward, you'll reach the second of Ambalavao's majestic churches in the form of the Betela Fanasina Church (built in 1906). On the same road,

 WHERE TO STAY IN RANOMAFANA ───────────────

Hotel Manja
There's a steep walk up to the bungalows but the valley views make it worthwhile. **$**

Setam Lodge
More spacious than average bungalows in the area and ideally located near the park entrance. **$$**

Hotel Thermal
Best town-centre hotel has a pleasant boutique feel, with lovely timber rooms and thermal hot tubs. **$$$**

THE GUIDE

CENTRAL MADAGASCAR

Tuk-tuk, Ambalavao

200m north, turn into the Atelier Papier Antaimoro, where beautifully decorated handmade paper is produced from tree bark. You could call a refreshment break if you're getting peckish because the atelier shares its location with the excellent Aux Bougainvillées Restaurant (and hotel) or you could head a few kilometres north on RN7 to the junction near Soavita Vineyard (closed at the time of writing). Here you will find – signposted as 'Point de vente du vin local' – a whole cluster of little stalls where you can sample local wine, flavoured rum and traditional snacks.

Foudia Trekking (WhatsApp: +261 34 84 964 79) can arrange Bajaj tours – and a whole range of activities – around Ambalavao.

Meet Madagascar's Famed Lemurs

MUCH MORE THAN 'JUST' LEMURS

Madagascar's most successful community-run wildlife reserves lies 12km south of Ambalavao, at the foot of the granite monoliths known as 'the Three Sisters'. It is, in part, this rocky landscape that has made the reserve so successful, since the large population of supremely confident ring-tailed

AMBALAVAO ZEBU MARKET

Every Wednesday and Thursday morning, a dusty hill 1km west of Ambalavao becomes the setting for one of Madagascar's two biggest zebu markets. There's a huge enclosure packed with massive bovine beasts and hundreds more – of every size, shape and colour variation – gathered across the open space. Keep an eye out for handy boltholes behind the sturdy timber fence posts because young bullocks occasionally break free for an impromptu gallop through the crowd.

Apart from being a wonderful social occasion, it's an important source of economy; prime zebu breeding stock reaches prices well in excess of US$800.

Sadly, many of the zebu that arrive here are destined to be shuttled onwards to the big abattoir in Fianarantsoa.

BEST CRAFT CENTRES IN AMBALAVAO

Soalandy Atelier
Learn how to convert silk from wild cocoons into silk scarves, coloured with natural dyes.

Atelier Papier Antaimoro
Handmade paper or card is pressed with leaves and flowers, so each sheet is unique.

Traditional Market
You'll find woven Betsileo hats and baskets along with household items and decorative pieces.

LUCA NICHETTI/SHUTTERSTOCK ©

Ring-tailed lemur

RING-TAILED LEMURS OF ANJA

Population estimates vary wildly, but there are actually around 600 ring-tailed lemurs in Réserve d'Anja. When the reserve was founded in 2001 there were about 120 (in about five troops), but with the population growing each year, it takes careful management to keep pace.

Initially some lemur groups were habituated to humans with supplementary food (bananas) and, although the diet is now completely wild, you'll be enchanted to see these elegant, and very vocal, creatures coming almost within arm's-reach. Lemurs have a charm that monkeys (higher primates) rarely seem to possess and Réserve d'Anja might be the best place in the world to interact closely with them in a completely wild environment.

lemurs have a particularly photogenic habit of sunning themselves on the warm rocks in the morning.

Visitors who arrive expecting picturesque lemur sightings are never disappointed, but if you take an opportunity for a guided walk uphill along the forested trails and among the boulders you'll find that Anja also offers unexpected appeal of a historical and cultural sort. There are rock-walled *valan omby* (zebu compounds) where Betsileo fugitives once hid their herds from Bara cattle rustlers. There are caves and overhangs where the local tribe hid from Merina (and later French) oppressors. There's a great, walled-in burial-cavern where, even today, mourners access via a rope so that remains are protected from tomb-raiders.

The community's guides – well-trained, knowledgeable and enthusiastic – will explain medicinal plants that are still widely used today and unexpected natural sightings in the form of Oustalet's chameleon (the second-biggest species) and Brookesia (the smallest).

The reserve is managed by Anja Miray village association with over 700 members. To keep pace with the lemur's rapidly increasing population (see sidebar), each of the members in this visionary organisation must plant 15 trees on the boundary of the park each year. With the addition of more

 HOW TO VISIT RÉSERVE D'ANJA

Less Than One Hour
The shortest trail is ideal for small children...and you're still guaranteed to see lemurs.

Two Hours
An overlooked trail running through the forest and over, under and between a rocky labyrinth.

Half Day
The longest hike (four to five hours) crests the top of the highest hill, offering wonderful views.

than 10,000 extra trees each year (and visitor numbers of around 14,000 annually) Réserve d'Anja is often cited as a global example of how a community reserve should be run.

Parc National Andringitra Hike

TREK THROUGH BREATHTAKING MOUNTAINS

Locals will tell you that Andringitra is increasingly difficult to access with each year that passes. However, it's worth all the trouble several times over for what are some of the most spectacular mountain landscapes in Africa. The most popular route is the three- or four-day hike around the northern edge of the national park. Depending on your itinerary, 18km days are not unusual, and steep ascents from 900m to over 2100m can make for long, hot slogs. Cultural insights from well-trained and enthusiastic local park guides (not always fluent in English) add to the fascination.

Most visitors tend to start from relatively accessible Tsaranoro Valley (you can make it here in 3hrs from Fianarantsoa, by *taxi-brousse* follwed by taxi, preferably 4WD). There's a lovely camp at the head of the valley and it's possible to get to **Pic Boby** (Madagascar's second-highest peak at 2658m) on day two. Then you can exit via Andranriampotsy Camp or (further down) Belambo Camp. This is such a stunning area that you'll wish you could stay longer. Belambo Camp – near two spectacular waterfalls and located beside the house of a very welcoming Betsileo farming family – would be reason enough to visit Andringitra.

A Guided Walk Through Tsaranoro Valley

TSARANORO'S SACRED FOREST

Tsaranoro Valley gets a good part of its scenic attraction from the dominating Massif de l'Andringitra and part from the dramatic Tsaranoro cliff face, which rises in a sheer 800m wall (making it one of the most spectacular rockface challenges for climbers).

Camp Catta, close to the base of the cliff, is most well-known as the eastern departure point for treks into Parc National Andringitra and Pic Boby. Few people tend to stay more than a single night in Tsaranoro Valley at the beginning or end of their hike, but this beautiful area is worth taking some extra time to explore. This valley is a cultural melting pot where the northern Betsileo farming community intermingles with the Bara pastoralists of the south. The Bara make no bones about their once notorious

HOW TO HIKE PARC NATIONAL ANDRINGITRA

Until 2010 it was possible to drive right to the main entrance of Parc National Andringitra in 1.5 hours in a regular saloon car on a well-maintained French-built road. A cyclone in 2022 destroyed several crucial bridges, effectively cutting the Betsileo communities of Andringitra off from the outside world. It now takes five hours to reach the park entrance. This is still preferable to starting your hike from the more accessible eastern side, where Tsaranoro Valley can be accessed via a *taxi-brousse* and a 10km trek. The climb into the mountains from Tsaranoro is nothing short of brutal.

Foudia Travel (madahelptravel.com) can arrange tours and advise on the best options.

WHERE TO EAT IN AMBALAVAO

Résidence du Betsileo
French cuisine with a Malagasy twist in city centre. The bar is great for aperitifs. **$$**

Tsieniparihy
Primarily famous as a bakery, but you'll also find the typical chicken and zebu specialities. **$**

Zongo Hotel
Large dining room with pleasant terrace for a hearty lunch featuring Malagasy and Western staples. **$$**

reputation as cattle rustlers, and the *valan omby* of both tribes are embedded with *fanafody* (talisman) to protect the precious herds from cattle thieves. Take a guided walk around the village and the sacred forest at the foot of Tsaranoro cliff for a unique insight into the lifestyles and beliefs of these two tribes. A local guide (obligatory and arranged through the community tourism office) will point out the difference between ornately balconied Betsileo homes and sturdy Bara bungalows.

The sacred forest is – thanks to official protection – now home to a large population of elegant ring-tailed lemurs (once considered a food source by both Bara and Betsileo). A guided wander around the sacred forest offers a great chance to learn about botany and traditional medicines and also an unexpectedly clear insight into Betsileo burial traditions. Two tombs were opened sometime in the past, perhaps by raiders searching for the valuable silk burial *lambas*. It's possible to look into the tombs as long as you observe *fady* – removing hats and refraining from pointing with the index finger – with their scattered human skulls and bones.

Rattle Along Madagascar's Most Renowned Railway

AN INCREDIBLE RAILWAY JOURNEY

The **Fianarantsoa-Côte Est Railway (FCE)** runs – as the name implies – from Fiana to the East Coast. There are 67 bridges and 48 tunnels along the way, including the 1074m-long Tunnel Ankarapotsy. Remote rail-side communities with names that seem to echo the clatter of steel wheels on the 130-year-old German rails – Andrambovato, Manampatrana, Sahasinaka – are home to communities of Betsileo, Tanala, Antaimoro, Antaisaka and Antaifasy people for whom the FCE is the only link with the outside world.

It is estimated that more than 30 workers had died (from malaria and accidents) during construction for each of the 163km of track by the time the railway was inaugurated on April Fool's Day 1936.

At the time of writing, the FCE was running three times a week on a reduced service (Tuesdays, Thursdays and Saturdays) but hopes were high that one of Africa's most evocative railways would soon be fully back 'on track'. Even at its most efficient, the journey has always been highly unpredictable. The 163km run (descending from 1100m at Fianarantsoa Station to sea level at Manakara) can take anything between

WHY I LOVE PARC NATIONAL ANDRINGITRA

Mark Eveleigh, writer

Two hours after leaving Ambalavao in a 4WD, a broken bridge (victim of a cyclone) brought me to a standstill. I shouldered my pack and forded the river before starting a further three-hour uphill hike...and this was before I even reached the entrance to Parc National Andringitra. Andringitra is worth the trouble many times over. Along with the awe-inspiring solitude of its peaks and valleys, this is also a cultural experience. Whether sleeping at local homesteads or pitching a tent in remote highland meadows, Andringitra is the best of all worlds.

 WHERE TO STAY IN AMBALAVAO AREA

Aux Bougainvillées
The best bet in central Ambalavao, with lovely suites and the town's finest restaurant. **$**

Camp Catta
Idyllic safari-style lodge in Tsaranoro Valley. Expect ring-tailed lemurs dancing on your roof at dawn! **$$**

Betsileo Country Lodge
Midway between Ambalavao and Réserve d'Anja delightful property with a swimming pool and mountain views. **$$$**

Village on Canal des Pangalanes

CANAL DES PANGALANES

Many people overlook Manakara (at the coastal end of the FCE) entirely and simply return to the highlands by road. This sleepy city – with its tin-roofed houses, sand roads and Caribbean atmosphere – is an ideal base from which to explore the famous Canal des Pangalanes by pirogue. The canal network (645km in total) was excavated in the 1890s by the French to create a sheltered waterway for a fleet of *boutre* (cargo boats).

With a degree of flexibility it is still possible to travel by *boutre*, although most visitors to Manakara content themselves with a guided full-day pirogue tour (organised through any hotel and, usually, including a lunch stop on a deserted beach).

12 and 48 hours. Take sufficient food and drink, and for the best views try to sit on the left side of the train when coast-bound (right if heading for the highlands).

Lac Hotel (right opposite the station in Sahambavy) has an agreement with the FCE Railway, making it potentially the most reliable local source of information on the erratic train schedule. It might make sense to begin or end your journey in Sahambavy anyway, since the hourlong rail journey to Fiana from here is the least interesting section.

GETTING AROUND

The famous FCE railway is the most renowned journey in Central Madagascar and most people tend to use it to get from the highlands (Fianarantsoa) to the coast (Manakara). Although it is possible to go in the opposite direction.

It's a 220km (roughly 4½ hour) drive from Manakara to the highlands and the junction of the RN7, and a further 40 minutes from there to Fianarantsoa (or two hours to Ambalao for access to Réserve d'Anja, Parc National Andringitra or Tsaranoro Valley). All of these locations are served by *taxis-brousses*.

Above: Parc Nacional Isalo (p92); right: Tsiandamba (p100)

SOUTHERN MADAGASCAR

CANYONS, CORAL AND WILDLIFE-RICH SPINY FORESTS

Madagascar's south draws visitors with its checklist of iconic sights: big-name national parks, beautiful beaches, bizarre plants and world-famous lemur reserves.

Southern Madagascar is a wide-open adventure among some of nature's most dramatic forms and the country's most stellar attractions. The stark desert canyons of Parc National Isalo, cut through with gurgling streams and natural rock pools, rival those of Arizona, while the southwest coast offers gorgeous fishing settlements that serve as gateways to the fifth-largest coral reef in the world.

And then there's the bizarre spiny forest, vast kilometres of an otherworldly habitat that contains some of the planet's strangest and most formidable flora: drought-resistant plants, thorny trees, sausage-shaped shrubs with toxic sap, and spindly topped baobabs. The spiny forest, and some 95% of the species within it, is found nowhere else on Earth.

There are cities in the south's bottom corners – scruffy Tuléar (Toliara) and languid Fort Dauphin (Taolagnaro) – but that's not why people come. Use them as a base to travel up and down the coast or into the dramatic hinterland, where tribal tombs dot the roadsides. The question is how to tackle a region of this size. For many people, a lodge in Isalo and a slice of white-sand beach are enough. But for others, the south is the perfect recipe for off-road exploration, when the security situation permits. After all, away from the RN7, it's strictly 4WD country, ripe for the adventure of a lifetime.

THE MAIN AREAS

PARC NATIONAL ISALO	PARC NATIONAL ZOMBITSE-VOHIBASIA	GREAT REEF	FORT DAUPHIN (TAOLAGNARO)
Wild walks among sandstone canyons. **p92**	Transitional forest with easy access. **p96**	Fabulous fish and Bounty ad beaches. **p98**	Remote, relaxed gateway to the southeast. **p106**

Morombé

Lac
Ihotry

Andavadoaka
Befandeva

Befandriana
Sud

Parc National Isalo, p92

The most popular national park
in Madagascar, and for good reason: ragged canyons, eroded rock
formations and natural pools.

Pa
Natio
Isa

Ambohitrabo

Piscine
Naturel

Bekodoy

Soahazo

Parc National
de Zombitse-
Vohibasia

Ranc

Salary

Antsevao

Andranolava

Parc National
de Zombitse-
Vohibasia

Ilakaka

Tsiandamba

Ankililoaka

Maninday

Tsifota

Ankasy

Ankilimalinika

Sakaraha

Manombo

Ambolimailaka

Mangily

Ifaty

Andranovory

**Parc National Zombitse-
Vohibasia, p96**

Trails in this little-visited park lead
through a transitional forest that
shelters wildlife from both western
and southern Madagascar.

Ambondrolava/Beravy

Tanile

Tuléar
(Toliara)

Arboretum
d'Antsokay

Baie
Saint
Augustin

Sarodrano

Onilahy River

Tongobory

Soalara

St Augustine

Nosy Ve

Anakao

Anakao

Ankilimivony

Betioky

Beheloka

Ankiririsa

Ambahita

INDIAN
OCEAN

Efoetsy

Parc National
Tsimanampetsotse

Sa
Amb

Besakoa

Ambola

Bekily

Great
Reef

Lac
Tsimanampetsotse

Antanandranto

Ejeda

Ama

Vohombe

Manakaralahy

Great Reef, p98

Turquoise seas house a
hive of marine activity, while
inland lies a great swathe of
the south's astonishing spiny
forest.

Linta River

Besosa

Amborompotsy

Itampolo

Ampanihy

Tranoroa

Etrobeke

Ankiliambany

Besakoa

Androka

Kilibory

Merarandra River

Ampalaza

Bevoalavo
Ouest

Tsiho

Find Your Way

Southern Madagascar is huge, covering an area twice the size of Scotland. Focus on the tail-end of the RN7, between Isalo and Túlear (Toliara) and the magnificent coastline either side of the city, or the area around Fort Dauphin.

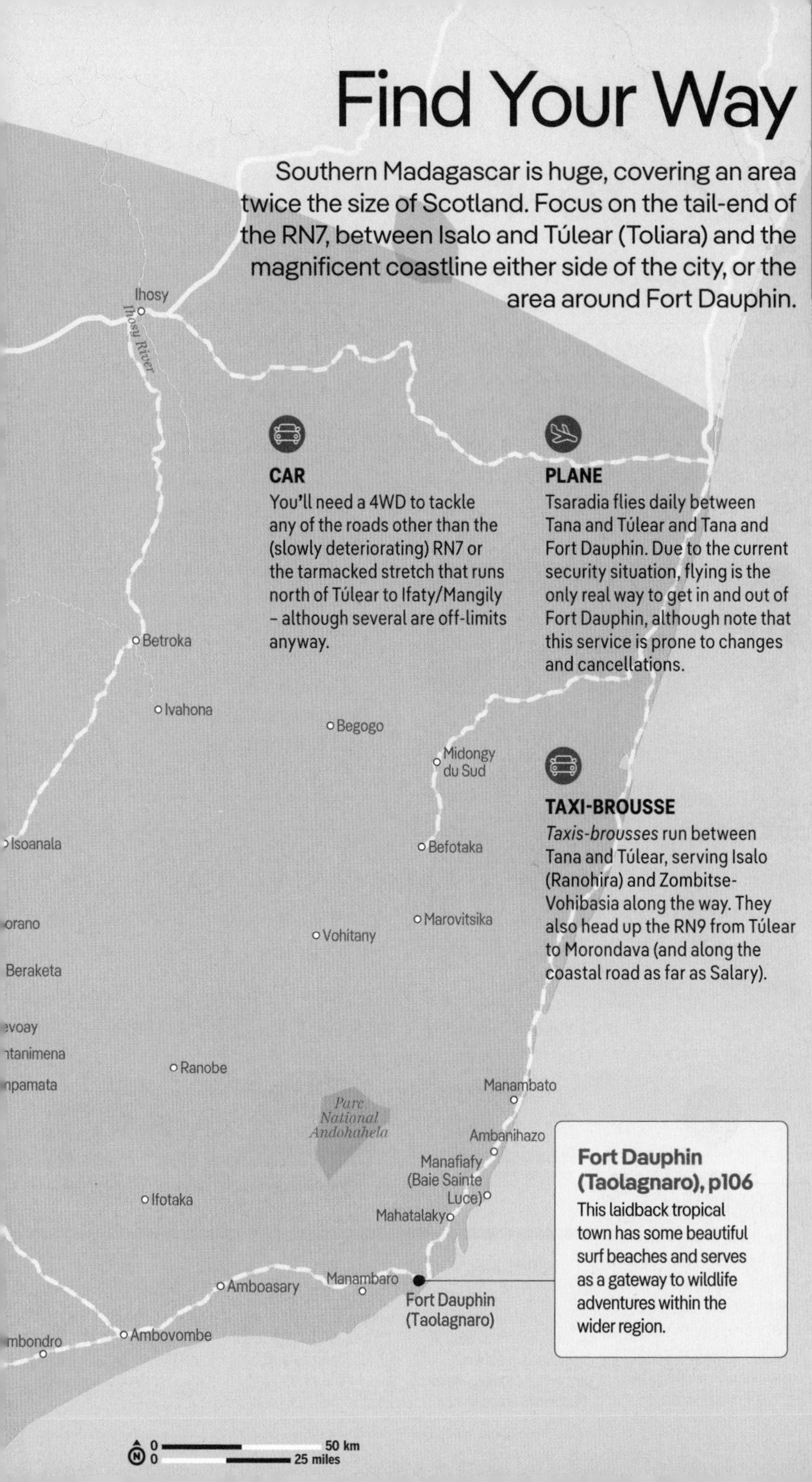

CAR
You'll need a 4WD to tackle any of the roads other than the (slowly deteriorating) RN7 or the tarmacked stretch that runs north of Túlear to Ifaty/Mangily – although several are off-limits anyway.

PLANE
Tsaradia flies daily between Tana and Túlear and Tana and Fort Dauphin. Due to the current security situation, flying is the only real way to get in and out of Fort Dauphin, although note that this service is prone to changes and cancellations.

TAXI-BROUSSE
Taxis-brousses run between Tana and Túlear, serving Isalo (Ranohira) and Zombitse-Vohibasia along the way. They also head up the RN9 from Túlear to Morondava (and along the coastal road as far as Salary).

Ihosy
Ihosy River
Betroka
Ivahona
Begogo
Midongy du Sud
Isoanala
Befotaka
orano
Beraketa
Marovitsika
Vohitany
evoay
ntanimena
npamata
Ranobe
Manambato
Parc National Andohahela
Ambanihazo
Manafiafy (Baie Sainte Luce)
Ifotaka
Mahatalaky
Amboasary
Manambaro
Fort Dauphin (Taolagnaro)
mbondro
Ambovombe

Fort Dauphin (Taolagnaro), p106
This laidback tropical town has some beautiful surf beaches and serves as a gateway to wildlife adventures within the wider region.

0 — 50 km
0 — 25 miles

Plan Your Time

Visit the national parks along the RN7 and the incredible spiny forest before hitting the Great Reef's beaches. With more time, you can also fly to Fort Dauphin, tucked away in the far southeast.

Parc National Isalo (p92)

If You Only Do One Thing

● Head for **Parc National Isalo** (p92), a wonderland of river-run canyons and denuded rock that's accessed either on the long drive down the RN7 from Antananarivo or a few hours' ride inland from Túlear.

● Hike to the **Piscine Naturelle** (p93) or the **Cascades des Nymphes** (p93) and try one of the park's off-road **mountain-bike circuits** (p95), or a **horse ride** (p94) through the surrounding grassy plains. There's plenty to do here, but make sure you allow for some downtime in the area's excellent hotels.

Seasonal Highlights

The ideal time to visit is between April or May and October. Otherwise, it can be very hot, while many of the dirt roads are impassable during the rainy season.

FEBRUARY

Elephant's foot, a kind of rotund miniature baobab, starts to bloom, its yellow flowers bringing colour to **Parc National Isalo** (p92).

APRIL

Easter is celebrated across the region, with large beach parties at Túlear, Anakao and Fort Dauphin.

MAY

With the rains over, the sandy **coastal track to Morombé** (p101) is back on the itinerary for 4WD adventurers.

A Few Days to Travel Around

● Take in **Isalo** (p92) and then head to the coast around Túlear, breaking up the journey with a stop at **Parc National Zombitse-Vohibasia** (p96).

● The **Great Reef** (p98), which spreads north and south of Túlear, provides access to some superb beaches. Top spots include the white-sand stretches around **Tsiandamba** (p100) and at **Salary** (p101), on the rough coastal road north to Morombé, and on both sides of the headland at **Anakao** (p104); you'll need a 4WD for the former, and possibly a driver-guide, but Anakao is an easy boat ride from Túlear.

If You Have More Time

● Spend a few days on the **Great Reef** (p98), snorkelling, diving and whale watching (in season), and mixing time on the beach with walks in the remarkable spiny forest that lies just inland; the guided tour of **Arboretum d'Antsokay** (p99) or **Reniala** (p103) is fascinating.

● Then either work your way north to **Morombé** (p101), a stepping stone to Morondava and western Madagascar, or fly (via Antananarivo) to **Fort Dauphin** (p106), where surf beaches, tropical waterways, iconic **lemur reserves** (p111) and **sacred forests** (p108) await.

JUNE
The best swells hit Madagascar during the austral winter (June to September). Ride the waves at **Anakao** (p104) or **Fort Dauphin** (p106).

JULY
It's prime time for watching humpback whales breaching in the turquoise waters off the **Great Reef** (p98).

OCTOBER
Head to **Berenty** (p111) for the best chance to see the reserve's ring-tailed lemurs and Verreaux's *sifakas* with their fluffy young.

DECEMBER
The four-day **Sambaraha Festival** in Fort Dauphin celebrates the culture and customs of the Anosy region.

PARC NATIONAL ISALO

ANTANANARIVO

Parc National
Isalo

Isalo is epic in every sense of the word. Rising from the savannah-like plains of the Ihorombe Plateau, this huge massif of continental sandstone is like a museum dedicated to the art of the desert canyon: sculpted escarpments; ochre rock walls; and deep river gorges shot through with lush vegetation and natural pools for swimming. It's no wonder this is Madagascar's most popular park.

Isalo is a sacred site for the Bara, who still bury their dead in permanent cave tombs high up in the cliff face; park trails lead past several of these funeral sanctuaries, as well as the Sakalava rockpile tombs that predate them. Hikers will also get a good taste of some of the area's incredible flora, such as the fire-resistant tapia tree, whose hard bark looks like crocodile skin, and the yellow flowering *Pachypodium rosulatum*, which resembles a miniature baobab tree and is often, understandably, called 'elephant's foot'.

TOP TIP

The buttons don't work at the once-interactive Maison de l'Isalo, 10km south of Ranohiro, but this little museum is still a good introduction to the history, culture and geology of the park. The amiable guides will be glad to have someone to escort around the information boards.

HIGHLIGHTS
1 Piscine Naturelle

SIGHTS
2 Canyon des Makis
3 Canyon des Rats
4 La Fenêtre de l'Isalo
5 La Reine de l'Isalo

ACTIVITIES
6 Circuit Malaso
7 Les Rênes de l'Isalo
8 Moyen Circuit
9 Namaza Circuit
see 6 Petit Circuit

SLEEPING
10 Le Relais de la Reine
11 ITC Lodge
12 Le Relais de la Reine

INFORMATION
see 13 Guides Association Office
13 MNP Office

MORE PERFECT PANORAMAS

There are more far-reaching views of Isalo's rugged canyons from the **mountain-bike circuits** (p95) that lead off the RN7 south of Ranohira, looping up to clifftops that tower above plains of Bismarck palms (*satrana*).

Parc National Isalo

Hit the Trails

CANYONS, LOOKOUTS AND NATURAL POOLS

One of the most popular trails in Isalo is the **Piscine Naturelle**, a 6km (return) hike to a beautiful natural pool. It's the picture of paradise, especially after a long, hot walk, with its gurgling waterfall tumbling into a deliciously clear pool fringed by ferns and pandanus plants. For an even finer walk, combine this with the **Circuit Crête** (Crest Trail), which branches off near the beginning of the Piscine Naturelle trail and loops for 5km along the ridgeline for sweeping views over Ranohira and the vast grasslands of the Ihorombe Plateau. The combined hike is 8km in total.

The best trail for spotting wildlife is the **Namaza Circuit**, which follows the course of a river gorge up to the dramatic Cascades des Nymphes; you're pretty much guaranteed to see ring-tailed lemurs hanging around the campsite about a kilometre in, sometimes Verreaux's sifaka and brown lemur, as well as the endemic Benson's rock thrush on the approach to the falls. The circuit is 3.5km, or 5km if you add the side trail to the Piscine Bleue and Piscine Noire; the 'Black Pool' is very deep (hence the colour) and very cold.

HIKING NEED-TO-KNOWS

You need to organise all your hiking in the park's gateway town of Ranohiro, preferably the day before, so you can make an early start and avoid the midday heat.

Entrance fees are paid at the MNP office, a right turn off the RN7 as it bends through town; if you're spending more than a day in Isalo (and you really should), it's cheaper to buy a multi-day pass.

The Guides Association Office, on the opposite side of the road, has a list of nearly 90 accredited guides, along with the languages they speak and their phone numbers.

 WHERE TO STAY IN PARC NATIONAL ISALO

Chez Alice
Convivial backpackers' hangout just north of Ranohira, with various wattle-roofed Bara-style bungalows. **$**

Le Jardin du Roy
Stunning property offering elegant stone bungalows and a gorgeous pool. Run by the Le Relais de la Reine owners. **$$$**

Isalo Rock Lodge
Stylish retreat with earthy-toned rooms, a spa and pool. The restaurant serves works of art. **$$$**

CRAIG3/SHUTTERSTOCK ©

La Reine de l'Isalo

North of Ranohira, you can follow a river up through lush pockets of forest in the Canyon des Makis. It's a nice walk, although parts of the canyon have suffered from wildfires in recent years and its namesake ring-tailed lemurs are harder to spot than they used to be. The nearby Canyon des Rats is a good place to see Bara tombs. The trails (closed December to April) are 2km and 4km long, respectively, and can be combined for a full-day hike.

Written in the Rock

SEEKING OUT SHAPES IN THE SANDSTONE

Time has sculpted many of Isalo's rocks into familiar figures. The most famous is **La Reine de l'Isalo** (Queen of Isalo), which appears on the back of the 1,000 Ariary note. It's 3km south of the Maison d'Isalo; you can only make out its regal form when heading north. A further 4km to the south, reached off the RN7, lies La Fenêtre de l'Isalo, a popular spot in the evening thanks to the way its natural rock window perfectly frames the setting sun.

You can also find several animal shapes in rock formations on the trails themselves. On the walk to the Piscine Naturelle, for example, look out for The Tortoise and, 850m further along, The Crocodile, while the 4WD and mountain-bike circuits further south pass by the Boot of Isalo and The Wolf.

A Trail for Cars

EXPLORING BY 4WD

A rough track leading off the RN7 10.5km south of Ranohira marks the start of the **Circuit Malaso**, a 4WD loop that is primarily intended to provide a window on the park for people with

---

 WHERE TO STAY IN PARC NATIONAL ISALO

ITC Lodge
Well-run place whose tidy garden bungalows offer excellent mid-range value. Home of Momo Trek. **$$**

Isalo Ranch
Sandy pathways tie this lodge's bungalows together into a welcoming little village, aided by a cosy restaurant. **$$$**

Satrana Lodge
Atmospheric wood-floored safari-tent rooms and endless desert views from its a majestic pool. **$$$**

impaired mobility but also provides a good way for trek-weary travellers to see places in the park that can't be reached on foot. The 42km route (guide from park office required) takes you across plains and to the edge of canyons, with the chance to see rock formations like the *Loup de l'Isalo*, a craggy outline that resembles a wolf. It's around a four-hour drive, with some optional walking on short trails.

On Your Bike

MOUNTAIN-BIKE TRAILS

Isalo is one of the best places in Madagascar for off-road mountain biking, with three official VTT (*vélo tout-terrain*) trails catering for most levels of rider. The **Petit Circuit** (30km) and **Moyen Circuit** (74km) cut through some spectacular scenery around 10km or so southwest of Ranohira. The former loops past the Boot of l'Isalo to link up with the 4WD Circuit Malaso , while the latter takes in grasslands studded with fan-shaped Bismarck palms (*satrana*) and climbs up to 1,000m for 180-degree panoramas of sculpted escarpments. For an even longer adventure, try the **Grand Circuit** (86km), which starts near Ilakaka and visits canyons, caves and Lac d'Andranovorikaolo, camping overnight along the way. You can rent mountain bikes from the MNP office; Le Relais de la Reine also rents bikes to guests.

Tackling an Iron Walkway

CLIMBING THE VIA FERRATA

An exciting way of gaining a different perspective of Isalo's landscapes is on a *via ferrata* (iron path); a protected route up the canyon cliffs where climbing aids have been bolted into the rock. The national park has created a 750m *via ferrata* within its boundaries, where fixed cables lead nearly 350m up a rock face near Andremanero, 27km northwest of Ranohira. Closer to town, Le Relais de la Reine hotel has its own 500m *via ferrata* (installed by professional climbers) in a neighbouring canyon. It's open to nonguests and offers tremendous views across to the national park. Both routes are suitable for people (aged 12 years and over) who have never climbed before, although anyone with a fear of heights should give it a miss. All equipment is provided.

ILAKAKA: SAPPHIRE MINING THE OLD-FASHIONED WAY

When sapphires were found near the Ilakaka River in 1998, what was then a simple village of two dozen huts erupted into a gemstone boom town of some 30,000 people. The lawless atmosphere of those early days is thankfully long gone, but **Ilakaka**, 28km southwest of Ranohira, is still one of the most fascinating sights in the south.

Gem dealers line the town's central street, where women with painted faces squat on the pavement, organising piles of stones by quality, but the main attraction is the open-cast mine itself – Color Line offers authentic one-hour tours, taking you out to the hand-dug mines that pockmark the area and explaining the whole process.

GETTING AROUND

Ranohira is on the *taxi-brousse* run between Antananarivo and Tuléar, around six hours south of Fianarantsoa. Public transport heading on to Tuléar usually arrives in town before 10am; heading north, it's generally between 10am and 1pm. Finding an empty seat can be tricky; each morning, one or two *taxis-brousses* connect Ranohira with Ihosy, two hours down the RN7,

from where there are more southbound options.

The trailheads for the main hikes in Isalo are all some distance from Ranohira; taking a car (available through most hotels) avoids the long, hot walk across open country from town.

Southbound *taxis-brousses* can get you to Ilakaka, although it's easier to arrange a transfer with your hotel.

PARC NATIONAL ZOMBITSE-VOHIBASIA

One of Madagascar's least known yet most accessible parks, Parc National Zombitse-Vohibasia protects 36,300 hectares of transitional forest. It's a stark example of the deforestation that has ravaged the country in the last 50 years; its forested pockets surrounded by a denuded landscape of sweeping grasslands and semi-desert. The park shelters eight species of lemur and a 72 bird species, almost half of which are endemic. Commonly sighted here are the giant coua, black parrot and blue vanga – and the real prize – the Appert's greenbul, which survives nowhere else on the planet. The protected area is comprised of three pockets of forest: Zombitse; the similarly sized Vohibasia; and the much smaller Isoky-Vohimena, which lies between them. Tourist activity is limited to the Zombitse section, which spreads either side of the RN7 at Ambakitany.

ANTANANARIVO ✪

Parc National
● Zombitse-
Vohibasia

Giant coua, Parc National Zombitse-Vohibasa

HAJAKELY/SHUTTERSTOCK ®

TOP TIP

Pay your fees at the barely functioning park office, just set back from the RN7, where guides wait by the roadside to take visitors along the short but rewarding network of flat trails; the four circuits here range in length from 15 minutes to two hours or so.

ARTUSH/SHUTTERSTOCK ©

Oustalet's chameleon

Hit the Trails

TRANSITIONAL FOREST OF LEMURS AND LIZARDS

The park's trails are in the Zombitse section, which spreads either side of the RN7. Perhaps the most rewarding for wildlife spotting is the **Madresy Circuit**, named after the strangler figs you'll see on the trail, which loops for 2.3km north off the RN7 and provides a good taster of what the park has to offer. Flora here includes rosewood trees, baobabs and Madagascar corkwoods, which the locals call *vazaha* (foreigner), due to the fact its bark peels in the dry season. You'll almost certainly see green geckos, three-eyed lizards and Oustalet chameleons – sizeable males and, if you're here at the right times of the year, females laying their eggs in the soft sandy soil by the side of the trail. Mandresy is also the best trail for lemurs, particularly Verreaux's sifaka and the oh-so-cute (and endangered) Hubbard's sportive lemur, which, for all intents and purposes, is endemic to the park; they're nocturnal but can be spied peering out of hollow tree trunks during the day.

The other three trails – the **Ritikala Circuit**, **Lobo Circuit and Velomianto Circuit** – start a couple of hundred metres behind the little roadside park office, on the southern side of the RN7. Bird-watching is fruitful on all of them, although you've got the best chance of spotting the locally endemic Appert's bulbul on the 850m Ritikala Circuit. The 2.7km Lobo Circuit and the 750m Velomianto Circuit are both worth exploring for their endemic flora; Velomianto, which takes just 15 minutes to walk, probably just edges it for its unusual orchids.

TRIBAL TOMBS

The tribes of Madagascar's south have some of the most elaborate tombs and memorials in the country. While the **Bara** bury their dead in decorative coffins high up in the cliffs of Isalo, the **Mahafaly**, **Sakalava** and **Antandroy** inter theirs in walled rectangular tombs that are covered with stones and scattered with the skulls of sacrificed zebu – the larger the structure, and the more zebu horns there are, the wealthier (and more important) the person was. Scenes from the life of the deceased are depicted in colourful paintings along the walls of the tomb and atop intricately carved wooden funerary posts (*aloalo*). In contrast, the **Antanosy** erect commemorative obelisks some distance from the tombs themselves.

GETTING AROUND

The park straddles the RN7, 90km southwest of Isalo and 145km northeast of Tuléar. *Taxis-brousses* between the two can stop here, although getting a seat may be difficult when it comes to moving on, as they don't tend to leave Tuléar or Ilakaka/Isalo until they're full.

GREAT REEF

ANTANANARIVO ✪

Great Reef ●

Stretching over 450km along the southwestern coast of Madagascar, the Great Reef is the fifth-largest in the world and the source of some of the best snorkelling, diving and whale watching in the country.

Raffish Túlear (Toliara), a sea of bicycle rickshaws at the end of the RN7, serves as its gateway. To the north, the tourist-saturated towns of Ifaty and Mangily give way to a gentle curve of white-sand beaches and Vezo fishing villages and a challenging coastal track that runs all the way to Andavadoaka, backed by a turquoise ocean that looks for all the world like paradise. To the south, the reef extends beyond idyllic Anakao, its best overall tourist destination and a top spot for surfing.

The area inland contains a vast spiny forest, the emblematic landscape of the south, which is best explored at a couple of private reserves either side of Túlear and in remote Parc National Tsimanampesotse.

TOP TIP

Although *taxis-brousses* depart Túlear in the early hours for the coast and up the RN7 towards Tana, and speedboats for Anakao also set off in the morning, you don't have to overnight in town, as there are some great places to stay – such as Auberge de la Table and Bakuba (p104) – nearby.

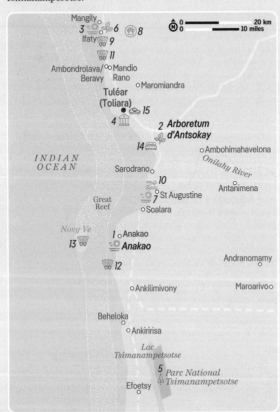

HIGHLIGHTS
1 Anakao
2 Arboretum d'Antsokay

SIGHTS
3 Ifaty and Mangily
4 Musée CeDRATOM
5 Parc National Tsimanampetsotse
6 Reniala
7 St Augustine's Bay
8 Village des Tortues

ACTIVITIES
9 Atimoo
10 Grotte de Sarodrano
11 Mangily Scuba
12 Nosy Satrana
13 Nosy Ve

SLEEPING
14 Bakuba

TRANSPORT
15 Túlear Taxi-brousse Station

PIERRE-YVES BABELON/SHUTTERSTOCK ©

Mahafaly tomb

FLORA OF THE SPINY FOREST

The spiny forest's flora – 95% of which is found nowhere else on Earth – has adapted in one ingenious way or another to survive in the semi-arid conditions: small waxy leaves avoid evaporation; spikes help to catch moisture; and bottle-shaped trunks store up water.

The most dominant flora is the *Didiereaceae*, or **octopus tree**, whose family includes the *Didierea Madagascariensis*, also known as the **compass tree** due to the way its branches always lean to the south. Also look out for the numerous species of **Euphorbia**, many of which have succulent, sausage-like branches devoid of leaves.

Funerary Art & Ancient Masks

MUSEUM OF TRIBAL CUSTOMS

If you're in Túlear with half an hour or so to spare, the interesting **Musée CeDRATOM** on Rue Flayelle is worth a browse. Run by the local university, the small, three-room Centre for Documentation and Research for Art and Oral Traditions of Madagascar features a few dusty exhibits on the cultural life of the Mahafaly, Sakalava, Bara and Antandroy peoples, including funerary art, scared rituals and an ancient mask with real human teeth.

An Arboretum with a Difference

A WINDOW ON THE SPINY FOREST

Founded in 1980 by a Swiss amateur botanist, the fascinating **Arboretum d'Antsokay** is essentially a 40-hectare distillation of the entire spiny forest in one place. It's a fantastic collection of 900 plant species, some 90% of which are endemic to the region. Take a one-hour guided tour to learn about the weird and wonderful flora on show here, including numerous species of octopus tree, a number of rare aloes and several different *Pachypodium*; you can't miss the *Pachypodium geayi*, or giant elephant's foot, which can grow up to 5m high.

ANOTHER PLACE TO STAY

One of the best places to stay near Túlear, further down the coast towards the Sarodrano Peninsula, is **Bakuba** (p104), a uniquely individual design hotel.

 WHERE TO STAY IN TÚLEAR

Chez Alain	**Hotel Moringa**	**Auberge de la Table**
Convivial budget option near the *taxi-brousse* station. Range of good-value rooms, plus quiet garden (with pool). **$**	In central Túlear, with smart, modern, spacious rooms and balconies overlooking a busy square. **$$$**	Fab value airy bungalows, especially the superior ones. Sun-trap pool and a very good restaurant. **$$$**

DRIVE

The Road to Morombé

The coastal road that runs for 240km north to Morombé is an epic off-road adventure; a bone-shaking journey between spiny forest and the sea, with only the occasional Vezo fishing village for company. You'll need a high-clearance 4WD to tackle the rutted sandy tracks, and even then the road is only passable in the dry season (April or May to October). Public transport, to some extent, also plies this route.

1 Ambolimailaka

Just 40km up the sealed road from Túlear, Ambolimailaka makes a pleasant get-away-from-it-all alternative to Ifaty/Mangily. The return of the fishing fleet – over 200 pirogues strong – at around noon each day is a spectacular sight.

The Drive: Heading on to the scattered village of Tsiandamba, 50km or so north of Ambolimailaka (around 1¾ hours) gives you your first taste of the rough, sandy track that constitutes a road around these parts.

2 Tsiandamba

There's a palpable sense of isolation along the Northern Reef around Tsiandamba – and a couple of terrific places to stay. Family-friendly Ankasy Lodge sits on a beautiful stretch of beach 7km before the village, while the luxurious Five Senses is perched on sand dunes 4km to the north, fronting an expanse of ocean that's perfect for kitesurfing.

The Drive: As you drive further north, the road gets worse; the stretch to Salary, 14km to the north, will see you spinning through loose sand.

PIERRE YVES BABELON/500PX ©

Canoes, Salary

3 Salary

The 7km stretch of pristine white sand at Salary is one of the most beautiful beaches in southwest Madagascar. Hole up at up-market Salary Bay and dive the shipwrecks offshore, including the *Nossa Senhora do Monte do Carmo*, a Portuguese warship that went down in 1774.

The Drive: The 65km drive to Andavadoaka is epic: deep, loose sand; bumps like a funfair ride; and possibly even shallow mangroves along the way. Allow at least three hours.

4 Andavadoaka

The remote and laid-back outpost of An-davadoaka, marking the northern edge of Ambatomilo Lagoon, is one of the most interesting spots north of Tuléar. Stunning Olo Be, on a rocky headland south of the village, is a gorgeous spot to spend a few days.

The Drive: The last 50km or so to Morombé ploughs through some deep sand, particularly the track just north of Andavadoaka. The remarkable baobab forest 14km into the journey is well worth a quick stop.

5 Morombé

The northern end of the Great Reef peters out at Morombé, 280km north of Tuléar. A half-hour drive northeast of town takes you to the biggest baobab in Madagascar, with a trunk measuring a whopping 29m in circumference. Locals call it Tsitakakanesa, which roughly translates as 'if you sing on one side, you cannot hear it on the other', a reference to its mighty girth.

DIVE OPERATORS IN IFATY & MANGILY

There are several quality operators in Ifaty and Mangily, offering everything from single-dive trips in the lagoon to multi-day safaris along the coast. Most also run whale-watching trips in season (mid-June or July to September).

Mangily Scuba
Widely regarded as one of the best dive operators along this stretch of coast, Mangily Scuba also organises excellent snorkelling trips.

Atimoo
This recommended outfit ranges further along the reef than other operators, and offers dives of the shipwrecks in Salary Bay.

Baobab, Reniala

The arboretum is home to birds such as bee eaters and red-capped couas, and reptiles like warty chameleons and Merrem's Madagascar swift; the recommended night tour reveals reddish-grey mouse lemurs and, if you're lucky, spiky tenrecs, plus scorpions and plenty of Madagascar hissing cockroaches.

There's also an ethnological trail and a small museum here, as well as a stylish restaurant and some excellent bungalows. The arboretum lies 12km southeast of town, a few hundred metres from the RN7. Take a taxi from Túlear; otherwise, any *taxi-brousse* heading towards Befety can drop you off at the junction.

MORE MARINE LIFE

There's more great snorkelling and diving in **Anakao** (p104), a boat ride from Túlear in the other direction, around two little islands just offshore, and the reef itself.

Mangroves & Mudskippers

BOARDWALK TRAIL THROUGH A THREATENED ECOSYSTEM

Since 2007, the tranche of mangrove forest that runs along the coast north of Túlear has been the focus of a unique initiative aimed at preserving this crucial but endangered habitat. Visitors can learn more about the Reef Doctor Honko Project at the **Mangrove Information Centre** (closed Wed), 12km up the RN9 from Túlear, where a

 WHERE TO STAY IN IFATY & MANGILY

Les Dunes d'Ifaty
Sea-view villas and pretty garden bungalows made of local stone. Beach security ensures privacy. **$$$**

Bamboo Club
Comfortable bungalows (thatched and brick) up from the beach, a small pool and excellent restaurant. **$$$**

Sur la Plage
Tidy, colourful bungalows, kept sparkling clean, and a first-rate restaurant. Bicycles for borrowing, too. **$$**

1km wooden boardwalk wends among mangroves littered with crabs and mudskippers; look for the 'VOI Mamelo Honko' sign of the community mangrove association that runs the reserve. Longer tours include (barefoot) walks through the mudflats and pirogue rides and kayak trips along a mangrove channel.

Meet the Fishes

SNORKELLING AND DIVING IN RANOBE BAY

The beach at **Ifaty and Mangily**, 25km north of Túlear, might be fairly scrubby and the shallows thick with seagrass, but the snorkelling and diving here is among the best along the Great Reef. A coral-planting project by the local NGO and the efforts of a fisherman's association to deter illegal fishing have resulted in abundant marine life.

The best snorkelling is at the Massif des Roses, a protected reserve in the middle of the lagoon, where you can see over 150 species of fish, from angelfish and snappers to goatfish and electric rays.

Most of the diving sites are clustered along the edge of the barrier reef. Large coral bommies at the South Pass host a variety of large pelagics such as trevally and barracuda, while the North Pass contains a famous network of sunken rocky arches known as the Cathedral. The most interesting site outside the lagoon, some 300m from the reef, is Bevato, a wall dive to 25m that is a reliable spot for groupers, huge wrasse, honeycomb rays and, occasionally, harmless reef sharks.

Meet the Mother of the Forest

LEARN ABOUT SPINY-FOREST PLANTS

Protecting a a 64-hectare parcel of extraordinary spiny forest, **Reniala** is the original and best of several similar reserves on the northern fringes of Mangily village. A couple of guided trails lead through the 1000-plus species of plant here, including some impressive varieties of baobab (*reniala* is the Malagasy name for baobab, translating as 'Mother of the Forest').

You'll learn how much of the spiny forest is still used in traditional medicine and everyday life – locals make a curative tea from the boiled branches of *Euphorbia stenoclada* (the silver thicket or coral tree), for example, while *Givotia madagascariensis* and *Commiphora lamii* are used to build the middle and outrigger parts of their pirogues.

There's also an on-site lemur rescue centre, which houses ring-tails in enclosures before releasing them in the reserve and, ultimately, back into the wild.

FAUNA OF THE SPINY FOREST

The spiny forest's unique environment provides a home for an equally unusual range of animals. Mammals you won't find anywhere else on Earth include the **white-footed sportive lemur** and **Grandidier's mongoose** (a giant striped mongoose that was only described by science in 1986 and is essentially restricted to Parc National Tsimanampesotse).

Of the seven bird species that are endemic to the spiny forest, the rarest are the **long-tailed ground-roller** and the **subdesert mesite**, while this ecoregion is also the only place you can hope to see the critically endangered **Belalanda chameleon** or the rare **radiated tortoise** and much smaller **spider tortoise**.

✺ WHERE TO EAT IN IFATY & MANGILY

Chez Freddy
Excellent place for well-executed grilled seafood. Live traditional music Saturday nights. **$$**

Sur la Plage
Feet in the sand, grilled fish fresh off the boat and expertly mixed cocktails. **$$**

Villa Maroloko
Great location on the beach, serving monster BBQ prawns, zebu brochettes and other lighter dishes. **$$**

The Tortoise & Its Care

TORTOISE RESCUE CENTRE

Just along the road from Reniala, the **Village des Tortues** protects over 3500 radiated and spider tortoises, which have been seized by police and brought here to be rehabilitated and returned to the wild. Although it's illegal to keep them as pets, some Malagasy believe that having a tortoise in the house keeps witchcraft away, while others think that their urine is a cure for asthma.

A guided tour of the grounds (in English) tells you the full story of these endangered animals – both of which are endemic to southern Madagascar – and how they are being conserved. The tortoises usually stay here for six months before being released in the far south of the country, where locals believe it is *fady* (taboo) to eat them.

Explore St Augustine's Bay

POOLS AND A PENINSULA

Arcing down to the mouth of the Onilahy River, **St Augustine's Bay** is just a short distance from Túlear but worlds away in every other respect. Near its southern end, about 25km from the city, lies the roadside Grotte de Sarodrano, a natural pool that's perfect for a refreshing dip; it is fed by tidal flow and inland springs, so contains both freshwater and saltwater fish.

Just beyond here, the hooked finger of the sandy Sarodrano Peninsula curls north into the bay. A drivable track runs along its length to the Vezo fishing village of **Sarodrano**, a cluster of grass huts and brightly coloured pirogues in a landscape of constantly shifting dunes. You can also take a pirogue across the bay from the Grotte de Sarodrano.

On the other side of the sandstone cliffs that mark the start of the peninsula, the little tropical town of **St Augustine** was the site of the very first English settlement in Madagascar in 1645–46 and later a safe harbour for pirates – Daniel Defoe, author of *Robinson Crusoe*, is said to have drawn inspiration from the location.

Anakao: Paradise Found

WHILE AWAY THE DAYS

Strung out along a series of perfect semicircles of white sand and looking out over turquoise waters, **Anakao** is laidback in the finest tradition of small seaside Malagasy settlements and the pick of places to stay along the Southern Reef. Days drift

---

 WHERE TO STAY IN ANAKAO

Auberge Peter Pan
Selection of eclectic bungalows in a yard of political art. Top food and a dynamic bar. Rates are half board. **$$$**

Lalandaka Ecolodge
Upscale beach shack with a laidback vibe. Classy central lodge and a variety of rustic-chic bungalows. **$$$**

Anakao Ocean Lodge
The premier resort along the Southern Reef. Beautiful bungalows, extremely helpful staff and superb food. **$$$**

by on near-empty beaches – at least, those either side of the village – watching Vezo fishermen sail their dugout pirogues back and forth across the lagoon. Sunsets here are magnificent.

Nearly all of the hotels in Anakao can arrange for local fishers to take you out to the picturesque **Nosy Ve**, a protected island that's home to a colony of red-tailed tropicbirds. You'll spend time snorkelling its fringing reef before landing to explore the island; the tropicbirds tend to nest among the low bushes (and under the boardwalk) at the southern end of Nosy Ve.

Around 7.5km south of Anakao village, around the headland, **Nosy Satrana** also offers some decent snorkelling on its reef-facing side. The island is connected to the mainland at low tide, and you'll often see zebu walking across the land bridge to graze.

Visit the Salt Lake of Tsimanampesotse

ANCIENT TREES AND BLIND FISH

One of the most extraordinary places in Madagascar, **Parc National Tsimanampesotse** spreads around the ancient salt lake of the same name; a milky blue body of water that is devoid of life (*tsimanampesotse* translates as 'there are no dolphins') bar the flamingos that congregate here between April and November.

Amid the spiny forest, look out for the 1600-year-old 'Grandmother', actually three separate baobab trees fused together over time. Trails also lead to a spectacular banyan tree whose curtain of aerial roots reaches down into a sinkhole in search of water and a sacred cave that's home to a species of pinky-white blind fish found nowhere else on Earth.

You can arrange a mandatory guide at the MNP office in the nearby town of Efoetse; the easiest way to visit Tsimanampesotse is on a tour from Anakao, 55km to the north (two hours' drive each way).

Red-tailed tropicbird

GETTING AROUND

Travelling north of Tuléar is best done in your own 4WD. *Taxis-brousses* from Túlear (Route de Manombo) run along the coastal road as far as Salary; for Andavadoaka, Morombé and Morondava, they take the quicker (but less interesting) inland route along the RN9. Daily *taxis-brousses* run south from Tuléar (Route d'Interet General) to Sarodrano and St Augustine, via the Grotte Sarodrano. Anakao is a seven-hour drive from Tuléar, along a rough road that cuts through dangerous bandit country, so nearly everyone arrives by speedboat; the enjoyable ride takes around an hour with Anakao Transfert (departs Marina Blue restaurant) or Anakao Express (further south along Rue Marius Jatop).

FORT DAUPHIN (TAOLAGNARO)

Fort Dauphin (Taolagnaro) could be one of Madagascar's premier resort towns if it weren't so far from everywhere else. The setting is superb, like a gateway to some tropical paradise, strung out along a peninsula between sea and mountains. And, if you've driven for days through the spiny forest to get here, or even if you've flown out over the trackless highlands of Madagascar's interior, this prosperous mining centre, with its sealed roads and street lights, looks for all the world like a mirage of civilisation.

There's little to see in Fort Dauphin itself apart from its beaches. But what beaches they are. Vast crescents of soft sand run unbroken for kilometres either side of town, while the headland is pocked by some lovely coves, including sheltered Libanona Beach. Hole up in one of Fort Dauphin's good hotels and strike out on day trips along the stunning coastline and into the dramatic hinterland.

TOP TIP

The atmosphere on Fort Dauphin's beaches is fun and friendly, but don't leave your belongings unattended, and be careful if visiting some of the more remote stretches of sand, as there have been reports of muggings, even during the daytime. Don't even think about wandering along the beaches at night.

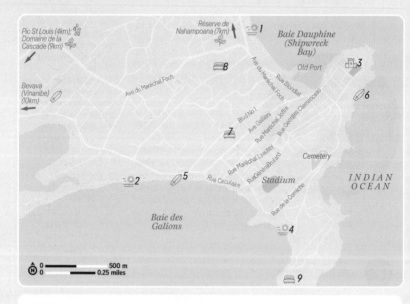

SIGHTS
1 Amparihy Beach
2 Ankoba Beach
3 Fort Flacourt
4 Libanona Beach

ACTIVITIES, COURSES & TOURS
5 Ampotatra Beach
6 Monseigneur Bay

SLEEPING
7 La Croix du Sud
8 Nepenthes
9 Talinjoo

Réserve de Nahampoana (p108)

Life's a Beach

COVES AND CRESCENTS

Fort Dauphin is blessed with some truly spectacular beaches. Head to beautiful **Ankoba Beach**, arcing west of town, and **Amparihy Beach**, which fronts Faradofay Bay to the north, for open expanses of seemingly never-ending white sand, where locals gather in the afternoons and at weekends to picnic and to play in the pounding waves. Delightful Libanona Beach and sociable, surfy **Monseigneur Bay**, on either side of the rocky headland that forms the peninsula's tip, are more intimate.

Holding Fort

MILITARY-BASE MUSEUM

Dramatically sited at the end of the headland overlooking Faradofay Bay, the small military museum (closed Sunday) at Fort Flacourt holds antique maps, old uniforms and some cannons used by the French. It's now a military base, so a guide is obligatory, and you might have to wait while the soldiers at the gate discuss whether or not to let you in, how much to charge and who should get the money.

Climb Pic St Louis

FORT DAUPHIN'S HIGHEST PEAK

The summit of Pic St Louis (529m), which you can see around 3km north of Fort Dauphin, affords great views over town and

THE BEST SURF BEACHES IN FORT DAUPHIN

Joe Kennedy Ravelo-manantsoa Toky (@joe_kennedy_surf) is the reigning National Surf Champion of Madagascar.

Ampotatra Beach
This beach break is probably the most consistent wave in Fort Dauphin. It's good for surfers of all levels, as prevailing offshore winds usually leave a glassy finish.

Monseigneur Bay
A fun, long right, perfect on a south-westerly wind for intermediate surfers looking to tighten their turns. The reef is mere centimetres beneath your fins, making for a spectacular (if nervy) view from the wave.

Bevava (Vinanibe)
Only for the most daring surfer. An unforgiving, hollow wave that works on a northerly wind. When this beach break is firing, you don't want to get caught inside, unless you're tucked tightly into the barrel.

🛏 WHERE TO STAY IN FORT DAUPHIN

Népenthès
Charming traditional-style Malagasy bungalows in a quiet garden setting in the centre of town. $

La Croix du Sud
An attractive hotel with something of a plantation-house feel. Some of the cheery rooms have balconies. $$$

Talinjoo
Gorgeous boutique hotel of dark-wood interiors, built into cliffs near Libanona Beach. Beautiful pool, too. $$$

along the coast as far as Lokaro. Allow around two hours or so to climb the rocky tack up the mountain's southern side and another 1½ hours to come back down. Start early, before the going gets too hot or windy, and take a guide – ask in town, or contact Dadamanga.

Forest Reserves

CULTIVATED GARDENS AND A REFORESTATION PROJECT

There are a couple of excellent, but very different, forest reserves within easy reach of Fort Dauphin. The **Réserve de Nahampoana**, 7km to the north, enjoys an exotic tropical setting: a tranquil, scented garden of tall trees and bamboo thickets, backed by green mountains. Founded in 1870 as private botanical gardens, the 50-hectare reserve became a kind of horticultural testing ground under the French, and then a government nursery. It is now home to a varied lemur population, including ring-tailed, Verreaux's sifaka and grey bamboo species. Trails lead through strands of kaffir lime, cinnamon and lemon eucalyptus before you're paddled down the slow-moving Lakandava River – you're likely to see malachite kingfishers and water lizards, and locals washing and fishing in the narrow channel.

Sandy tracks lead to gorgeous **Domaine de la Cascade**, 9km west of Fort Dauphin, on the road to Ambovombe. The park (closed Monday) adjoins the last patch of primary humid forest in southern Madagascar and has been set up as an educational and environmental project, restoring and protecting the forest while providing an alternative income for locals. The *domaine* covers 136 hectares and consists of a nursery set in a paradisiacal valley with several walking trails, including one where you can swim in natural pools and take a dip at a pretty waterfall.

Both reserves have bungalows if you want to stay the night (there are night walks at Nahampoana) or are looking for a peaceful alternative to staying in Fort Dauphin.

MORE PECULIAR PLANTS

There's a fantastic collection of spiny-forest flora at the **Arboretum d'Antoskay** (p99) and in **Parc National Tsimanampetsotsa** (p105). You can also explore this wacky habitat at **Berenty** (p111) and the **Ifotaka Community Forest** (p111).

GETTING AROUND

The airport is just 4km west of Fort Dauphin, a short taxi ride away. The centre of Fort Dauphin (and its nearest beaches) is very walkable, although taxis within the wider town are cheap. To get to Nahampoana and the Domaine de la Cascade, grab a taxi from Fort Dauphin (agree a fee, including waiting time, beforehand) or arrange a transfer, either through your hotel or directly with the reserves themselves.

Beyond Fort Dauphin

Ifotaka

Parc National
Andohahela
Nosy
Lokaro
Lac Lanirano
The Lokaro
Fort Dauphin Peninsula
(Taolagnaro)

Venture beyond Fort Dauphin for rugged
peninsulas and wildlife reserves home to
unusual plant life and tribal tombs.

Beauty comes in many forms in the corner of southeast Madagascar that surrounds Fort Dauphin (Taolagnaro). Scenic waterways wend their way east to the sandy coves and fishing villages of the Lokaro Peninsula, while west of town the humid forests of the Anosy region merge into the spiny forests of Androy in Parc National Andohahela. Further west of here lies Berenty, a historic reserve that was the biodiverse byproduct of its owners felling the surrounding spiny forest in order to establish a sisal plantation. Further on still, the fascinating Ifotaka Community Forest is home to the ancestral tombs of the local Antandroy tribe and best explored from a nearby luxury camp.

TOP TIP

Keep an eye out for the decorative cenotaphs of the Antanosy tribe (p97), clustered together in groups by the side of the RN13 west of Fort Dauphin.

Verreaux's sifaka, Ifotaka Community Forest (p111)

PORT_FOLIO/SHUTTERSTOCK ©

PIERRE-YVES BABELON/SHUTTERSTOCK ©

Evatraha

Hop on a Boat to the Lokaro Peninsula

SCENIC WATERWAYS AND A HIKE-FRIENDLY HEADLAND

The Lokaro Peninsula is a spectacular and well-preserved area of inland waterways, green hills and barrier beaches. It lies about 15km northeast of Fort Dauphin along the coast (by far the more interesting way to get here), or about 40km by road.

Half the fun of visiting Lokaro is the journey there. Excursions from Fort Dauphin begin with a short drive to **Lac Lanirano**, where you board a motorised outrigger to navigate the snaking channel – lined by ravinala palms and sprouting pandanus plants – that the lake tapers to. Boats dock at the fishing village of **Evatraha**, at the end of Lac Ambavarano, from where it's half an hour on foot over the hills to lovely **Mahanoro Beach**. It's another 30 minutes' walk on to beautiful **Lokaro Bay**, where an hour's stroll along the beach leads to **Nosy Lokaro**, a rugged little island (accessible on foot at low tide) with good snorkelling.

Explore Parc National Andohahela

THREE PARKS IN ONE

The 72,500-hectare Parc National Andohahela, around 40km northwest of Fort Dauphin, is one of Madagascar's most diverse. It protects some of the last remnants of rainforest in the south,

 WHERE TO STAY BEYOND FORT DAUPHIN

Tsimelahy Village
Cheap and extremely basic hotels and guesthouses provide early morning access to Andohahela. $

Berenty
The concrete bungalows here are comfortable but a bit tired. Book well in advance; it's popular. $$$

Mandrare River Camp, Ifotaka
Luxury safari-style tents overlooking the Mandrare, superb food, and top-notch guided excursions. $$$

as well as spiny forest and a small but extremely important parcel of transition forest – the only place in the world where the rare triangular palm is still found in its natural habitat. In all, the park boasts a remarkable 12 species of lemur, more than 120 species of bird, and a variety of amphibians and reptiles, including crocodiles.

The best lemur-viewing is in Malio, in the park's rainforest section, while the trails in Ihazofotsy-Mangatsiaka get you up close and personal to Andohahela's spiny forest. The most popular area, however, is Tsimelahy, the bird-rich and botanically unique transition zone just off the RN13, where an excellent 3km trail follows the Tarantsy River through a pink sandstone canyon.

Join the Primatologists at Berenty

HOME OF THE DANCING LEMURS

Arguably the most famous private reserve in Madagascar, **Berenty** contains nearly one-third of the remaining tamarind gallery forest in the country. American primatologist Alison Jolly put Berenty on the map with her studies into ring-tailed lemur behaviour here in the early 1960s, and it once drew nearly 8000 yearly visitors.

The reserve, 82km west of Fort Dauphin, was founded by the de Heaulme family in 1936 and is still run by their descendants today. Visitors can walk forest paths unguided in search of six species of lemur, in particular the large groups of extremely habituated ring-tailed and Verreaux's sifakas – Berenty's famous 'Dancing Lemurs', who side-skip across open ground between the trees.

Explore Ifotaka Community Forest

SACRED FORESTS OF THE ANTANDROY

The remote Ifotaka Community Forest, 130km west of Fort Dauphin, preserves around 22,000 hectares of spiny and gallery forest – sacred places to the local Antandroy people, as they house the tombs of their ancestors. Protected first by taboos and now by the local community association, the forests are home to an extraordinary array of flora and fauna: tamarinds and octopus trees; ring-tailed lemurs and Verreaux's sifakas; crested *couas* and scops owls. **Ifotaka** is best explored with the knowledgable guides from Mandrare River Camp, who will give you a fascinating introduction to Antandroy culture and customs.

SISAL

As the RN13 runs towards Amboasary and the Mandrare Valley, the landscape morphs into nothing but sisal. This spiky agave plant, introduced to Madagascar from Mexico in the 1930s, runs in uniform rows to the horizon – what used to be thick spiny forest is now back-to-back plantations stretching for 30,000 hectares.

Sisal's long, thin fibres are mostly used to make carpets, and rope for shipping. The plants can't be harvested until they're four years old, and each one only has a few years before it's no longer commercially viable. The industry provides a vital source of income for more than 15,000 local families, although work in the fields is tough: the fronds are razor sharp and workers must harvest 3000 leaves a day in order to get paid.

 GETTING AROUND

You can hire a 4WD in Fort Dauphin to visit Lokaro, but the boat journey is half the fun of getting here: Dadamanga, Lavasoa and Nepenthès can all organise trips. You can also hire a 4WD to get to Andohahela, or take a *taxi-brousse* to Tsimelahy and hike the 8km from the RN13 (check the security situation before setting out), but it's far easier to visit on a trip with Dadamanga. Visiting Berenty and Ifotaka is best done directly (La Croix du Sud for the former, Mandrare River Camp for the latter).

WESTERN MADAGASCAR

UNFORGETTABLE ADVENTURES OUT WEST

Western Madagascar is all that's good about Madagascar: a world of baobabs, otherworldly landscapes and isolated national parks.

This is a region that rewards those who follow their curiosity to the end of the road, and then go on a little further.

Yes, you could still see a lot if you stick to the paved road, although paved roads in Madagascar (between Antsirabe and Miandrivazo, for example) can be pretty appalling. Without straying from the tarmac, you could experience the wonderful wildlife of Parc National Ankarafantsika or the quiet coastal charms of Majunga (Mahajanga). You could even visit an ecotourism project in the mangroves and (if you ignore the last 6km of dirt road) surround yourself with the image that has come to define a nation's wild beauty: the Allée des Baobabs.

But the end of the paved road is very often the start of a whole new adventure. Head north and northwest of Morondava to look for fossa in the Réserve Forestière de Kirindy. At one point on the journey you'll cross a river on a ferry pulled by people as in centuries past, before having lunch at Mad Zebu (where the cuisine is cutting-edge contemporary) on your way to the stunning Parc National Bemaraha. Around Majunga, it's a similar story; visit lakes and wetlands, deep subterranean caverns, and national parks so remote that maps of the 'road' network are speculative at best.

ELENA SKA/SHUTTERSTOCK ©

THE MAIN AREAS

MAJUNGA (MAHAJANGA)
Agreeable city by the sea.
p116

MORONDAVA
Baobabs, beaches and ecotourism.
p124

DENNIS CAN DE WATER/SHUTTERSTOCK ©

Above: Malagasy man and zebu on Allée des Baobabs (p125); right: *Tsingy*

Find Your Way

The area around Morondava is vast, and you may need to backtrack via Morondava to get between attractions (eg Bemaraha and the Tsiribihina River). Having your own 4WD is the best way to go.

Majunga (Mahajanga, p116)

Enjoy oceanfront Corniche, visit radiant Cirque Rouge, then escape across the water to the fishing village of Katsepy.

FERRY

Don't be fooled by short map distances into thinking you'll get anywhere quickly. The road north of the Morondava region involves a number of river crossings where you'll wait for a car ferry to get across.

Morondava (p124)

Relaxing on beaches, admiring the world's most beautiful baobabs, and getting immersed in local community life at the Kivalo Soa Honko.

4WD

A 4WD (preferably with driver) is the best way to get around this part of western Madagascar, partly because some roads are terrible, but often it's the only way. Arrange via tour operators/ guides in Morondava.

Cirque Rouge

Katsepy   Majunga
Namakia   Mitsinjo   Pare National
Soalala   Ankarafanisika
Vilamatsa   Lac   Bekoratsaka
            Kinkony Bekipay Ambondromany
Ambohipaky
            Andranomavo
Besalampy
                        Maevatanana
Berevo-
sur-Ranobe   Maria
Tambohorano   Kandreho
                                Mahatsinjo
Andrea   Morafenobe
Maintirano Andafiha
            Beravina
                                Ankazobe
Tsianaloka Antsalova
            Parc   Tsiroanomandidy Mahitsy
Mozambique National
Channel   Bemaraha   Miarinarivo
Tamotamo   ANTANANARIVO
        Bekopaka

        Behamotra
                Mahajilo River
            Ankotrofotsy
Allée des   Beroboka Nord
Baobabs   Réserve Forestière
Morondava de Kirindy
                        Malaimbandy
Belo-
sur-Mer Parc National
        Kirindy Mite
    Antevamena

0 — 50 km
0 — 25 miles

PIERRE-YVES BABELON/SHUTTERSTOCK ©

ARTRUSH/SHUTTERSTOCK ©

Manambolo River, Tsingy de Bemaraha (p129)

Plan Your Time

Majunga (Mahajanga) and Morondava are the two main towns in the west, but they're separated by vast tracts of wilderness; to get between them, you'll need to travel via Tana.

Ten Days to Explore

Drive from Tana to **Morondava** (p124), breaking up the journey in **Miandrivazo** (p132); if you fly there and back you could do this route in a week. In Morondava, visit **Allée des Baobabs** (p125) and **Kivalo Soa Honko** (p126), then look for fossa in the **Réserve Forestière de Kirindy** (p128). Lunch at **Mad Zebu** (p129) then spend three nights in the otherworldly **Parc National Bemaraha** (p129).

A Week in the Northwest

Break up the journey north in the biodiversity hot spot **Parc National Ankarafantsika** (p121) on your way to **Majunga** (p116), which is worth a couple of days to soak up the seaside atmosphere and visit **Katsepy** (p118) and **Cirque Rouge** (p118). Don't miss the **Grottes d'Anjohibe** (p120) and mount a two-day expedition to **Parc National Baie de Baly** (p123).

Seasonal Highlights

APRIL TO OCTOBER
The dry season, this is the busiest time of year and the only months to explore the *tsingy* (limestone pinnacle formations) at Parc National Bemaraha.

NOVEMBER
There's nothing quite so compelling (or disconcerting) as hearing fossas mate; it all happens in the Réserve Forestière de Kirindy in November.

DECEMBER & JANUARY
A mini high season over Christmas and New Year, December and January are generally busy all over the west.

MARCH & APRIL
Wet seasons are relatively light, but trails north of Morondava may be impassable. Prices are generally lower. It's good for wildlife in Parc National Ankarafantsika.

MAJUNGA (MAHAJANGA)

Majunga

ANTANANARIVO

One of the largest cities in Madagascar's west, Majunga (Mahajanga) is both an attractive waterside city and a gateway to a whole portfolio of natural attractions, from stunning caves and rock formations to sacred lakes and bird-rich wetlands. Yes, the city sprawls a long way back from the water. But it possesses one of the lovelier waterfronts of Madagascar's seaside cities, and it has its sprinkling of attractions.

The city also has an interesting human story. The waterfront here has been a trading crossroads since Arab, Swahili and Gujarati merchants used it as a thriving commercial base between the Malagasy highlands, East Africa and the Middle East from the 13th century onwards. These days, Majunga has large Comoran and Indian populations, not to mention surviving historical connections with mainland Africa. It all adds up to one of the most ethnically diverse places in Madagascar.

TOP TIP

Spend at least two days in and around Majunga; one to enjoy Cirque Rouge and the sunset along Majunga's Corniche, the other to spend a day in Katsepy. Katsepy's Chez Mme Chabaud has seven tidy bungalows that make a quieter alternative to busy Majunga.

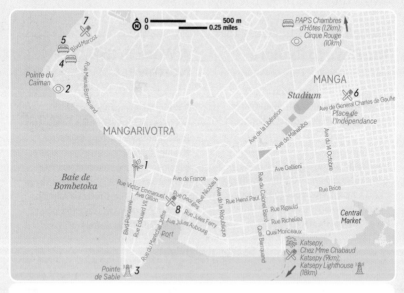

SIGHTS
1 Baobab Tree
2 Corniche
3 Lighthouse

SLEEPING
4 Hôtel du Phare
5 Karibu Lodge

EATING
6 Chez Madame Chabaud
7 Fishing Residence
8 Parad'Ice

Tuk-tuks, Majunga

Wander the Waterfront
Majunga (Mahajanga)

JOIN THE LOCALS TO PROMENADE

With no major downtown port to crowd out the loveliness, Majunga's inhabitants have claimed the city as their own, especially along the palm-lined **Corniche** (Blvd Poincarré and Blvd Marcoz) that borders the sea.

If you've travelled at all around Madagascar, where the country's charm all too rarely resides in urban areas, you'll understand just how special late afternoons in Majunga really are. As sunset nears, the sea breeze arrives and evening takes over, locals flock to the waterfront from all across town to sip a soft drink or nibble kebabs from numerous street carts. Not far from the waterfront, look for shady arcades and arches, and walls draped with gorgeous bougainvillea. Exquisitely carved wooden doors adorn some of the houses in these arcades; they date back to the city's prosperous 19th-century heyday.

In the thick of the Corniche's most popular stretch, at the T-junction with Ave de France, there is an enormous **baobab tree**, with a circumference of 21m! Believed to be well over 700 years old, the tree is a real Majunga landmark: locals believe it is *fady* (taboo) to touch it. Right down at the southern end of the Corniche is another icon of Majunga's skyline: the **Lighthouse** that guides boats in from Pointe de Sable.

TOURS BEYOND MAJUNGA (MAHAJANGA)

Aventure & Découverte
Specialises in quad-bike excursions to nearby attractions. Also organises 4WD and pirogue (traditional dugout canoe) trips, including to Parcs Nationaux Baie de Baly et Tsingy de Namoroka. Contact via Facebook.

La Ruche des Aventuriers
In addition to tours in and around Majunga, it also offers tours out into the wild, covering all of the main sights around Majunga – including three-day camping trips to hard-to-reach Lac Kinkony. Contact via Facebook.

Rivo
Local guide Rivo (032 45 839 28), who speaks basic English, can organise a two-day visit to Grottes d'Anjohibe, with a night of camping by the pool. Facilities are basic and meals are simple.

 WHERE TO STAY IN MAJUNGA (MAHAJANGA) ———————

Hôtel du Phare
Overlooking the Corniche, this place has simple, spacious and spotless rooms, with a nice garden. **$$**

Karibu Lodge
Fifteen duplex suites with sea views and terrace/balcony. Pool and bar-restaurant overlook water. **$$$**

PAP'S Chambres d'Hôtes
Just three rooms, but they're smart and stylish, and public areas are just as delightful. **$$$**

As you wander the length of the Corniche, you'll find yourself never wanting the evening to end, and finding a way to stay longer so you can enjoy it all over again.

Explore Rainbow-Coloured Cirque Rouge

ENJOY THE EARTH COLOURS

You can't visit Majunga without a detour to **Cirque Rouge**, a dramatic place that's one of western Madagascar's most famous sights. At its best around sunset – plan to arrive mid- to late afternoon and stay until the sun goes down – this amphitheatre of eroded rock glows in a rainbow hue of colours, including red, pink, ochre and white for much of the day. But it's the warm hues of the setting sun that really set the rock walls ablaze in spectacular fashion. In addition to just admiring the view and watching as the colours change from one minute to the next, take the lovely 10-minute walk by the stream that runs along the bottom of the valley and down through a small canyon to the sea.

Cirque Rouge is 12km north of the city but almost on the edge of Majunga's urban sprawl. Charter a taxi for the afternoon and make sure they wait to bring you back to town after dark.

Escape the Big City

BEACHES, LIGHTHOUSE AND FINE FOOD

Whether you're en route to Kinkony or looking for a day trip from Majunga, **Katsepy** (pronounced *kah-tsep*), just across the waters of Bombetoka Bay, is a fine little excursion. Take the early morning boat and, if you're lucky, you'll arrive just as the fishers are hauling in their catch from the night before. Relax on one of the pretty local beaches, head for **Katsepy's Lighthouse** (charter a taxi or walk there for two hot hours from the village) for fabulous views of Bombetoka Bay and Mozambique Channel, then take lunch at the fabulous Katsepy outpost of **Chez Mme Chabaud**, Majunga's best restaurant. Otherwise, soak up the atmosphere of this small, sleepy fishing village.

WHERE TO EAT IN MAJUNGA (MAHAJANGA)

Parad'Ice
Cheerful cafe-restaurant serving simple meals, including *ravitoto* (pork stew with manioc greens) or zebu stew. $

Chez Madame Chabaud
Small and intimate Majunga institution producing divine fusion cuisine mixing Malagasy, Creole and European influences. $$

Fishing Résidence
Hotel-restaurant noted for exquisite seafood, such as calamari and prawns in *combava* (wild lemon) sauce. $$

GETTING AROUND

You can get to Majunga from Tana by air or by road (bus or car). Once you're here, tours, upmarket hotels and car rental companies can take you out into Majunga's attraction-rich hinterland. In the town itself, apart from along the Corniche where you'll want to spend most of your time getting around on foot, a taxi is your best bet; expect most rides around town to cost at least Ar10,000.

Car-and-passenger ferries to Katsepy leave from the port at 7.30am daily, then return from Katsepy around 9am. If there's sufficient demand, it sometimes does a second trip back from Katsepy in the afternoon. Private motorboats cross in both directions a few times a day until about 3pm.

Beyond Majunga (Mahajanga)

Majunga

Parc National
Baie de Baly

Grottes
d'Anjohibe

Mahavy-Kinkony
Wetland Complex

Parc National
Ankarafantsika

Combining the remote with the accessible, the area around Majunga is like a bucket list of Madagascar's best.

Imagine a world of vast subterranean caves and grottoes, of internationally recognised wetlands, or of remote national parks that could be yours alone. Throw in one of Madagascar's most interesting bird- and lemur-rich national parks, and you could easily spend a week or more exploring the area.

What gives the area such appeal is the sheer diversity of attractions. Yes, you can see lemurs, and stay in remote luxury deep in the wilderness. But with the Grottes d'Anjohibe, the Mahavy-Kinkony Wetland Complex, and national parks as varied as Baie de Baly, Ankarafantsika, Baie de Baly et Tsingy de Namoroka, the world beyond Majunga really does have an embarrassment of riches.

TOP TIP

Allow more time than you think you may need for exploring the region: some of the attractions here are major expeditions.

Parc National Ankarafantsika (p121)

ARTRUSH/SHUTTERSTOCK ©

TIPS FOR GROTTES D'ANJOHIBE

How to Get There?
It takes a good 3½ hours to get to Anjohibe from Majunga. To do it as a day trip, you'll need to leave at first light to be back by sunset.

Stay Overnight?
Local guide Rivo can make the arrangements for an overnight camping stay by the pools: if you have the time, it's a unique experience to stay after the day-tripping crowds have gone for the day.

When to Go?
The track to the Grottes d'Anjohibe is passable only between April and October and requires a 4WD.

Pal tree spikes, Parc National Ankarafantsika

Discover a Magical Subterranean World

EXPLORE UNDERGROUND

Stepping into the **Grottes d'Anjohibe** – which are 80km, or a 3½-hour drive from Majunga – is like discovering another, altogether more magical subterranean world, one that bears no resemblance to the one above ground. Extending over 5km, this succession of caverns takes many forms. Some call to mind great cathedrals, others some strange fantasy forest, with stalactites and stalagmites of varying shapes and sizes strewn around. As you walk through this miraculous world, rays of light from passageways and holes in the ceiling cast an eerie, almost sepulchral light upon the scene. Even if you've seen your share of caves elsewhere, these really are something special.

The complement to all of the below-ground magnificence are the natural pools that frame the entrance to some of the caves; some of the caverns also have pools with pitch-black waters. Cast in deep emerald shades, the external pools are a superb place for a swim. You'll be in the shadow of high cliffs and *ravinala* palm trees whose leaves sway in the breeze like parading ostriches. The first pool you come to near the entrance to the site is shallow and inviting, but

WHERE TO STAY IN MAJUNGA (MAHAJANGA)

Hôtel Chez Chabaud	**Baobab Tree Hotel & Spa**	**Coco Lodge**
Rooms here may lack character but the whole place is immaculate, and it's terrific value. **$**	Majunga's most luxurious option: stylish rooms, an excellent restaurant, a bar, spa and priceless views. **$$$**	Well-designed, personable little hotel, Coco Lodge has huge rooms, a pool, a bar, and restaurant. **$$$**

better things await you a little further on. The second pool sits at the base of a spectacular waterfall and is ideal for your first swim.

Hike a Forest Oasis

HIKING AND WILDLIFE

They should declare **Parc National Ankarafantsika** (114km, or a two- to three-hour drive from Majunga) a national treasure. One look at everything that surrounds it should tell you why: Ankarafantsika is an island of dry deciduous forest, the last of its kind in Madagascar. And whether you're arriving from Tana to the south or from Majunga in the north, the contrast is stark: there isn't a tree in sight for hundreds of kilometres. What makes Ankarafantsika's survival so incredible is its accessibility: the park sits astride the RN4 and is one of few parks in the country that you can reach by public transport.

The best way to explore this fascinating place is on foot. Eight short circuits fan out across the park, and together they make up a network that shows you the best the park has to offer; you could easily combine two or three of these trails to create a half-day traverse.

If you're hiking out in the park's western reaches, don't be surprised if it gets sandy underfoot as you cross a thickly forested plateau. Most of the park's eight lemur species are found here: watch in particular for Coquerel's sifaka, brown lemurs and four nocturnal species (sportive, woolly, grey mouse and the unfortunately named fat-tailed dwarf lemur). The birdlife is exceptional in these parts, too. The scenery out west is similarly rewarding, with a dramatic canyon reached via a grassland plateau where tall, golden grasses sway in the breeze.

Trails also crisscross the northern half of the park, and you'll get a representative sample of what the park has to offer only if you visit the north as well as the west. Here you'll skirt the pretty lake and pass beneath baobabs. The birdwatching is excellent here (and completely different from the south). The north also has more reptiles, including crocodiles.

In addition to a fine portfolio of lemurs, Ankarafantsika also shelters 129 different bird species across its entirety, as well as 70 species of reptiles, such as small iguanas and a rare species of leaf-tailed gecko. But perhaps the park's most celebrated resident is the critically endangered ploughshare tortoise. For the past three decades, the Durrell Wildlife Conservation Trust (durrell.org) has overseen a hugely successful captive-breeding program. The species remains in peril and security is high: you can only watch the tortoises through a chain-link fence.

WILDLIFE OF ANKARA-FANTSIKA

Rhinoceros Chameleon
Gets its name from the male of the species that sports a large, curious-looking, bulb-like proboscis.

Madagascar Fish Eagle
The latest UN estimates put the number of fish eagles at just 40 breeding pairs; only found along Madagascar's northwest coast.

Sickle-Billed Vanga
Found only in Madagascar, this bird has an extravagant beak and announces its presence with raucous calls.

Mongoose Lemur
Critically endangered, and one of only two lemur species to live beyond Madagascar (in the Comoros Islands).

Golden-Brown Mouse Lemur
Nocturnal and one of the smallest of all lemurs; it was only discovered in 1994 and lives only in and around the park.

WHERE TO STAY IN PARC NATIONAL ANKARAFANTSIKA

National Park Campsites
Expect basic shared facilities at Ankarafantsika's park-run campground; there's not much shade. **$**

Gîte d'Ampijoroa
The national park's privately run accommodation. Large, simple bungalows; surprisingly good restaurant. **$$**

Blue Vanga Lodge
Some 5km from park entrance, with large, spotless bungalows; meals available if ordering ahead. **$$$**

PARCS NATIONAUX BAIE DE BALY ET TSINGY DE NAMOROKA

This isolated protected way out west of Majunga would be a major Madagascar attraction if it were easier to reach. That's because it's home to dense forests of peculiarly Madagascan *tsingy*, jagged rocky pinnacles interlaced with deep canyons, streams and lush, green trees. Trails meander among the rocks, and its possible to cross some canyons on rope bridges custom-laid for the purpose. There are three day-trip circuits through the park, each of which combines hiking with a 4WD expedition.

Count on four days round trip from Majunga, plus time you spend here. **Aventure & Découverte** (p117) is a Majunga operator that can organise trips. The park is only accessible from May to October.

ARTRUSH/SHUTTERSTOCK ©

Paradise flycatcher

Go Birding at Mahavy-Kinkony Wetland Complex

COUNT THE WATERBIRDS

Madagascar's incredible diversity is on show at the **Mahavy-Kinkony Wetland Complex**; it's a one-day drive to get here from Majunga. Where elsewhere it's all about the lemurs, here it's the birds that take centre stage. So grab your binoculars, head out into this area where very few other travellers go, and be prepared to add large numbers of birds to your Madagascar bird list.

The complex extends over a large area, with marine bays, rivers, a delta and 22 lakes. The latter includes Madagascar's second-largest lake, **Lac Kinkony**, with its 143 recorded species; it's the only place where all of western Madagascar's waterfowl species can be seen. In between all of this water, the protected area also encompasses ecosystems as diverse as dry deciduous and gallery forests, savannah grasslands, marshlands, mangroves, and even caves.

This is an adventurous undertaking, and is all the more enjoyable because of it. As is so often the case out in these parts, roads are incredibly rough and it can be slow-going.

 WHERE TO STAY IN ANJAJAVY

Anjajavy le Lodge
Relais & Châteaux property with luxurious guest villas, fine dining and lots of activities. **$$$**

La Maison de Marovasa-Be
Exquisite villas and suites, each with balcony. The whole place has a lost-world, sustainable feel. **$$$**

Antsanitia Beach Resort
Isolated ecotourism gem with lovely bungalows, gorgeous pool, open-air bar, and fabulous restaurant. **$$$**

Talk to any Majunga tour company to see what's possible, but count on at least three days to get there and back from Majunga, including time while there.

Explore a Remote Park

MADAGASCAR'S GARDEN OF EDEN

There's remote. And then there's **Parc National Baie de Baly**. Crowning Madagascar's western bulge, this isolated park is a place of incredible biodiversity and wonder; it really does have an earth's-first-morning quality about it. And remember this sobering thought: most of Madagascar once looked like this.

Best known as the home of the critically endangered ploughshare tortoise, this remote park has it all: dense dry, bamboo and mangrove forests; sand dunes and beaches; lakes and rivers. Such is the variety of habitats that it can feel as if all that's good about Madagascar's natural world has been compressed into this one park. Inhabiting these different habitats are eight forest-loving lemur species; Decken's sifaka and brown lemurs are most commonly sighted. Also within the park, this time on the beaches, are the nesting grounds for green, hawksbill, Madagascar big-headed and loggerhead turtles. More than 120 bird species have also been recorded here.

Getting around is itself an adventure, and the four different circuits (each lasting from one to six hours) combine walks with 4WD trails and, for the longer circuits, getting around in a pirogue (traditional dugout canoe). Wherever you find yourself in the park, stop often, listen to the silence and to the birdsong, and look up or look around you: a visit here is a genuine feast for the senses.

Most Majunga tour operators can arrange a visit, although access to the park is only possible from May to October. To get here, you'll travel via Soalala, 150km southwest of Katsepy on a two-day 4WD expedition from Majunga.

WHERE MAMMALS BEGAN?

In 1999, Dr John Flynn, now of the American Museum of Natural History in New York, and his team unearthed one of the earliest known mammal fossils south of Majunga. The 167-million-year-old fossil belonged to a primitive mammal species known as *Ambondro mahabo*. It lived at a time when Madagascar, much of Africa, Australia, India and South America were joined as part of the giant supercontinent Gondwana.

Until 2022, when a review of existing fossils was undertaken, paleontologists believed that modern mammals originated in the Northern Hemisphere. Now they're not so sure, and the Madagascan fossil (the second-oldest mammal fossil ever found) may give a clue to where we all came from.

GETTING AROUND

Public transport is rare to nonexistent in these parts. Only Parc National Ankarafantsika, which lies along the RN4, is accessible by buses or *taxis-brousses* travelling between Tana and Majunga. For everywhere else, you'll need to organise a tour through a Majunga (or possibly even an Antananarivo) travel agency. You'll save time if you make the necessary arrangements in advance of your visit.

MORONDAVA

Where the road from Tana and Antsirabe runs into the ocean, Morondava is a wonderfully relaxed place. Most places to stay and eat line the sandy Rue de l'Indépendance, a narrow north–south thoroughfare lined with gently decaying clapboard houses occupying a narrow spit of land between the beach and a mangrove canal. In addition to being a gateway to numerous attractions to the north and northwest, Morondava has two main attractions just outside the town itself: the renowned landmark and utterly spectacular Allée des Baobabs and Kivalo Soa Honko, a fine ecotourism project in the mangroves near town.

There's not much to do in the town itself, but it does have good places to stay and eat. And you'll really love being here when the afternoon sun loses its sting and you nurse a drink with locals at an outdoor table along Rue de l'Indépendance.

TOP TIP

Every vehicle that visits the Allée des Baobabs times their arrival to coincide with sunset. Sunrise can be an eerily quiet alternative, when there's barely another tourist in sight; it also offers the best views of the baobabs from across the lily pond.

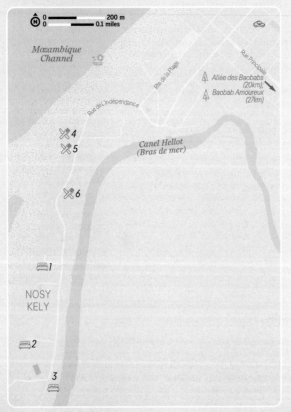

SLEEPING
1 Chez Maggie
2 Hôtel Palissandre Côte Ouest
3 Trecicogne

EATING
4 Bleu Soleil
5 La Gargote Valisoa
6 Restaurant Le Corail

Allée des Baobabs

Watching Sunset at Allée des Baobabs

BAOBAB ALLEY TURNS GOLDEN

There are baobabs through Madagascar, but nowhere do they come together in such a magical way as they do at **Allée des Baobabs**. The trees, some of which may be more than 1000 years old, flank either side of the RN8 between Morondava and Belo-sur-Tsiribihina. At any time of the day, their huge, gnarled branches fan out at the top of their trunks as if the trees have been planted upside down; baobabs have been nicknamed the 'roots of the sky'. But as the sun nears the horizon, the trunks turn golden, the colours of the trees and surrounding earth deepen, and the long shadows cast weirdly wonderful shapes across the landscape. Some of the best views of the actual sunset are from the large lily pond; a trail leads along the pond's north side to the best viewing area. But also don't forget to look away from the sun to see the baobabs turn magnificent.

The local community has set up a gift shop selling local handicrafts, lemur field guides, and baobab jam or oils. There's also a coffee shop/bar, super-clean toilets and a small breakfast restaurant beneath a tamarind tree near the southern

BAOBABS IN LOVE

Providing inspiration for many a Malagasy wood sculptor, two *Adansonia grandidieri* baobab trees known as **Baobab Amoureux** have twisted themselves into a perfect lovers' embrace, earning them the sobriquet of 'Baobabs in Love'. The entwined lovers are around 3km off the Morondava–Kirindy road, just north of the Allée des Baobabs – look for the Kivalo signpost. It's worth visiting before a sunset trip to Allée des Baobabs, or as a detour on your way between Morondava and Réserve Forestière de Kirindy or Belo-sur-Tsiribihina.

 WHERE TO STAY IN MORONDAVA

Trecicogne
This lovely Italian-run guesthouse has polished wooden floors, spotless rooms and open-air restaurant. **$$**

Chez Maggie
Well-appointed bungalows and chalets, garden, breezy restaurant; Chez Maggie is fabulous value. **$$$**

Hôtel Palissandre Côte Ouest
Morondava's premier address; supremely comfy bungalows, restaurant and pool. **$$$**

entrance to the site. The whole complex opens at 5am and closes after the last sunset visitors leave.

The Allée des Baobabs is 20km from Morondava; the turn-off is 14km east of town, in the village of Marofototra.

Visit a Mangrove Ecotourism Project

LEARN ABOUT COASTAL VILLAGE LIFE

Most travellers hurry through Morondava, staying overnight before launching a trip to Parc National Bemaraha. But **Kivalo Soa Honko** is one of the best things you can do in Madagascar's west.

Begun as a partnership between the local community and the World Wildlife Fund for Nature (WWF Madagascar) in 2017, the project is an opportunity for a more human-centric experience. You'll begin around 7am for the drive to a roadside village named Antsakoameloky, then walk cross-country with a guide in the cool of morning to Mangily village, where you'll receive a traditional local ceremony of greeting, accompanied by much song and dance. From here, the program can vary in terms of the order in which things happen. Over the course of the day, you'll take a 90-minute walk to the ocean shore, explore the mangroves with a local guide in a pirogue, tick off as many of the 50 bird species as you can, keep an eye out for the grey mouse lemurs, join the locals as they go crab-fishing, visit the local boat-making area, eat a specially prepared local meal and maybe even plant a tree. At the end of the day, you'll drive back to Morondava via the Baobab Amoureux and sunset at the Allée des Baobabs.

The whole experience costs Ar145,000, which covers all activities, plus Ar255,000 if you need to rent a vehicle for the day. Ask at the Association des Guides Agréé de Morondava (AGAMO; 033 9601 610) or any of the tour operators in Morondava.

The project has been such a success that two similar, if smaller, projects have begun nearby: **Lovobe** (south of Morondava; Ar95,000 per person plus vehicle) and **Kimony** (close to Kivalo; Ar135,000 per person plus vehicle).

GAEL RAKOTOVAO/SHUTTERSTOCK ©

Grilled Madagascar shrimps

WHERE TO EAT IN MORONDAVA

La Gargote Valisoa
This place is simplicity itself, with tasty local specialities (fish, zebu, soups) at good-value prices. $

Chez Maggie
House specialities in this thatch-roof bar-restaurant include steak, jumbo shrimp or catch of the day. $$

Restaurant Le Corail
Recommended for Malagasy cuisine, with international dishes, fresh seafood and excellent *romazava* (stew). $$

Bleu Soleil
With the best beach views in Morondava, this breezy place mostly does pizza and cocktails. $$

GETTING AROUND

You could walk from one end of Morondava to the other, but the sun beats down for much of the day. Take a taxi (rarely more than Ar10,000) instead.

To reach Kivalo or the Allée des Baobabs, you'll need your own wheels; either rent a vehicle for the day, charter a taxi, or visit en route between Morondava and Belo-sur-Tsiribihina.

Beyond Morondava

The area north and northeast of Morondava is filled with attractions, from fine dining to extraordinary wildlife and landscapes.

You could easily spend weeks exploring the many attractions around Morondava and still not see it all. The national parks and other protected areas in these parts – Bemaraha, Kirindy, Kirindy-Mitea – combine stirring natural beauty with some exceptional wildlife watching, from fossas and lemurs to incredible birdlife. Among the many activities you can join are multiday river trips along the Tsiribihina and Manambolo rivers, hiking amid the limestone pinnacles of Parc National Bemaraha, and snorkelling off a coral island near Belo-sur-Mer. And wherever you find yourself, you'll want to keep an eye on the lunch clock and plan your day around the stellar cooking of Mad Zebu, in Belo-sur-Tsiribihina.

TOP TIP

Many companies reserve Mad Zebu tables in advance; do likewise or be prepared to wait. Lunchtime peak is around 11.30am.

Parc National Bemaraha (p129)

ZARUBA ONDREJ/SHUTTERSTOCK ©

MORONDAVA TOUR OPERATORS & GUIDES

François Vahiako
Vahiako (visk_fr@yahoo.fr) is head of the Morondava Guides Association and organises 4WDs (with driver) for trips to Parc National Bemaraha, Belo-sur-Mer, or coastal pirogue trips. Look for him at Les Bougainvilliers.

Jean le Rasta
Charismatic Jean le Rasta (032 04 931 60 or 020 95 527 81), or Rasta Jean, speaks English, owns a 4WD, and runs tours in the region. Look for him at L'Oasis.

Remote River Expeditions
(remoterivers.com) Runs sustainable-travel-focused trips down Mangoky, Mahavavy and Manambolo rivers, as well as trips across western Madagascar. Find them at Chez Maggie.

Loic Tours
(contact@loictours.com) Has an office across the road from the water in Morondava. Offers full portfolio of activities, from 4WD rental to national-park trips.

Fossa

Find Fossa: Réserve Forestière de Kirindy

FOSSAS IN THE FOREST

As you drive north (60km, or 1½ hours) from Morondava, out beyond the Allée des Baobabs, the 125-sq-km **Réserve Forestière de Kirindy** looms on the horizon like a mirage. An island of dense forest surrounded by a denuded landscape of cattle, tree stumps and burning piles of vegetation, the Kirindy Forest is both sad and precious at the same time.

An oasis of biodiversity, Kirindy is home to 45 recorded bird species, including the crested ibis, the white-breasted mesite and the Madagascar pygmy kingfisher. Of the 32 different reptiles, watch for tenrecs and the giant jumping rat.

But nowhere in Madagascar do you stand a better chance of seeing the fossa (*Cryptoprocta felix*), the country's largest predator. This puma- or dog-like creatures with oversized ears and strangely elongated bodies can be seen year-round, but the best time to see them is in mating season (September to November). And seeing them is not even difficult, as long as you stay for longer than a passing visit around Ecolodge, where they're easily seen sleeping under the wooden cabins or stealing goodies from the kitchen and rubbish dump.

There are also eight different lemur species, but most are nocturnal, so make sure you take a guided night walk as well as

WHERE TO STAY IN RÉSERVE FORESTIÈRE DE KIRINDY

Ecolodge de Kirindy
Basic wooden bungalows with mosquito nets, uncomfortable mattresses, a restaurant, and fossas in the vicinity. **$$$**

Le Camp Amoureux
Run by the local community. An hour's drive south of Kirindy. Simple accommodation, night walks. **$$$**

Relais du Kirindy
Among the most pleasant places to stay with tidy, elevated wooden bungalows, restaurant, pool. **$$$**

daytime excursions. After dark, watch for the grey mouse lemur, red-tailed sportive lemur, fork-marked lemur, fat-tailed dwarf lemur, Coquerel's giant dwarf lemur and the Madame Berthe's mouse lemur; the latter is the world's smallest primate and weighs around 30g. By day, you'll likely see Verreaux's sifaka and the red-fronted brown lemur.

Enjoy Haute Cuisine at Mad Zebu

WESTERN MADAGASCAR'S BEST RESTAURANT

When you think of the great kitchens of Madagascar, the dusty settlement of Belo-sur-Tsiribihina (100km, or three to four hours north of Morondava by road) probably doesn't spring to mind. But it should. Getting here can also be half the fun. If you're coming from the south, you'll have to cross the river on a cable ferry that is guided across the current by a team of swimmers.

The restaurant itself sits along Belo's main street. The dining area is relaxed and laid-back: think slightly rickety tables, plastic chairs and plastic gingham tablecloths. But dishes seem to come straight out of a Michelin-starred restaurant (the chef trained in prestigious kitchens in Madagascar and Europe), with exquisite creations such as pan-fried shin of zebu; prawn medallions; or snapper fillet with peanuts, risotto and coconut sauce; all elaborately presented. Vegetarian options are available too, and make sure you save room for dessert.

Tackle the Tsingy of Parc National Bemaraha

HIKE/CLIMB IN OTHERWORLDLY BEAUTY

The landscapes of the Unesco World Heritage-listed **Parc National Bemaraha**, which lie 195km or a six- to eight-hour drive from Morondava, are at once quintessentially Madagascan and seem to spring from the surrealist imagination of Salvador Dalí. At its heart is the *tsingy*, the jagged, serrated limestone pinnacles that can rise hundreds of metres into the air. They were formed over centuries by the movement of wind and water.

The park is very well set up for visitors, smoothing the rough edges and making accessible some astonishing places that would be otherwise unreachable. This is done through the use of *via ferrata* (mountain routes equipped with fixed cables, stempels, ladders and bridges), rope bridges and walkways. You won't need any technical climbing experience for any of the routes: you just wear a harness, which you clip to cables and ladders as you go.

Spread over a large area, the park has two main areas worth exploring, the Petit Tsingy and the Grands Tsingy.

PREPARING TO EXPLORE THE TSINGY

Although there are a few 4WD circuits, you'll miss the best bits if you don't explore the park on foot. We recommend *at least* a day in the Petits Tsingy and a day in the Grands Tsingy.

Much of the walking in the *tsingy* can be strenuous and requires careful conversations with your guides before setting out: some of the routes are better for wildlife, others for views, some are strenuous, others an easy stroll, and so on. Anyone with a low level of fitness or vertigo might find exploring the *tsingy* challenging, particularly the Grands Tsingy, where hauling, squeezing, crawling and pulling are all part of the experience.

FOR MORE TSINGY

You can also see this uniquely Madagascan landform at the **Parcs Nationaux Baie de Baly et Tsingy de Namoroka** (p122), a remote park west of Majunga.

 WHERE TO STAY IN BELO-SUR-TSIRIBIHINA

Hôtel Ravinala
Dirt cheap in the truest sense of the word. Large, grimy rooms; no mosquito nets. **$**

Hôtel-Restaurant du Menabe
Old, colourful colonial building with an okay restaurant. Simple, airy rooms with huge double beds. **$**

Hotel Karibo
Cell-like rooms in main building; better, pricier ones out the back, and a good restaurant. **$$**

ZARUBA ONDREJ/SHUTTERSTOCK ©

Tsingy, Parc National Bemaraha

WILDLIFE OF PARC NATIONAL BEMARAHA

Parc National Bemaraha protects 11 lemur species. Watch for Decken's sifaka and the red-fronted brown lemur while hiking in the Petits Tsingy, as well as fat-tailed dwarf lemurs and grey mouse lemurs sleeping in tree hollows. The park also has two endemic lemur species that are found nowhere else: Cleese's woolly lemur (or Western woolly lemur) and the Sambirano lesser bamboo lemur.

Of the more than 100 bird species present, highlights include the critically endangered Madagascar fish eagle, as well as Henst's goshawk, Madagascar sparrowhawk, Madagascar harrier, crested ibis and Madagascar grey-throated rail. Some 45 reptiles and amphibians round out an impressive portfolio; watch for the Antsingy leaf chameleon and Madagascar iguana.

The **Petit Tsingy**, close to Bekopaka, is the most accessible section of the park, and has plentiful hiking trails. There are seven in all, ranging from an easy 1½-hour walk with walkways and easy bridges to a hardcore six-hour circuit requiring you to abseil a 30m cliff. Many of the trails in this area come with the added bonus of including a section by pirogue through the stunning Manambolo River gorges.

The largest and most impressive expanse of limestone pinnacles, the **Grands Tsingy** lie around 40km north of Bekopaka; it's a two-hour drive on a bad road, so start your day early. Most visitors drive to the start of the two circuits (four hours each), which follow a fantastic via ferrata through (and up and over) the pinnacles.

Rest in Belo-sur-Mer

SAND DUNES, SNORKELLING AND SUNSHINE

If **Belo-sur-Mer** were anywhere else on earth other than this isolated Madagascan shore, it would be known as a world-famous getaway; it's 95km, or a three- to four-hour drive from Morondava. There's not a whole lot to do here, but that's the point. Sand dunes almost drown the village, and at midday Belo-sur-Mer bakes in the sun with all the charm and glare of an over-exposed photograph. Just inland, vast salt marshes burn white like a hallucinatory void. But come sunset, it is

 WHERE TO STAY IN PARC NATIONAL BEMARAHA

Tanankoay Friendly hotel offering everything from camping to spacious en-suite bungalows, gardens and restaurant. **$**	**Camp Croco** This shaded tented camp offers epic sunsets by the Manambolo River and bare canvas tents. **$$**	**Orchidée du Bemaraha** Choice of both tents and rooms. Also two pools, a lovely bar, and beautiful grounds. **$$$**

Belo-sur-Mer

TAKE YOUR TIME

Joachin (Zo) Randriamahefa, driver

I've been driving the roads of Madagascar for many years and I know how bad they can be. The once-excellent road between Antsirabe and Miandrivazo (220km), for example, used to take four hours, but now takes six. I see lots of tourists get frustrated when it takes so long to arrive, but in Madagascar you can never really predict the condition of the roads. Often, it will be better to break up a long day journey with an overnight stop along the way. When making plans, and to avoid late-night arrivals, ignore the number of kilometres and ask an experienced local how long it really takes.

an entirely different place: climb to a sandy summit for golden views, and the whole scene seems suddenly magical. In the early morning and late afternoon, wander amid the fishers and their boats as they haul in their catch or mend their nets by the sea. Or watch as the skilled boatbuilders of the village craft the pirogues and *boutres* (single-masted dhows used for cargo) Belo-sur-Mer is still famous for. Or just look for beautiful shells on the beach.

And when it's too hot on land, take to the sea and the string of uninhabited, coral-fringed islands, some semi-submerged, that lie just offshore. All of the hotels can arrange pirogue-and-snorkelling excursions out to Nosy Andrahovo. Take a picnic lunch to enjoy under the palm trees and you're all set for paradise.

Trek Remote & Wildlife-Rich Backcountry

WALKING IN SEARCH OF WILDLIFE

Not many people make it out here. Their loss. Deliciously remote, and not to be confused with the better-known Réserve Forestière de Kirindy, the 722-sq-km **Parc National Kirindy-Mitea**, 90km (or three to four hours by 'road') south of Morondava and which surrounds Belo-sur-Mer, is wild and beautiful.

🛏 **WHERE TO STAY IN PARC NATIONAL BEMARAHA**

Le Soleil des Tsingy
The park's best base, with wilderness views from the restaurant, infinity pool, and lovely bungalows. **$$$**

Le Grand Hôtel du Tsingy du Bemaraha
Brick bungalows with good bathrooms and a decent restaurant. **$$$**

Olympe du Bemaraha
Set in leafy grounds, a well-run place with nicely spaced bungalows, a good restaurant and pool. **$$$**

BEST KIRINDY-MITEA HIKES

Circuit Ambondro–Sirave (3km, two hours)
Champion of the hikes. Fantastic Ambondro-Sirave passes amid sand dunes, spiny forest, baobabs, and a gorgeous beach.

Circuit Agnolignoly (2km, one hour)
A low-key stroll through mangroves and coastal estuaries, watching for waterbirds as you go.

Circuit Maetsakaloe (4km, two hours)
Baobabs, birds, dry forest and lemurs await you along this walk, with birdlife another highlight.

There's no tourism infrastructure to speak of. What that means in practice is there's no luxury to be found. But it also promises a more personal experience in an environment rarely disturbed by visitors. Out here it's all about sand dunes, mangroves and untouched coastline, with some fine wildlife viewing to animate the fine landscape.

Make sure you bring your hiking boots. Three short circuits traverse the park and it's the best way to get a taste of what Kirindy-Mitea has to offer. Along most of the walks, there's a chance that you'll see Verreaux's sifaka, the red-fronted brown lemur and the ring-tailed lemur. But greater sightings await you after dark, when your guide can help you track down nocturnal species like Madame Berthe's mouse lemur, fork-marked lemur, grey mouse lemur, Coquerel's dwarf lemur, fat-tailed dwarf lemur and red-tailed sportive lemur. If you're really lucky, you might even see the fossa. The birdlife, too, is spectacular, with 58 recorded species in total, a remarkable 18 of which are endemic to the region.

And if you have the time, ask your guide or Morondava tour operator to arrange a pirogue trip along the estuary and through the mangroves.

A River Trip Down the Tsiribihina

TRAVEL OFF-ROUTE AND DOWNRIVER

One of the most memorable things you can do in Madagascar is take a boat trip down the Tsiribihina River: there's nothing quite like drifting down a remote river, far from the world and its noise.

Most river journeys begin close to the town of **Miandrivazo** (*Mee-an-dree-vaaz*), which lies along the main RN34 road around halfway between Antsirabe and Morondava (265km, four to five hours). And it usually takes 2½ days to cover the 146km to Belo-sur-Tsiribihina (where you'll arrive around lunchtime on day three). You'll travel in a wooden pirogue (paddled by a local) or a larger motorised barge-like boat called a chaland. The former is a more sustainable way to travel and more in keeping with the backcountry silence of the journey at its best.

Almost as soon as you set out on day one, you're enveloped in scenery that is both beautiful and varied: the river passes through country that is in turns broad in the plains and narrow through the Tsiribihina gorges, with vast sandbanks converted to paddy fields alternating with tall, red cliffs and beautiful deciduous forest. You might see wildlife along the way – there is excellent birdwatching along the river, as well as the chance to spot lemurs, crocs and chameleons. But it's more about the scenery, about witnessing as it's lived far from the nearest

 WHERE TO STAY IN BELO-SUR-MER

Ecolodge du Menabe
Belo's best accommodation option, with 12 beachside bungalows, good food and activities, too. **$$**

Tsara Belo
Simple thatch bungalows, just off water's edge, are a good choice. Closes January and February. **$$**

Hôtel Entremer
Excellent choice, with great food, nice seaside bungalows, strong community ties, activities and solar power. **$$$**

The road from Morondava to Tuléar is only passable in dry season (usually May to October) and it takes three bone-shaking days – more if you linger along the towns of the Northern Reef. The reward? Beautiful landscapes, remote villages, makeshift ferries and heavenly beaches.

Your first day out of **1 Morondava** (p124) should take around six to eight hours. The tracks here are not as rough as those further south, but there are five wide, shallow rivers to cross and numerous streams to ford. At the end is **2 Manja**, a lively provincial town with a pretty church. The only place to stay is Kanto Hotel, a friendly spot with a surprisingly good restaurant, but basic rooms with shower water that barely trickles from the wall. Try to avoid weekends when the downstairs bar bumps and grinds until the wee small hours.

Day two is a long and punishing day in the saddle, and the actual route changes from one year to the next, depending on the rains. As with day one, it's a day of off-road driving, with a rickety vehicle ferry crossing at **3 Bejoavy**. You'll have to set off at first light, carry a picnic lunch, and count on ten hours to **4 Morombé**.

On day three, you'll pass along the splendid stretch of coastline that shadows Madagascar's Great Reef **5 Andavadoaka**, followed by the toughest section of road, a 30km, baobab-lined stretch of sand south of town. There are numerous gorgeous hotels and lots of good snorkelling and diving, so you may want to split this into two days as you head for **6 Tuléar (Toliara)**, which will feel like a grand metropolis, considering where you've been.

MANAMBOLO RIVER TRIPS

The Manambolo River is an alternative to the Tsiribihina, but there are pros and cons. The Tsiribihina is easy to reach from Miandrivazo, but to reach the Manambolo involves a rough, day-long 4WD trip from the capital. Then again, the Manambolo descent has the advantage of leaving you in Bekopaka, which is more convenient for Parc National Bemaraha.

The Manambolo descent is the more spectacular of the two, especially for its final passage through the Manambolo Gorge, and the Manambolo is generally quieter than the Tsiribihina, with far fewer groups making the trip downriver. Organise your Manambolo expedition through **Remote River Expeditions** (remoterivers.com).

Morondava ferry

road: this is some of the most remote country on the planet. You'll encounter locals fishing or attempting to cross the river with their loaded zebu carts, washing clothes by the riverside, and children playing and swimming.

Day one generally finishes with a visit to lovely waterfalls, where you can have a paddle (this will be your shower for the day). Camp is set on sandbanks every night, complete with campfire and prime viewing of the Milky Way; most operators will organise short walks and visits to local villages. In some cases, they'll invite local musicians and dancers to provide entertainment one evening, which can turn into quite a party if villagers join in!

Motorboats arrive at the ferry landing in Belo, but pirogues generally stop 40km upstream and travellers finish the last stretch either by zebu cart or 4WD.

When it comes to practicalities, the main time for river descents is from April to November. During the rainy season, you'll sleep in villages rather than on the sandbanks. And most river-trip packages include all camping equipment, food, (nonalcoholic) drinks, a guide and, of course, the boat.

You can organise the trip in Miandrivazo, a town that's full of operators and river guides, or in advance through **Remote River Expeditions** (remoterivers.com), **Mad Caméléon** (madcameleon.com) or **Espace Mada** (madagascar-circuits.com).

GETTING AROUND

Infrequent public transport (ie *taxis brousses*) connects Morondava with the main towns like Miandrivazo (for river trips) and Bekopaka (for Parc National Bemaraha), but from there you'll need your own wheels. Far better to arrange a car and a driver, or an all-inclusive tour, through one of the many operators in Morondava. Booking in advance will save you days of waiting around.

Manambolo gorge

Above: Moorish idol fish, Nosy Be (p142); right: Vanilla flower

NORTHERN MADAGASCAR

PLANTATIONS, BEACHES AND WILDLIFE

Madagascar's tropical north is a wild frontier that is still surprisingly accessible thanks to the handy airports at Nosy Be and Diego Suarez (Antsiranana).

The rugged north serves up the full Madagascar package – endless beaches, teeming coral reefs, historic townships, emerald-green cocoa, coconut, ylang-ylang and vanilla plantations, and national parks alive with lemurs, birds and chameleons. If you want a sampling platter of the best the island has to offer, without vast distances between stops, fly to Nosy Be or Diego Suarez (Antsiranana) and arrange a vehicle and driver to explore.

The cluster of islands around Nosy Be is the focus for beach lovers, with some of Madagascar's best resorts, superior diving and snorkelling, and an accessible national park with a full scorecard of Madagascan wildlife. Ferries provide easy access to the mainland, where a hired vehicle or *taxi-brousse* can whisk you to the stunning beaches and national parks around Diego Suarez or remote Sambava, capital of the Sava region and the hub for Madagascar's thriving vanilla trade.

Distances in the north are small, but roads are often diabolical, with the exception of the RN5a from Ambilobe to Vohémar – formerly one of the worst roads in the country but now as smooth as a billiard table. Linking Diego Suarez and central Madagascar, RN6 is in a bad way, and the tracks to many national parks are inaccessible during the rainy season. Don't be too ambitious about how much ground you can cover in a day as you roam the tropical north.

ARTUSH/SHUTTERSTOCK ©

THE MAIN AREAS

NOSY BE
Diving, snorkelling and stunning sands. p142

DIEGO SUAREZ (ANTSIRANANA)
Beaches, fine food and pristine nature. p154

SAMBAVA
Vanilla, wild beaches and national parks. p165

50 km

25 miles

FERRIES & PIROGUES

Motorised pirogues (small outrigger boats) between the islands operate like taxis-brousses, leaving when enough passengers gather, but services wind down after lunch, so getting back may involve paying extra for a 'special' trip. Ferries and pirogues also buzz from Nosy Be to Ankify on the mainland.

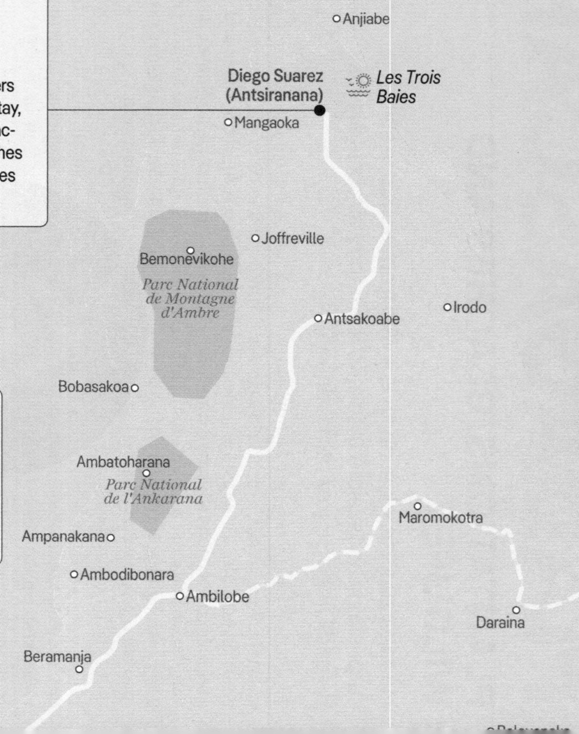

HIRED 4WD

Hiring a 4WD with a driver is the best way to explore the mainland, and it's the only way to reach many of the national parks, unless you're happy to add on several more hours walking to and from the highway.

TAXIS-BROUSSES

Regular taxis-brousses link the towns on the mainland, including Ankify, the port for ferries to Nosy Be and neighbouring islands. However, with the poor condition of the roads, journeys can be slow and services often fizzle out in the afternoon.

Diego Suarez (Antsiranana), p154

This historic town offers appealing places to stay, great food, and easy access to glorious beaches and adventure activities in the hinterland.

Nosy Be, p142

Madagascar's beach capital has stunning sands, thriving coral reefs, tropical jungles and superior places to stay and eat; more island escapes lie just offshore.

Anjiabe

Les Trois Baies

Diego Suarez (Antsiranana)

Mangaoka

Irodo

Joffreville

Antsakoabe

Bemonevikohe

Parc National de Montagne d'Ambre

Bobasakoao

Ambatoharana

Parc National de l'Ankarana

Ampanakano

Ambodibonara

Ambilobe

Beramanja

Maromokotra

Daraina

Vohémar

Nosy Faly

Hell-Ville

Nosy Be

Andilana

Dzamandzaro

Parc National Marin de Nosy

YUG/SHUTTERSTOCK

o Ampijoroana

o Ampanefena

o Tanambao

o Bemanevika

● Sambava

o Farahalana

o Antalaha

o Maromandia

o Ambohimitsinjo

o Andranofotsy

Sambava, p165

Madagascar's vanilla capital is a base for plantation visits, beach days, and trips to some of the north's most impressive national parks.

Tsaratanana Massif

o Zarambavy

Maromokotro

o Matsaborimadio

o Ambararatabe-Nord

o Béalanana

o Sandrakota

o Doanyo

Andapa

Parc National de Marojejy

o Antetezantany

Marojejy Massif

o Matsoandakana

o Ambanja

o Ankaramibe

o Maromandia

o Ambaliha

o Ambolobozo

Find Your Way

International and domestic flights serve Nosy Be and Diego Suarez and taxis-brousses link the major towns via rutted RN6, passable RN3b and recently upgraded RN5a, but you'll need a hired vehicle to access most national parks.

Plan Your Time

Arrange your time around lazy days on tropical islands, snorkelling and diving trips, hikes into stunning national parks, plantation tours, and bumpy drives and boat trips getting between these attractions.

Ambatozavavy, Nosy Be (p142)

IRS/SHUTTERSTOCK ©

Island-Hopping

● Nosy Be is northern Madagascar in miniature, and many people are happy to settle into a resort and day-trip to surrounding islands, without ever visiting the mainland.

● Start your explorations in historic **Hell-Ville** (p143) and buzz along the coast to **Ambatoloaka** (p148), the hub for snorkelling and diving trips to nearby islets and sandbars. The island's best strip of sand is in the north at **Andilana** (p148) and you can pop over to idyllic **Nosy Sakatia** (p148) on the way.

● For wildlife encounters, take a pirogue to **Nosy Komba** (p152), or arrange a tour to lovely **Parc National Lokobe** (p150), just east of Hell-Ville.

Seasonal Highlights

Northern Madagascar is a dry-season destination; many national parks and beach areas are reached via dirt tracks that become impassable during the rains from November to April.

APRIL

The end of the rains ushers in the tourist season across the north, though remote reserves can be tricky to reach till May.

MAY

In the third week of May, the **Zegny'Zo Festival** brings street theatre and traditional music to Diego Suarez (Antsiranana).

JUNE

The spirited **Donia festival** in Hell-Ville welcomes bands and singers from Madagascar, Comoros, Réunion and Mauritius.

BYVALET/SHUTTERSTOCK ©, GOLDEN BROWN/SHUTTERSTOCK ©, BYVALET/SHUTTERSTOCK ©

A Week in the Tropical North

● **Nosy Be** (p142) is the logical start point. Get your fill of beaches and diving, then head over to Ankify and work your way north to explore the wildlife-thronged *tsingy* (limestone pinnacles) at **Réserve Spéciale Ankarana** (p163).

● Swing into the dramatic **Tsingy Rouges** (p164) on your way north to **Diego Suarez (Antsiranana)** (p154).

● Devote several days to the beaches at **Les Trois Baies** (p160) and the hiking trails on **Montagne des Français** (p161).

● To finish up, escape the tropical heat with a hike in lovely **Parc National Montagne d'Ambre** (p162), where refreshingly cool rainforests hide lemurs, chameleons and more.

Two Weeks of Beaches, Wildlife & Vanilla Country

● You'll need a few weeks to take in all the highlights of the north. Starting in **Nosy Be** (p142), make time for a dive trip to spectacular **Nosy Mitsio** (p153).

● Buzz over to the mainland and visit the plantations near **Ambanja** (p152), then track down some of Madagascar's most enigmatic animals in the reserves around **Diego Suarez** (p154).

● Turn south and branch east at Ambilobe to spot Tattersalli *sikafas* at **Loky Manambato Protected Area** (p171). Use vanilla-scented **Sambava** (p165) as a base to explore wildlife-crammed **Parc National de Marojejy** (p167), then cruise south to Andapa for more creature encounters at **Réserve Spéciale Anjanaharibe-Sud** (p172).

AUGUST

The prime time for national park visits; humpback whales begin to arrive on the northwest coast.

SEPTEMBER

The height of the dry season, meaning easier bird-spotting in dry-forest reserves such as **Réserve Spéciale Ankarana** (p163).

OCTOBER

Whale sharks cruise the northwest coast from October to November, visiting many dive sites around Nosy Be.

NOVEMBER

Visitor numbers fall as the rains arrive, but you can spot adorable baby lemurs before the tracks to reserves become impassable.

NOSY BE

Nosy Be

ANTANANARIVO ✪

The largest of more than 20 tropical islands basking off the north-west coast, Nosy Be – literally 'big island' – crams in some big experiences. There are blissful beaches, rainbow-coloured reefs, volcanic summits, wildlife-mobbed jungles, and even a taste of city living in Hell-Ville (Andoany), the island's historic capital.

With regular flights from Réunion and Antananarivo and seasonal charters from a growing number of European cities, this languorous isle is the perfect start to a trip to the north. Indeed, many holidaymakers spend all their time in Madagascar basking on the beaches of Nosy Be and its fringing islands.

But the mainland lies within easy reach, so this could just be the start of a circuit taking in the national parks around Diego Suarez (Antsirana) and Sambava. If you're planning a wider trip, set aside some time to do nothing at all on Nosy Be's beaches – it's what the island is famous for.

TOP TIP

Most visitors stay on the beach, but resorts tend to be a long way from the main round-island road (made up of Route de l'Ouest and Route de l'Est), meaning you'll be dependent on tours to explore. For easy access to public transport, base yourself in Hell-Ville or Ambatoloaka.

Nosy Be

ARTUSH/SHUTTERSTOCK ©

Municipal Theatre, Hell-Ville

Take a Wander Round Historic Hell-Ville

NOSY BE'S HISTORIC CAPITAL

The island's largest town, Hell-Ville (Andoany) takes its name from the 19th-century French governor Admiral de Hell, but it's actually rather a pleasant place to explore. For a walk with history, start at Hell-Ville's art deco **Marché de Hell-Ville**, with its spice-stacked stalls and check out the adjacent **Municipal Theatre** next door, another fine deco building from 1954.

Follow Blvd de l'Independence south, passing the historic offices of export company **A M Hassanaly et Fils** (look for the star and crescent motifs above the arches). Continue southeast to the junction with Rue Passot (Cours de Hell) and check out the grand wooden mansions housing the restaurants **Le Papillon** and **Nandipo** on adjacent side streets. In the park in front of Le Papillon, there's a modest **monument for the Morts pour la France**, commemorating local soldiers killed during WWII.

Continue east past the **church of Sts Pierre et Paul**, a stately heirloom from 1870, and the time-worn town **Tribunal**. Around the town's petanque court lie half a dozen 19th-century government buildings flanked by rusting cannons. This was the centre of colonial Hell-Ville – the grandest structure is the **Prefecture of Police** overlooking the port, with its shady terrace and balconies.

Finish up by walking past the modern harbour to the **Vieux Port**, where traditional dhows unload freight in front of handsome old warehouses built from volcanic stone.

WHY I LOVE NOSY BE

Joe Bindloss, writer

The thing I love best about Nosy Be is island-hopping. Motorised pirogues provide easy access to fringing islands that feel a million miles from the busy main island. Bring a mask and snorkel and flit over to Nosy Sakatia, where green turtles teem offshore from the main village, or head to Nosy Komba, where lemurs frolic close to the landing beach at Ampangorinana. For diving, I recommend the marine park at Nosy Tanikely for rainbow shoals, turtles and big groupers, or Grand Banc and Rosario for encounters with sharks and other megafauna (including whale sharks in October and November).

There's good food in Nosy Be too; make time for a lavish modern-European lunch at Papillon in Hell-Ville.

WHERE TO STAY IN HELL-VILLE

Tamana Hostel
Colourful murals, comfy dorms and sea views mark out this central hostel; check ahead to make sure they're open. **$**

Hôtel Belle Vue
Close to the market, this friendly hotel has clean, bright rooms, some with views over the leafy backstreets. **$$**

Les Terrasses d'Ulysse
Huge, tastefully decorated apartments beside the bay, with big windows to let in the sea breezes. **$$$**

NOSY BE

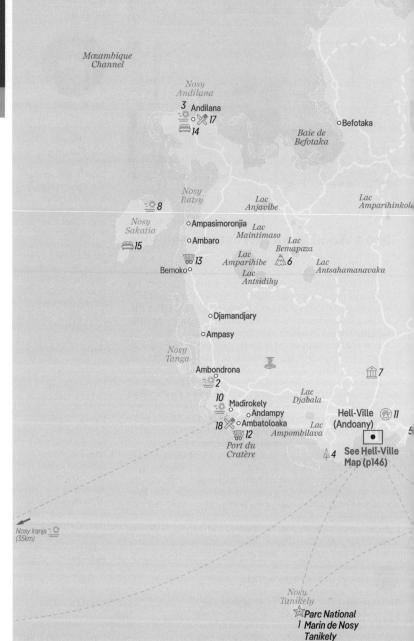

Mozambique
Channel

Nosy
Andilana

3 Andilana
17
14

Befotaka

Baie de
Befotaka

Nosy
Ratsy

Lac
Anjavibe

Lac
Amparihinkole

8

Nosy
Sakatia

○ Ampasimoronjia
○ Ambaro

Lac
Maintimaso
Lac
Bemapaza

15

13
Bemoko○

Lac
Amparihibe
6
Lac
Antsahamanavaka

Lac
Antsidihy

○ Djamandjary

○ Ampasy

Nosy
Tanga

Ambondrona
○
2

10
○ Madirokely
○ Andampy
18
○ Ambatoloaka
12

Lac
Djabala

Lac
Ampombilava

7

Hell-Ville
(Andoany)

11

●

5

Port du
Cratère

4

See Hell-Ville
Map (p146)

Nosy Iranja
(35km)

Nosy
Tanikely

Parc National
1 Marin de Nosy
Tanikely

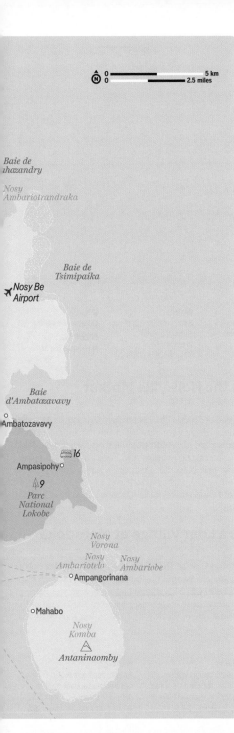

Baie de
ihazandry

*Nosy
Ambariotrandraka*

Baie de
Tsimipaika

✈ **Nosy Be
Airport**

Baie
d'Ambatozavavy

○
Ambatozavavy

Ampasipohy ○

△ **9**
*Parc
National
Lokobe*

*Nosy
Vorona*

*Nosy
Ambariotelo* *Nosy
Ambariobe*
○ **Ampangorinana**

○ **Mahabo**

*Nosy
Komba*
△
Antaninaomby

○ **16**

HIGHLIGHTS
1 Parc National Marin
de Nosy Tanikely

SIGHTS
2 Ambondrona
3 Andilana Beach
4 Arbre Sacré
see 8 Danae Beach
5 Marodoka
6 Mont Passot
7 Musée de Nosy Be
8 Nosy Sakatia
see 1 Nosy Tanikely
9 Parc National Lokobe
10 Plage de Madirokely
see 1 Tanikely Lighthouse

**ACTIVITIES, COURSES &
TOURS**
see 10 Forever Dive
11 Lemuria Land
see 10 Les Baleines Rand'Eau
12 Mada Scuba
see 13 Madaplouf
see 12 Nosy Be Fishing Shop
see 12 Oceane's Dream
see 15 Oisodo
13 Sakalav' Diving
see 12 Tropical Diving

SLEEPING
14 A Casa di Giorgia
15 Sakatia Lodge
16 Zara Village

EATING
17 Cacao Beach by Loulou
see 18 Chez Mama
18 Karibo
see 12 Parad'Ice
see 3 Shorefront Malagasy
Restaurants

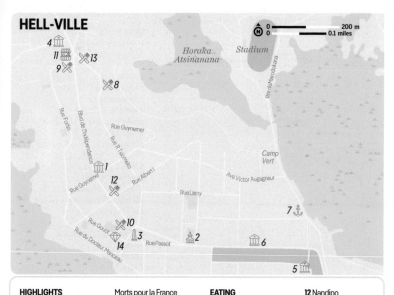

HELL-VILLE

Horaka Atsinanana

Stadium

Camp Vert

HIGHLIGHTS
1 A M Hassanaly et Fils
2 Church of Sts Pierre et Paul
3 Monument for the

4 Municipal Theatre
5 Prefecture of Police
6 Tribunal
7 Vieux Port

Morts pour la France

EATING
8 Brochette Food Stall
9 Chez Sity Halal
10 Le Papillon
11 Marché de Hell-Ville

12 Nandipo
13 Restaurant Manava

SHOPPING
14 Le Jardin des Sens

GO FISH

The waters around Nosy Be teem with marine life, including giant trevally, dogtooth tuna, barracuda, amberjack, grouper, red snapper, sailfish and black marlin.

Specialist operators such as **Tropical Fishing** offer premium trips led by expert fishing guides; they also have a fishing lodge on Nosy Mitsio for multiday fishing safaris.

For a low-cost alternative, pick up a rod and tackle at the **Nosy Be Fishing Shop** in Ambatoloaka.

Browse the Hell-Ville Market

STOCK UP ON SPICES

At the north end of Blvd de l'Independence, the historic **Marché de Hell-Ville** is abuzz with activity in the mornings, as traders set up stalls piled high with tropical fruit, vegetables, dried fish, baskets, spices, cocoa beans and bundles of vanilla pods. It's an atmospheric place for a wander – and a good place to buy spices and vanilla packaged to travel. Look out for vendors selling kola nuts and stalks of the narcotic shrub khat in front of the marketplace.

Explore a Lost Village at Marodoka

UNCOVER NOSY BE'S SEAFARING PAST

A few kilometres east of Hell-Ville, sleepy **Marodoka** marks the site of an ancient Swahili trading port, settled by Arab traders in around 800 CE. The village is dotted with the ruins of grand stone and stucco mansions, including the House of the Ghosts, former home of wealthy Indian trader, Karim Djikak.

WHERE TO EAT IN HELL-VILLE

Casa Mofo
Hell-Ville's favourite breakfast stop serves freshly baked pastries, fresh juices, strong coffee and tasty ice cream. **$**

Les Siciliens
Proper Italian pizzas with proper Italian toppings, served in a calm dining room off Blvd de l'Independence. **$$**

Nandipo
An atmospheric wood-framed bar and restaurant on Rue Albert 1er, with Spanish Civil War photos on the walls. **$$**

Inland lie the island's oldest mosque (founded around 1700) and an overgrown 19th-century cemetery. The Ravinala Association des Femmes arranges cultural programmes featuring traditional dances and island cuisine. Charter a tuk-tuk in Hell-Ville to get here.

For more insights into Nosy Be's past, visit the overlooked **Musée de Nosy Be**, north of Hell-Ville on the airport road, with dusty household objects, traditional costumes, tools and machinery, and old photos of Hell-Ville through the ages. You'll have to track down the attendant to open the doors.

Unwind with a Massage

RELAX WHILE EXPLORING HELL-VILLE

Massages are offered everywhere in Nosy Be, including by wandering masseurs on the beaches, but the presence of sex tourists means you need to be cautious about agreeing to a massage. One place you can be sure there'll be no shenanigans is **Le Jardin des Sens** on Rue de Fortin; as well as selling essential oils and health products, the shop has a calm therapy room for relaxing massages and reflexology treatments.

Visit the Sacred Banyan Tree

NOSY BE'S MOST SACRED SITE

On the coast west of Hell-Ville, reached via a bumpy track from the village of Mahatsinjo on Route de l'Ouest, the **Arbre Sacré** is Nosy Be's most important animist shrine. Wrapped in red and white cloth, this vast, tangled banyan tree was planted by Queen Tsiomeko of the Sakalava tribe in 1836, and it's a popular place to leave offerings. The current Queen of Nosy Be makes an annual pilgrimage here to sacrifice a zebu and gain benediction (look for the zebu horns dangling from the roots). Shoes must be removed and you must cover your legs with a wrap, and enter and leave the compound putting your right foot first.

Go Diving

ENTER NOSY BE'S UNDERWATER WONDERLAND

The marine environment around Nosy Be and surrounding islands is exceptionally rich, despite some bleaching of hard corals. Soft corals such as gorgonians are thriving, green turtles are common, and fish and seashells are abundant. Drop-offs on the edges of reefs see plenty of visiting megafauna, including manta rays, hammerheads and whale sharks from October to November.

Parc National Marin de Nosy Tanikely has three impressive dive sites, rammed with fish, turtles and invertebrate

HELL-VILLE'S TOP TABLE

Set in a gorgeous, time-seasoned wooden mansion near the south end of Rue de l'Independence, Hell-Ville's best restaurant is only open for lunch (except Sundays), but what a lunch!

Eclectic art fills the walls of **Le Papillon** on Rue Gallieni and diners spill out onto the terrace, enjoying delectable modern-European cooking featuring fresh island ingredients. Think rich zebu-meat bourguignon and grilled fish with Réunion-style *rougail de tomate* and coconut rice, and you'll be on the right track. Their partner restaurant – **Karibo** in Ambatoloaka – is also worth a visit for creative cooking; it's open in the evenings, Monday to Saturday.

 WHERE TO SHOP IN HELL-VILLE

Trésors des Îles
The best souvenir shop on the island, full of wood-carvings, zebu-horn ornaments and cute toys made from recycled cans.

Le Jardin des Sens
A great place to stock up on beauty products made with local essential oils; next-door La Vaniala is also good.

Bijouterie L'Ecrin Lapidaire
A cave of Madagascan gems, minerals, fossils and jewellery, affiliated with the Société Tropicale Minière.

species. For whale shark encounters, try your luck at Rosario or the varied sites around Nosy Sakatia (also good for 'macro' encounters with crustaceans, nudibranchs and seahorses). Mantas often swing by the submerged plateau at Manta Point, while hammerheads and reef sharks cruise by Grand Banc. The 25m trawler *Mitsio* is the region's best wreck dive.

Dive companies are dotted around the island; reliable operators include **Oceane's Dream**, **Tropical Diving** and **Mada Scuba** in Ambatoloaka, friendly **Forever Dive** at Madirokely, and **Madaplouf** and **Sakalav' Diving** at Ambaro. Most companies offer one- and two-dive day trips, multiday packages and dive certification courses.

Bask on the Beach

FIND SAND, SEA AND SERENITY

Nosy Be is circled by stunning beaches where the sand is so fine it whispers underfoot, but you'll have to follow winding dirt tracks to reach the public beaches.

Most people start at **Ambatoloaka**, where the attractive main beach is backed up by bars, restaurants and ice-cream parlours, including the spectacular **Parad'Ice** – purveyor of indulgent tamarind, ginger, guava and passion fruit sorbets. Ambatoloaka has a slightly sleazy feel after dark, with plenty of lone men seeking paid-for romance, so it's best enjoyed in the daytime.

Running north towards the headland, **Plage de Madirokely** is more relaxed; there's another fine, broad strip of sand just north at **Ambondrona**. As you move north along Route de l'Ouest (the island's main road), you'll pass numerous side tracks running to beach resorts and public sections of beach.

Head to the end of Route de l'Ouest to reach eye-wateringly beautiful **Andilana Beach**. The pale golden sand here seems to go on forever and you can enjoy some of the island's best food under an airy canopy at **Cacao Beach by Loulou**. For a low-cost alternative, follow the dirt track by **A Casa di Giorgia** to the shorefront, where a cluster of simple **Malagasy restaurants** will grill up the catch of the day (anything from tuna to octopus and lobster) for a bargain price.

Live the Desert Island Dream on Nosy Sakatia

TURTLES, SEASHELLS AND SUBLIME SANDS

To find your own island in the sun, head to Ambaro, where motorised pirogues buzz over to gorgeous **Nosy Sakatia**, a low-lying island ringed by sparkling sands, just 1.5km offshore. Local agencies offer organised tours, but it's easy to arrange a day

CLIMB MONT PASSOT

At 329m, the extinct volcano of **Mont Passot** is Nosy Be's highest point, and it's easily reached by rented motorcycle or quad bike or on an organised tour. Ringed by blue crater lakes, this lofty vantage point offers sweeping panoramas, particularly at sunset, but the viewing area is hemmed in by souvenir stalls and thronged by tour groups.

To get here, turn off Route de l'Ouest near the village of Dzamandzar along a rutted dirt road; lone travellers have been robbed in the area in the past, so be sure to drive back before it gets dark.

It's also possible to hike a 6km circuit around the peak with a guide, visiting the sacred lake of Amparihibe – note that fishing and swimming in the lake is *fady* (taboo).

 WHERE TO STAY IN AMBATOLOAKA AND MADIROKELY

Le Coucher du Soleil
Uphill from the beach strip (follow the path behind the mosque), with cosy bungalows in a lush garden. **$$**

Hôtel Gérard et Francine
A gorgeous resort on Ambatoloaka's main beach, with a strong stance against sex tourism. **$$$**

L'Heure Bleue
Set amongst the trees on Madirokely beach, with saltwater and freshwater pools and attractive bungalows. **$$$**

Andilana Beach

trip with one of the boat owners by the Chanty Beach Lodge (signposted off Route de l'Ouest).

Most trips start on the outrageously beautiful, seashell-strewn beach on the north coast, before moving on to the Malagasy village at the south end of the island for lunch. At high tide, turtles congregate immediately offshore from the village – you can rent snorkelling gear, kayaks, paddleboards and sea scooters at **Oisodo** on the beachfront.

To visit on a budget, you can board a shared pirogue, but you may face a long wait for enough passengers to gather. For an overnight stay, try the castaway-style **Danae Beach**, with inviting wooden bungalows behind that gorgeous northern beach, or the lovely **Sakatia Lodge**, a great hub for snorkelling and diving, with appealing garden bungalows and family villas facing the island's turtle sanctuary.

Go Whale Watching

MEET GIANTS OF THE DEEP

From August to October, migrating humpback whales cruise through the waters off Nosy Be, and local boat operators ferry travellers out to observe these magnificent animals breaching. One of the best companies is **Les Baleines Rand'Eau**, based at the Chez Senga hotel at Madirokely, where guides insist on responsible interactions with cetaceans and trips support the conservation work of the Mada Megafauna Association. Boats run to see turtles and whale sharks once the humpbacks move on from Nosy Be.

SPICE ISLAND

Aside from tourism, Nosy Be does a lively trade in spices, cane sugar and essential oils, with ylang-ylang, cocoa, vanilla and sugarcane plantations sprawling over the rolling hills inland from the beach. If you're exploring the island by motorcycle, it's worth stopping when you spot an ylang-ylang plantation – these artificially stunted trees are a favourite hangout for reptiles such as the rainbow-coloured panther chameleon.

Tour agencies can arrange trips to visit ylang-ylang plantations and observe the process of extracting essential oils, used in the production of beauty products and perfumes (Indian Ocean ylang-ylang is a key ingredient in Chanel No 5). You can also visit the ylang-ylang distillery at the **Lemuria Land** animal park outside Hell-Ville, but this is more a petting zoo for tame lemurs than a proper conservation project.

WHERE TO STAY ON THE WEST COAST

A Casa di Giorgia
A low-cost alternative to package-tour hotels, with apartments and rooms behind Andilana's stunning beach. **$$**

La Case Sakalava
A calm escape behind Ambaro beach, with uncluttered bungalows powered by solar energy. **$$$**

Vanila Hôtel
A top-class resort, with boutique rooms full of local art, poised beside a lovely section of Ambaro beach. **$$$**

149

To sample real Malagasy food on Nosy Be, eat where locals eat. In Hell-Ville, try family-run **Chez Sity Halal** beside the market, where Malagasy dishes of the day are chalked up on the blackboard, or friendly **Restaurant Manava**, which cooks up a hearty bowl of *romazava* (tomato, mustard greens and meat stew) alongside a range of European dishes.

After dark, head to the no-name **food stall** beside Hôtel Belle Vue for tasty *brochettes* (grilled skewers) served at bench tables. In Ambatoloaka, local-style **Chez Mama** opposite the Safari Safari bar serves up good Malagasy food made with market-fresh ingredients. On outlying islands, and at Andilana, seek out simple *gargotes* (local restaurants) behind the beaches, serving seafood so fresh you can taste the sea spray.

Dive into the Forest in Parc National Lokobe

MAXIMUM WILDLIFE ENCOUNTERS

For close encounters with local wildlife, **Parc National Lokobe** preserves a dense area of coastal rainforest to the east of Hell-Ville, accessible from the village of Ambatozavary. On walks through the forest, you can see black lemurs (and the brown female of the species), grey-backed sportive lemurs, boa constrictors, huge spiders, leaf-tailed geckos, and myriad chameleons, including the spectacular panther chameleon. Move quietly and you may also spot mouse lemurs and long-eared owls.

Most people visit on an organised tour, paddling around the headland from Ambatozavary by pirogue (which may involve a hike across muddy mangroves) and stopping for a filling buffet lunch at the village of Ampasipohy. Most tour agencies can make bookings, but you may have to discourage guides from disturbing lemurs to create photo opportunities. For an overnight stop, try pretty **Zara Village** at Ampasipohy, with tidy bungalows and a pool set in a lush tropical garden.

Boat Trips from Nosy Be

EXPLORE THE ISLANDS

It's easy to arrange boat trips to neighbouring islands in Nosy Be; Ambatoloaka has the biggest choice of operators. Boats typically leave around 8.30am and return mid-afternoon, after a seafood barbecue lunch in a local village.

The most popular destinations for day trips are Nosy Komba (p152), with its interesting museum, craft stalls and lemur park, and **Nosy Tanikely**, a tiny wedge of rainforest and sand, fringed by a beautiful marine park. This is the area's best spot for snorkelling. You can also climb the historic **Tanikely Lighthouse**, which has been guiding ships since 1908.

You can arrange trips to Nosy Sakatia near Ambaro (p148) and gorgeous **Nosy Iranja**, a pair of tiny islets linked by a postcard-perfect 1.5km-long sandbar frequented by nesting turtles. Most people visit Nosy Mitsio (p153) on multiday diving, whale-spotting and fishing trips arranged through upscale boat operators such as Madavoile, Ulysse Explorer and Tropical Fishing.

GETTING AROUND

Nosy Be's Fascene Airport is an 11km taxi ride from Hell-Ville. Explore the island using organised tours, taxis or tuk-tuks – shared tuk-tuks charge a fixed fare in downtown Hell-Ville; negotiate a fare to reach Ambatoloaka. In Ambatoloaka, it's easy to rent mopeds, motorcycles and quad bikes. Vehicles have basic insurance, but ride carefully as you'll be liable for damage. Check vehicles over and keep your fuel tank filled – the only

petrol stations are in Hell-Ville and near Ambatoloaka. Shared pirogues run from Hell-Ville's Petit Port to Nosy Komba, and from Ambaro to Nosy Sakatia. To reach Ankify on the mainland, take a slow car ferry or fast motorboat from Hell-Ville's Grand Port. Boats leave when full, but services fizzle out after lunch when the crossing becomes choppy; book at the ticket office, not through touts.

Beyond Nosy Be

Pirogues and charter boats run out from Nosy Be to idyllic neighbouring isles where you can escape the crowds.

Nosy Be is just the beginning of the island experience. From the port in Hell-Ville – and from beaches all over the island – you can arrange boat transfers to smaller islands in the archipelago, where fishing villages offer a glimpse of the Nosy Be of 30 years ago.

Often, island stays mean simplicity and solar power, but there are some charming resorts that strike the perfect balance between seclusion and castaway comfort. Head to Ankify on the mainland for plantation tours and onward travel to the rest of northern Madagascar.

For a day trip, Nosy Komba is the best choice, with stalls piled with local crafts and a lively lemur park just minutes inland from the beach.

Nosy Mitsio

Nosy Be

Ampangorinana
Nosy Komba

Ankify

Ambanja

TOP TIP

For island day trips, get an early start; shared pirogues take a while to fill up, and services peter out in the afternoon.

Nosy Komba (p152)

LENISECALLEJA PHOTOGRAPHY/SHUTTERSTOCK ©

AMBANJA & ANKIFY

Surrounded by mango, cashew, ylang-ylang, vanilla, cocoa and spice plantations, **Ambanja** is the nearest town to **Ankify**, the port for boats to and from Nosy Be.

Plantation Millot, off the Ankify road in Andzavibe, offers tours of its cocoa and ylang-ylang groves and stands of pepper vines and vertiver grass, followed by a lunch prepared with home-grown ingredients (book through their parent company, Cananga).

For an overnight stay, try friendly Palma Nova, with tidy rooms and a good restaurant off Ambanja's main road, or the appealing Le Baobab, with bungalows spilling onto a pretty beach just north of Ankify.

For a truly sustainable escape, try 100%-solar-powered Eden Lodge, west of Ankify near the remote village of Anjanojano and only accessible by boat (usually from Nosy Be).

ALESSANDRO PIERPAOLI/SHUTTERSTOCK ©

Lemurs, Nosy Be

Lemurs & Local Life on Nosy Komba

SAND, SEAFOOD AND BONUS LEMURS

An 8km boat ride from Nosy Be, the island of **Nosy Komba** is an isolated volcanic cone that towers 622m over the bay, its slopes enveloped in dense jungle. Villages and resorts hug the beaches dotted around the coast, and steep trails climb into the rainforest, offering almost guaranteed sightings of black lemurs, chameleons and other wildlife.

To reach Nosy Komba, you can come on a tour or take a pirogue from the Petit Port in Hell-Ville. Most people land at **Ampangorinana**, the sprawling village at the north end of the island, which is dotted with relaxed places to stay and inviting *gargotes* (local restaurants), set in palm-thatched Malagasy houses.

The main lane through Ampangorinana is lined with crafts stalls, specialising in local wood carvings and ocean-themed lace, and above the village is a popular Lemur Park, where black lemurs have learned to associate visitors with a free banana meal. To minimise your impact, politely decline if guides offer to lure lemurs onto your shoulders for photo opportunities.

 WHERE TO STAY ON NOSY KOMBA

Chez Yolande
A friendly, family-run lodge in Ampangorinana, with a cosy restaurant and inviting rooms, some with terraces. **$$**

293 on Komba
Set among mango trees above Ampangorinana's beach, with graceful, art-filled rooms and a spring-fed infinity pool. **$$$**

Tsara Komba
A bougainvillea and palm-studded garden, with just eight rooms in elegant, palm-thatched lodges. **$$$**

Close to where pirogues from Hell-Ville land, the interesting Lovako Museum has some thoughtfully laid-out displays on island history, culture and customs, including a detailed exploration (in French) of the impact of colonialism. To see more of Nosy Komba, arrange a guide in Ampangorinana and follow the steep trail to the summit (allow five sweaty hours).

For meals, recommended **Gargote Vanille** at the east end of the village has an extensive chalkboard menu of local seafood and Malagasy favourites. Perched atop the headland east of the main beach, **Le Maki Lodge & Restaurant** offers good food, sublime sea views and cooling sea breezes. For a tropical cocktail, **Malala Beach Bar** has seating on two levels overlooking the sand and a full-sized pool table.

Take the Island Experience Upmarket on Nosy Mitsio

SWIM WITH THE BIG FISH

About 55km northeast of Nosy Be, offshore from Cap St Sebastien on the mainland, **Nosy Mitsio** is the largest island in a beautiful archipelago that offers a true escape from it all. Beachfront villages dot the coast of Nosy Mitsio, but other islands in the group are uninhabited and the marine environment is pristine.

The archipelago's volcanic origins are obvious from the columnar basalt formations on the coast – most notably, the towering Organ Pipes, accessible by boat from the islands' two resorts. Sport fishing is another lure; specialist operator **Tropical Fishing** runs multiday fishing safaris in search of giant trevally, black marlin, dogtooth tuna, sailfish, barracuda and more, with an emphasis on catch-and-release.

Below the surface are spectacular (and deep) dive sites, attracting pelagic megafauna such as scalloped hammerhead sharks, manta rays and whale sharks (from October to November). Humpback whales are also spotted from August to October. The outlying outcrops, known as the Tétons and Four Brothers, and the shark-thronged Banc du Petit Castor are the most popular dives.

It takes two hours to reach Nosy Mitsio by boat from Nosy Be or Ankify – if you're staying on the island, your lodge will arrange transfers. Most of Nosy Be's dive and boat charter companies offer multiday liveaboard trips to the Mitsio archipelago.

THE BEST PLACES TO STAY ON NOSY MITSIO

Constance Tsarabanjina
On its own private island in the west of the archipelago, with a barefoot luxury ethos, exquisite wooden bungalows, and masks, snorkels, kayaks and paddleboards for guests, plus a respected dive centre. There's a four-night minimum stay. $$$

Mitsio Lodge
Run by Tropical Fishing, with a petanque court, a massage room, a bar and restaurant, and appropriately tropical wooden bungalows with palm roofs. Most visitors come on multiday fishing safaris with daily sport-fishing excursions. $$$

GETTING AROUND

Nosy Komba can be reached in about 20 minutes from Hell-Ville's Petit Port (book at the concrete ticket office). Motorised pirogues leave when full, but they take a while to fill up, and services tail off after lunch. If you come on a day trip, set out early; you may need to arrange a more expensive 'special' ride to get back to Nosy Be. Alternatively, take a boat tour with a local agency.

To access Nosy Mitsio, you can arrange a multiday diving or fishing tour from Nosy Be, or stay with one of the island resorts, who will arrange transfers by boat from Nosy Be or Ankify.

DIEGO SUAREZ (ANTSIRANANA)

The capital of Diana Region, Diego Suarez (Antsiranana) takes its European-sounding name from the Portuguese explorer Diogo Soares de Albergaria, who sailed into the bay in 1543. A colonial air still lingers in the centre – particularly along Rue Colbert, with its column-propped verandas – but these days the mood is firmly French and Malagasy.

With direct international flights from Réunion and Comoros, and domestic flights from Antananarivo and Sambava, Diego is a handy starting point for touring the far north, but it's worth lingering to explore the stunning coastal landscapes around Baie de Diego Suarez, the world's second-largest bay.

Despite a lingering sex tourism scene, most visitors are drawn to Diego by adventures in the surrounding hills, and the stunning beaches around Les Trois Baies. Diego is also an easy base for trips to the gorgeous natural reserves at Ankarana and Montagne d'Ambre.

TOP TIP

Get an early start from Diego for trips to Les Trois Baies and Montagne des Français – the heat builds quickly and the tracks crossing the Oronjia Protected Area to the Trois Baies beaches and the Anosiravo reserve pass through scrub forests without much actual shade.

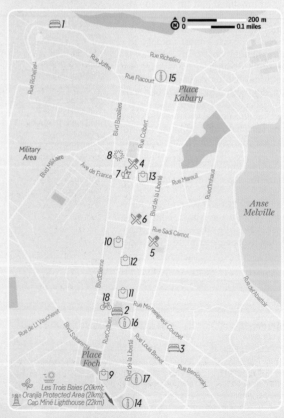

SLEEPING
1 Allamanda Hôtel
2 Grand Hotel
3 La Belle Aventure

EATING
4 La Cambusa
5 Rosticceria
6 Tsara Be Vaovao

DRINKING
7 La Vahinée Bar

ENTERTAINMENT
8 Taxi Be Nightclub

SHOPPING
9 Boutique Chocolat
10 Jewelers By Bleu Nuit
11 Kalidas
12 La Natura
13 La Société Tropicale Minière

INFORMATION
14 Association Fanamby
15 Diana Region Tourist Offices
16 Evasion Sans Frontière
17 Madabest

TRANSPORT
18 Diego Raid

Go Shopping in Diego

BROWSE THE NORTH'S TOP SHOPS

Diego Suarez is the best place to pick up souvenirs in the north. In the centre, Rue Colbert is dotted with colourful shops selling T-shirts, wood carvings, zebu-horn ornaments, model boats, baobab models, toys made from recycled drink cans, local *rhum arrangé* (rum infused with spices and fruit) and other portable souvenirs.

For something more glamorous, drop into bijou **Jewelers By Bleu Nuit** for tasteful jewellery, dinky trinkets and chic handbags. Gleaming silver, gold and gemstone-inlaid rings, bangles and necklaces are on offer at **Kalidas** near the Grand Hotel, one of the town's ritziest jewellers.

Several stores stock beauty products and eatables sourced from northern Madagascar's plantations. On Rue Colbert, **La Natura** has essential oils, creams, soaps, shampoos and health cures made from local plants. For tasty local chocolate and cocoa, see if **Boutique Chocolat** is open at the south end of the strip – if not, try the well-stocked **Score** supermarket near the Grand Hotel.

At the north end of Rue Colbert, **La Société Tropicale Minière** is a treasure house of jewels, gems, crystals and fossils – interesting buys include Madagascan rubies, emeralds and star sapphires, petrified wood and pieces of copal (ancient tree resin) containing preserved insects.

Take a Tour of the Oronjia Protected Area

BEACHES, SCRUB FORESTS AND MILITARY RELICS

The **Oranjia Protected Area** encompasses most of the peninsula to the east of Diego Suarez, preserving an important area of scrub forest alive with birds and chameleons, and some of the north's finest beaches at Les Trois Baies. Most people arrange 4WD tours to Oranjia with Diego travel agencies such as **Evasion Sans Frontière** and **Madabest**, focusing on the peninsula's gorgeous coastline.

For maximum immersion in this evocative, sun-baked landscape, arrange to be dropped off with a guide at Baie de Sakalava and walk along the coast via Baie des Pigeons to meet your vehicle at Baie des Dunes. Alternatively, hike around the north end of the peninsula from Baie des Dunes to Ramena, passing the **Cap Miné lighthouse** and the ruins of old gun emplacements, barracks and fortifications that saw heavy action as the French Vichy government attempted to fend off the Allies during WWII.

CAMP ANDRAFIAMENA-ANDAVAKOERA

Around 80km south of Diego Suarez, close to Réserve Spéciale Ankarana, the **Andrafiamena-Andavakoera Protected Area** preserves an important area of dry and semi-humid forests that provides a vital refuge for the critically endangered black *sifaka* (*Propithecus perrieri*).

Association Fanamby in Diego Suarez maintains the appealing Camp Andrafiamena-Andavakoera, with inviting en-suite bungalows on a ridge overlooking the forest. You can arrange guide-led walks to search for *sifakas*, birds and reptiles and explore limestone *tsingy* formations, caves and natural pools.

To get here, turn off the RN6 at Marotaolana, 64km northeast of Ambilobe, then follow a rough, rutted road for around 20km towards the village of Anjakahely. The protected area is inaccessible during the rainy season from November to April.

 WHERE TO STAY IN DIEGO SUAREZ

La Belle Aventure
Laid-back La Belle Aventure has a quiet location, mural-filled hallways, and the best rooms nab a sea view. **$$**

Grand Hotel
Elegant, colonial-style rooms surround a gorgeous pool at Diego's most prestigious hotel, and there's a busy bar. **$$$**

Allamanda Hôtel
With oodles of style, this is the place to come for fine food, a seaside pool and stupendous bay views. **$$$**

WALKING HISTORIC DIEGO SUAREZ

It's well worth setting out on foot to explore the history and heritage of downtown Diego Suarez. Start out at the Centre Hospitalier Universitaire de Place Kabary at the northeast end of town, where a green gate at the back of the grounds leads to the curious **1 Japanese Monument**, recalling the Japanese submarine crews who fought alongside Vichy French troops before the British and Allies gained the upper hand in WWII.

From here, stroll west along Rue Richelieu, passing a striking **2 pink house** with minerals and crystals set in its walls, to reach the handsome, late 19th-century **3 Résidence**, formerly the home of the French governor and now the offices of the Diana regional government. Just west lie the crumbling Moroccan arches of the ruined **4 Hôtel Palace de la Marine**, a once-lavish hotel constructed by gold-mining entrepreneur, Alphonse Montages. Across the road, the **5 Mosquee Jacob** was construct-ed by Muslim migrants from India, Mauritius and the Comoros in the 1920s. Turn back to Rue Colbert and go south past the **6 Tribunal** – Diego's eye-catching courthouse, constructed in 1908 – to reach the **7 Alliance Française**, set in a striking iron-framed building from 1925 that once housed the Diego Suarez market.

Continuing south, you'll pass more fading colonial-era buildings, including the red-and-yellow **8 Prefecture d'Antsiranana**. Note the star and crescent logo on many of the veranda-fronted shops – these graceful buildings were constructed by 19th-century Muslim migrants from the Indian subcontinent. The grandest structure is the column-fronted **9 Maison Cassam Chenaï**, built by a Gujarati family in 1925 (today, it's the BMOI bank). Finish up the walk with a coffee, juice or cold beer in the bar at the inviting, modern deco-style **10 Grand Hotel**.

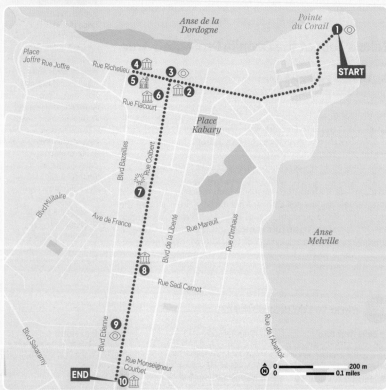

For bonus fun, arrange a tour by quad bike or mountain bike through **Diego Raid** on Rue Colbert, exploring some of the less-visited tracks meandering around the peninsula (look out for the chunky trunks of baobab trees beside the trails). The same company rents out mountain bikes for independent exploring, but it's safer to go with a guide. For more ideas, swing into one of the two **Diana region tourist offices** on Rue Colbert.

Visit the Mer d'Emeraude

MESMERISING GREEN WATERS

The waters around Baie de Diego Suarez are an intense shade of blue, but you'll notice a vivid colour change to aquamarine at the appropriately named **Mer d'Emeraude**, a shallow, sandy-bottomed lagoon protected by small islands near the mouth of the bay. With Evian-clear waters, it's a heavenly spot for a splash, and many Diego travel agencies offer organised boat trips, including a fish barbecue lunch on one of the idyllic, sand-dusted beaches flanking the lagoon. **Diego Raid** on Rue Colbert offers trips using traditional *boutre* dhows. You can also arrange boat trips independently at the jetty in Ramena, south across the bay from Mer d'Emeraude.

Have a Wholesome Massage

RELAXATION WITHOUT THE FUNNY BUSINESS

You'll see signs advertising massages all over Diego Suarez, but at **La Natura** on Rue Colbert, you can be confident that a relaxing pummelling is all that is on offer. Trained masseurs provide 45-minute massages in the clinic next to the boutique using La Natura's natural health products (except on Sundays). Swing into the shop afterwards to stock up on herbal remedies, creams and cosmetics.

Use the Pool at the Grand

ESCAPE THE HEAT IN STYLE

Several of Diego's top hotels have pools for guests, but the **Grand Hotel** on Rue Colbert throws open its lovely, landscaped pool to nonguests for a fee from noon to 6pm daily. It's a lovely spot to escape the afternoon heat, screened off from the street and shaded by palm trees, and towels are provided. Afterwards, grab a post-swim drink in the hotel bar and stake out a vantage point for people watching on the veranda on Rue Colbert.

GETTING THE BEST FROM DIEGO

Driver **Charlain Zara** shares his top tips for getting the best from the Diego Suarez area.

The Best Beach
Go to Baie des Dunes. It's beautifully quiet – there are no villages or resorts – and the fine sandy beach is protected by rocks.

The Best Place to Swim
For swimming, I'd pick Baie des Pigeons. You can only get here by walking, and the water is perfectly clear.

The Best Views
For views, climb Montagne des Français. You can see in all directions, from Diego Suarez town to the Mozambique Channel and the Indian Ocean.

The Best Place to see Wildlife
Montagne d'Ambre – the local climate is lovely and you can see loads of wildlife species and forest waterfalls.

WHERE TO EAT IN DIEGO SUAREZ

La Rosticceria
A friendly Italian restaurant serving freshly made pasta in tasty sauces, inside or out on the veranda. **$$**

La Cambusa
An expat favourite full of *Pirates of the Caribbean* murals, serving meaty French and Malagasy dishes. **$$**

Tsara Be Vaovao
Diego's gourmet address fuses Malagasy, French and Asian flavours with real panache. **$$$**

ASSOCIATION FANAMBY

If you're planning to visit Camp Andrafiamena-Andavakoera south of Diego Suarez or the Loky Manambato Protected Area near Vohémar, visit the offices of the non-government organisation **Association Fanamby** in the Ny Havana building near the junction of Rue Colbert and Ave Lally Tollendal.

This pioneering NGO has been managing and promoting new protected areas in Madagascar since 1997, and friendly staff can take bookings and provide information on the areas they manage (including progress on plans to restore the camp for visitors at Loky Manambato).

Hôtel Palace de la Marine (p156)

Sample Diego Nightlife

MUSIC AFTER HOURS

Like many Madagascan towns, Diego is busy in the morning, quiet in the heat of the day, and lively again from afternoon to evening. As the sun dips towards the horizon, locals and visitors promenade along Rue Colbert, examining chalkboard menus to choose a spot for dinner, before attention shifts to bars such as **La Vahinée Bar** on Rue Colbert and the **Taxi Be Nightclub** behind the Alliance Française. While you may have to fend off some unwanted attention from sex workers, there's *rhum arrangé* on the menu and often live Malagasy music. Big-name Malagasy bands often play special nights at Taxi Be.

GETTING AROUND

Diego Suarez's Arrachart airport is served by direct Air Austral/Ewa Air flights from Mayotte in Comoros and St-Denis in Réunion, with easy connections from the French mainland. There are also domestic Tsaradia flights to Sambava and Antananarivo.

Travelling by road, *taxis-brousses* run to Joffreville, Sambava, and towns along the RN6 towards Antananarivo, including Ambilobe (for Réserve Spéciale Ankarana) and Ambanja, where you can swap to a local *taxi-brousse* to

reach the ferry port at Ankify and Nosy Be.

For more comfort, arrange a vehicle and driver through **Evasion Sans Frontière** at the Grand Hotel or the friendly and affordable **Madabest**, just off Rue Lally Tollendal, near the Ny Havana building.

Tuk-tuks charge a fixed fare for trips around the centre; for longer trips to the airport, Montagne des Français, Ramena or Les Trois Baies, negotiate a fare with one of the town's yellow Renault 4 taxis.

Beyond Diego Suarez

Using Diego Suarez as a base, you can easily explore some of the north's most interesting natural reserves and loveliest beaches.

Northeast of town, the gleaming Baie de Diego Suarez is the world's second-largest bay, second only to Rio de Janeiro Bay in Brazil. This protected anchorage made Diego Suarez vitally important during the colonial period, and the bay became a battleground during WWII.

Spending a few days exploring the bay is one of Diego's great pleasures. The focus is on the wonderful beaches at Les Trois Baies, on the east coast of the Oranjia peninsula, and the walking trails that climb the Montagne des Français massif. South of Diego along RN6 lie a string of wonderful natural reserves, accessible with a vehicle and driver, or with a bit more effort, by *taxi-brousse*.

Les Troies Baies
Diego Suarez (Antsiranana)
Baie des Français
Anosarivo Natural Reserve
Joffreville
Ramena
Parc National Montagne d'Ambre
Tsingy Rouges
Réserve Spéciale Ankarana

TOP TIP

It's best to explore the area around Diego Suarez with a guide, as it's easy to get lost and there have been muggings in remote areas.

Antsiranana Bay, Diego Suarez

DAMIAN RYSZAWY/SHUTTERSTOCK ©

OPERATION IRONCLAD

During WWII, Madagascar was ruled by the Vichy government of France, placing the country on the Axis side in the battle for control of the Indian Ocean.

Fearing that Japanese troops would gain a foothold on the island, allowing easy raids on merchant shipping, Winston Churchill initiated Operation Ironclad – an amphibious assault on the port of Diego Suarez in May 1942.

Despite fierce French resistance and the formidable fortifications around the bay, British forces gained control of the port, extending the campaign to seize the entire island of Madagascar by the end of 1942.

Relics from this forgotten battle can still be seen all around Baie de Diego Suarez, including the tunnels leading to the summit of Montagne des Français and the crumbling gun emplacements on the Oranjia peninsula.

French cannon, Diego Suarez

Bask on the Trois Baies Beaches

SAND, SEA, SURF AND SILENCE

Around 12km east of Diego Suarez, Les Trois Baies are little snippets of paradise, enveloped in bird-filled scrub forests and sprinkled with some of the finest sand you'll find anywhere in Africa. The largest of the bays, **Baie de Sakalava**, has a string of top-notch kitesurfing resorts behind its golden sands; it's the easiest beach for a day trip as there are plenty of places to stop for lunch.

From Baie de Sakalava, a rough trail (navigable by 4WD, quad bike or mountain bike) runs around the headland to beautiful **Baie des Dunes**, a strong contender for Madagascar's best beach, with a gorgeous sweep of undeveloped sand, a cluster of wooden shacks where you can arrange a grilled seafood lunch, and good snorkelling around the rocky outcrops bookending the bay.

From here, you can stroll east across the headland to **Baie des Pigeons**, a serene and undeveloped bay with a perfect crescent of sand and a clear, reef-sheltered lagoon. Alternatively, you can walk west around the top of the Peninsula to Ramena, passing the Cape Miné lighthouse and the ruins of French military fortifications that last saw action during WWII.

 WHERE TO STAY AT BAIE DE SAKALAVA

Kite Paradise Madagascar
The liveliest of Baie de Sakalava's kitesurfing camps, with a mix of rooms, luxe bungalows and safari tents. **$$**

Filao Eden
A low-key kitesurfing camp, with simple, cosy bungalows linked by sand-floored paths through the casuarinas. **$$**

Sakalava Lodge
By a fine stretch of sand, this attractive resort has garden bungalows and beachside Malagasy cabins. **$$$**

Tour agencies in Diego Suarez arrange beach trips to Les Trois Baies as well as guided walking, cycling and quad bike trips. Alternatively, make arrangements through taxi drivers in Ramena.

Kitesurf at Baie de Sakalava

MADAGASCAR'S KITESURFING HUB

The shallow, reef-protected bay at Baie de Sakalava is transformed into an aquatic playground from April to November, as strong winds whoosh along the east coast, creating perfect conditions for kitesurfing. Indeed, the winds can be so powerful, they'll pluck the sunglasses off your face. All of the beach resorts at Baie de Sakalava have kite centres renting out gear and offering courses for beginners and improvers.

Kite Paradise Madagascar is the most fun outfit – the owners are kitesurfing-obsessed, rooms have a touch of style, and the restaurant lounge has a stage with instruments for impromptu jam sessions after a day on the bay. Kite Alizé at the Mada Kite Camp is another reliable operator. Out of season, the winds drop, and the bay is perfect for swimming, snorkelling and sunbathing.

Climb Montagne des Français

DIEGO SUAREZ'S BEST VIEWPOINT

Between Diego Suarez and Les Trois Baies lies curving **Baie des Français** (Baie d'Andovobazaha), a broad crescent lined with mangroves and mudflats that were once used for harvesting sea salt. Offshore is the island of Nosy Lonja, a sacred site where Malagasy people perform *fijoroana* ceremonies to honour their ancestors, and behind the mangroves looms 400m-high Montagne des Français, named for the French soldiers who used the summit as a lookout during the colonial period.

Today, the mountain is protected as the **Anosiravo Natural Reserve**, with a string of walking trails leading to viewpoints and natural features. The short Vallée des Baobabs circuit (1km) visits some robust baobab trees and small shrines used by Christian pilgrims, while the Vallée des Perroquets (8km) circuit takes in viewpoints, forest trails, limestone caverns and rocky outcrops with dozens of bolted sport climbing

ASSOCIATION FANAMBY

Association Fanamby in Diego Suarez oversees operations at **Camp Andrafiamena-Andavakoera** (p155), 60km south of Diego Suarez, and **Loky Manambato Protected Area** (p171) between Ambilobe and Vohémar.

ESCAPE THE RUSH IN RAMENA

On the northwest side of the Oranjia peninsula, the sleepy village of **Ramena** is an agreeable place to escape from the world. Inexpensive *taxis-brousses* buzz between Diego Suarez and Ramena throughout the day and the village beach is clean and good for families.

Malagasy seafood restaurants line the waterfront, taxi drivers offer trips to Les Trois Baies and Montagne des Français, and boat trips run from the main jetty to the Mer d'Emeraude.

For an overnight stay, the appealing **Le Chti Près** has a superior seafood restaurant, beach beds and parasols for rent and cosy sea-facing rooms. Just inland, **Badamera Park** has rooms and bungalows dotted around a pretty exotic garden, and there's a popular Sunday buffet lunch with live music.

WHERE TO STAY AT BAIE DES FRANÇAIS (ANDOVOBAZAHA)

Le Suarez
Behind the mangroves, with gorgeous, thatched adobe bungalows in a forest garden by a waterhole-style pool. **$$$**

Meva Plage
A tasteful collection of bungalows around a pool behind the beach at the northeast end of the bay. **$$$**

Jungle Park
A true original, with jungle activities, eco-domes and treehouses around a forest pool off the Ramena road. **$$$**

routes (contact the Jungle Park/New Sea Roc offices on Rue Colbert in Diego Suarez for supported climbing excursions).

The most popular walk is the steep and tiring Tours 360° circuit (5.5km), which climbs to a panoramic lookout at the top of the massif, following 650 steps through a series of French-excavated tunnels through the mountainside. Arrange mandatory guides at the reserve entrance, and keep an eye out for lemurs, chameleons, snakes, tortoises and birds. Note that relieving yourself in some parts of the reserve is *fady* (taboo) – your guide can advise.

Find a Cooler Wilderness at Parc National Montagne d'Ambre

LEMURS, CHAMELEONS AND GENTLER CLIMES

The first thing you'll notice as you approach **Parc National Montagne d'Ambre** is the agreeable temperature. This rainforest reserve sprawls across the slopes of an extinct volcano near **Joffreville** (Ambohitra) and the temperature is consistently 10°C cooler than on the coast – ideal conditions for exploring! It rains on the mountain almost every day, but as you explore trails bursting with lemurs, snakes, frogs and chameleons of all shapes and sizes, we suspect you won't mind.

The reserve is home to the elusive fossa, alongside more frequently spotted ring-tailed mongooses and crowned and Sanford's lemurs. Keep your eyes peeled for rarer inhabitants, such as the rufous mouse lemur, dwarf and northern sportive lemurs, aye-ayes and the Montagne d'Ambre fork-marked lemur. This is also one of the best places to spy tiny *Brookesia* chameleons, some of the world's smallest reptiles, which can be found in the leaf litter on the forest floor.

Many people day-trip to the park from Diego Suarez or Joffreville, taking walks from the campsite at Station des Roussettes, about 2.5km east of the park headquarters (where you'll need to pay park entry fees and arrange a guide). Trails wind through the Voie des Mille Arbres (Path of a Thousand Trees), a copse of exotic tree species planted by French colonial horticulturalists, to scenic waterfalls such as the Cascade Antankarana and Cascade Sacrée, where local Malagasy people leave offerings to animist spirits.

Longer trails visit serene crater lakes (created during the last eruptions of the Montagne d'Ambre volcano some two million years ago) and the summit of the mountain (1475m), reached via an 11km trail from the park entrance. Many groups stop overnight at the small campsite at Grand Lac before tackling the summit trail.

 WHERE TO STAY AT JOFFREVILLE (AMBOHITRA) ————

Monastère de Joffreville
The friendly nuns at this Benedictine monastery offer tasty meals, local crafts, and simple, tidy rooms. **$$**

Nature Lodge
A stylish ecolodge with wood-lined bungalows dotted around generous grounds, perched above epic views. **$$$**

Litchi Tree
Elegant rooms in the former home of French war hero Joseph Joffre; owner Hervé Dumel cooks up a feast. **$$$**

Réserve Spéciale Ankarana

Explore Surreal Landscapes at Réserve Spéciale Ankarana

ROCKY OUTCROPS AND ABUNDANT WILDLIFE

Most people visit the dry forests and karst outcrops of **Réserve Spéciale Ankarana** en route to or from Diego Suarez, but you can also stay close to the reserve headquarters or in nearby Ambilobe. Wherever you stay, you're in for a treat. This easy-to-reach reserve takes in wildlife-filled forests, dramatic caves and canyons, subterranean rivers and fortress-like formations of serrated limestone *tsingy* – eroded karst pinnacles that play an important role in local folklore.

The name *tsingy* literally means 'walking on tiptoes' – a reference to the legend that the Antakarana people of northern Madagascar took to their tiptoes to flee across these limestone spikes to escape raids from the Merina people of the central highlands during tribal wars in the 18th century.

Most people concentrate on the trails leading through the eastern ranges of the park, accessible from the park headquarters at Mahamasina on the RN6. *Petit* circuits (two to

ANKARANA'S WILD WONDERS

The diverse terrain of Réserve Spéciale Ankarana provides a home for a remarkable diversity of wildlife. In all areas of the park, listen out for the call of hunting fish eagles, sparrowhawks and harrier hawks, and scan the canopy for crowned, Sanford's and northern sportive lemurs, and the undergrowth for hedgehog-like tenrecs and ring-tailed mongooses.

In Ankarana's caves, look up to spot 14 different bat species. The dry forests and *tsingy* also throng with giant land snails and scorpions, and 90 species of birds, including blue *vangas*, *vasa* parrots and the striking crested *coua*.

Alongside many other reptile species, look out for leaf-tailed geckos, blending in perfectly with the tree trunks they sit on and always angled head down so avian predators can't see their eyes.

WHERE TO STAY AT RÉSERVE SPÉCIALE ANKARANA

Chez Aurélien
A homey option right by the park headquarters, with simple bungalows and home-cooked meals. **$**

Ankaranana Lodge
Minutes from the park entrance, with a great pool and smart bungalows set amongst the trees. **$$$**

Kozobe Hotel
Ambilobe's most stylish hotel offers cavernous rooms, arranged around a resort-style landscaped pool. **$$$**

three hours) visit the Perte des Rivières, where a seasonal river plunges underground into a vast natural sinkhole, and eye-catching *tsingy* formations at Tsingy Rary, Tourelles and Tsingy Meva, and the stalactite- and stalagmite-filled Grotte des Chauves-Souris (home to eight species of bats, including Commerson's leaf-nosed bat).

Moyen and *grand* circuits lasting five to nine hours continue to the stalactite-filled Boucle Benavony cavern, a rope bridge dangling over jagged *tsingy* formations, and the impressive viewpoint at Ambohimalaza (with views as far as Nosy Be and Montagne d'Ambre). The main lure of the park's remote western ranges (only accessible from June to December) is the chance to wriggle around the dramatically eroded caverns of Grotte Squelette, Grotte d'Andrafiabe and Grotte Cathédrale.

See Nature as Art at the Tsingy Rouges

SURREAL ERODED LANDSCAPES

About 45km south of Diego Suarez, a rough 4WD track branches off RN6 to the remarkable **Tsingy Rouges**, a deep valley lined with eroded laterite pinnacles, like an army of petrified soldiers. These striking formations were created by the action of wind and rainwater and the site is constantly changing and evolving with natural erosion. The iron-oxide-rich soil of the valley provides vivid ochre, vermillion and magenta pigments that were once used for face paints and natural dyes.

Today the site is protected, but each monsoon sculpts the pinnacles into new shapes and configurations. You'll need a 4WD to reach the Tsingy, but you can then explore without a guide, following clear trails. Close to the main grouping of pinnacles is an elevated platform offering views of more *tsingy* in a deep, narrow valley. Most people arrange a visit through a tour agency in Diego Suarez; note that the access road can be impassable during the rainy season (December to April).

GETTING AROUND

Most people explore the area around Diego Suarez with a rented vehicle and driver; Madabest, Diego Raid and Evasion sans Frontière in Diego can make all the arrangements. To go it alone, *taxis-brousses* from Diego Suarez to Ramena pass the entrance to the Anosiravo reserve, while *taxis-brousses* to Ambilobe and points further south pass the headquarters for Réserve Spéciale Ankarana.

Taxis-brousses also run from Diego to Joffreville. If you come by public transport, stay at the cosy, inexpensive Relais de la Montagne d'Ambre just east of the main junction in Joffreville, a 3km walk from the national park entrance.

SAMBAVA

Sambava

ANTANANARIVO

Tucked away in the verdant northeast, Sambava is surprisingly af-fluent considering its hidden-away location. The capital of the Sava region is a vital hub for Madagascar's lucrative vanilla industry, and the centre is dotted with the ritzy offices of vanilla companies and processing plants that fill the air with a subtle scent of spice.

Vanilla, coconut, cocoa, clove and coffee plantations sprawl north and south along the coast, behind beautiful undeveloped beaches. Sambava is also notable for its sizeable Chinese population – the descendants of spice workers who came here in the 1930s – and 'Chinese soup' (wonton soup with noodles) is served all over town.

For visitors, Sambava is a handy base for trips to spectacular Parc National de Marojejy, or a staging post for trips further south to Andapa, Antalaha and Réserve Spéciale Anjanaharibe-Sud. Al-ternatively, you can tour local plantations and take advantage of some fine beaches, far from the tourist crowds.

TOP TIP

Sambava's golden beaches are sparsely developed and enticing, but currents are strong and sharks may be present in the murky waters around the mouth of the four rivers that converge here. For swimming, stick to the beaches away from the river mouth, towards the airport.

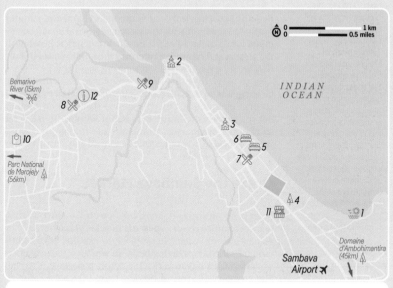

SIGHTS
1 Ampandrozonana
2 Church of St Thérèse
3 FJKM Filadelfia Church
4 Société Soavoanio

SLEEPING
5 Hotel Las Palmas
6 Hotel Orchidea Beach II

EATING
7 Boule D'Or Restaurant and Bar
8 Mimi Patisserie
9 Resto Ling

SHOPPING
10 Maison de la Vanille
11 Sambava Open-Air Marketplace

INFORMATION
12 Sava Tourist Office/Mimi Hôtel

SAMBAVA'S CHINESE HISTORY

One of the first things you'll notice when you reach Sambava is the Chinese influence – particularly the noodle dishes that pop up on restaurant menus.

The first Chinese migrants to Madagascar were imported by French general Joseph Gallieni in the late 19th century to help construct the roads and railways, but most of Sava's Chinese population arrived from Canton in the 1930s as workers for spice-harvesting companies.

While many of Madagascar's 'old Chinese' adopted Malagasy customs under French rule, Sambava's Chinese community follows a mix of religions, and the town has a number of prestigious Chinese schools. Get a taste of Chinese culture in Sambava at the excellent **Resto Ling** restaurant near the bridge in the centre.

Coconut sorting, Sambava

Hit the Beach

EMPTY, GOLDEN SANDS

Beautiful beaches trace the shoreline in Sambava, running south and north in a glorious sweep of gold. For safe swimming, locals make a beeline for the lovely public beach near the airport at **Ampandrozonana**, which is thronged by families on Sundays (there's even a decent surf break).

North of the river mouth, a seemingly endless curve of unblemished sand runs for more than 20km, backed by swaying coconut plantations. Currents are too strong for swimming, but you can walk for miles in peaceful solitude. To reach the start of the beach, head to the pirogue station just east of the river bridge, where boatmen can pole you across the river mouth to the sand.

Graze the Sambava Market

STOCK UP ON TROPICAL TREATS

After a fire destroyed Sambava's downtown market, stall-holders relocated to the **open-air marketplace** towards the airport. It's an atmospheric place to explore, with tightly tangled pathways weaving between wonky wooden shelters where villagers sell groceries, meat, fish, household essentials and an amazing array of tropical fruit – the local *corossols*

WHERE TO EAT IN SAMBAVA

Patisserie Mimi
The bakery at Mimi Hôtel is the place to grab a fresh croissant, pain aux raisins or pain au chocolat. **$**

Boule d'Or Restaurant & Bar
Sambava's best pizzas are served at this friendly place; there's also buttered popcorn for the kids. **$$**

Resto Ling
The best place in town for a filling bowl of *mine* (noodle) and wonton soup, right by the bridge in the centre. **$$**

(soursops) are particularly good. It's a great opportunity to see a Malagasy market aimed entirely at locals.

Take a Plantation Tour

DELVE INTO SAMBAVA'S SPICE HERITAGE

The friendly **Sava tourist office** at **Mimi Hôtel** can arrange trips to explore local vanilla, spice and coconut plantations, with guides who can explain (in French) how these exotic crops are raised, harvested and processed.

Close to Sambava, **Société Soavoanio** runs tours of its coconut plantation south of the centre on weekday mornings. Make bookings at their coconut-oil processing centre opposite the market. About 50km south of Sambava, **Domaine d'Ambohimantira** produces premium vanilla, alongside cinnamon, camphor, allspice and cloves. Book through the agency Soaland Discovery to enjoy a guided tour of the plantations and a posh lunch on the terrace; you can also stay overnight in stylish villas in the grounds.

For an accessible introduction to the vanilla industry, drop into the **Maison de la Vanille** on the highway west of Mimi Hôtel. During the peak harvest season (June to January), you can visit the busy warehouse behind the shop where workers process, sort and grade the day's deliveries from local plantations (a purchase from the shop is appreciated).

Go to Church

FEEL SAMBAVA'S SPIRITUAL RHYTHMS

Sundays in Sambava are quite an experience, as locals flock to the town's churches before hitting the beach. Lively Sunday services (with enthusiastic choral singing) take place at around 6am and 8.30am, often accompanied by special Sunday school events for kids and a banquet of snack foods for the congregation. The busiest churches are the angular, modernist **church of Sainte Thérèse** near the river bridge, and the Protestant **FJKM Filadelfia church** east of the centre near the beach hotels.

Dive into the Jungles of Parc National de Marojejy

TROPICAL FLORA, ABUNDANT FLORA

About 60km southwest of Sambava, off the RN3b, Parc National Marojejy is one of Madagascar's great undiscovered parks. Covering more than 550 sq km of pristine rainforest draped over the towering Marojejy Massif, this is a humid,

EXPLORING SAVA

Sambava hotelier **Bruno Lee** shares his tips for top things to do in Sava.

Best Day Out near Sambava
Tour the Bemarivo River, bordered by plantations of exotic crops, including vanilla. The whisper of wind, birdsong and the flow of water will rock you as you explore beautiful countryside.

Best Wildlife Experience
Prestigious Parc National de Marojejy spans low-altitude forests and humid mountain thickets with a high rate of endemicity – you can see 10 species of lemurs, including the spectacular silky *sifaka*.

Best Day Trip
North of Vohémar, a short excursion will take you into a stunning landscape around the village of Plaideau. In one space, we have forest, river and sea, plus canyons and panoramic views of the islets.

 WHERE TO STAY IN SAMBAVA ───────

Mimi Hôtel
Run by the Lee family, with cosy rooms and bungalows, a good restaurant and the regional tourist office. **$$**

Hôtel Las Palmas
A calm, family-run hotel, with art deco details and comfy accommodation in rooms and split-level bungalows. **$$**

Hôtel Orchidea Beach II
Quiet, shady, and facing a lovely stretch of beach, with expansive, airy rooms and stylish tiled bathrooms. **$$$**

CAMPING AT MAROJEJY

The three camps at Parc National de Marojejy can cater to trekkers with or without tents. Each has a cluster of simple cabins with tin or polythene roofs, space for tents, a covered eating area and camp kitchen, and a basic toilet block.

You will need to bring all your own food, and potentially food for your guides, porters and cooks – fees are lower if you provide meals for your whole group. There is plentiful water in the park, but carry purification tablets.

If you come on an organised trip, the agency will make all the arrangements; alternatively, you can organise things yourself (and pay the park fees, camping fees and fees for porters, cooks and guides) at the park headquarters in Manantenina on RN3b.

primordial jungle, where waterfalls thunder into hidden glades, tree roots writhe around moss-cloaked boulders and lemurs chatter overhead – including the critically endangered silky *sifaka*.

Designated a Unesco World Heritage Site in 2007, the Marojejy Massif is noteworthy for its extraordinary biodiversity, with 2000 types of plants, 148 species of reptiles and amphibians, 118 bird species, and 11 species of lemur. Hikes here weave through four levels of forest, before emerging in front of epic views over the mountains.

The classic route to the summit (2132m) takes four days, starting from the park interpretative centre and headquarters in the village of Manantenina (between Sambava and Andapa). You'll need to stop here to pay the park entry fees and arrange a guide, porters, cooks and equipment.

Day one involves a steep hike from the end of a 5.6km-long dirt road. You'll start amidst rice fields and vanilla plantations before entering a forest teeming with wildlife. Listen out for the rustle of birds, reptiles and lemurs and scan the forest floor for giant fire millipedes, pill millipedes (which can roll into a ball) and other crawly critters.

After a night at Camp Mantella (450m), where you can detour to pretty Cascade de Humbert or splash in a natural swimming hole, you'll spend night two at Camp Simporna (1250m). From here, it's a steep and strenuous scramble over

Parc National de Marojejy

Vanilla production, Sambava

slippery rocks and tree roots before you reach the summit and those spectacular views. You'll descend to Camp Marojejia (775m) for night three before exiting the park on day four.

The easiest way to visit is on an organised trek (try the Sava tourist office in Sambava), but it's also possible to visit on a long day trip from Sambava or Andapa. You'll need to arrange a car and driver for the day, and set off early so you have time to hike to Camp Mantella and get back to your hotel by nightfall.

GETTING AROUND

The tiny airport southeast of central Sambava receives several Tsaradia flights a week from Diego Suarez (Antsiranana) and Antananarivo; there's heavy demand for seats on these small turboprops, so book early for all routes.

You can hire a vehicle and driver on arrival through the Sava tourist office at the Mimi Hôtel. If you're driving from the west coast, you can reach Sambava via the significantly improved RN5a from Ambilobe in six to seven hours.

Regular *taxis-brousses* connect Sambava to Diego Suarez, Ambilobe, Antananarivo and towns in the Sava region. For short downtown trips, tuk-tuks and taxis charge a fixed fare, or you can charter the whole vehicle to reach the airport and local plantations and beaches.

Beyond Sambava

Sambava is the gateway to a string of little-visited towns and national parks scattered across Sava's emerald green vanilla country.

Beyond Sambava, RN5a traces the lush tropical coastline south to Antalaha, another vanilla-producing hub with its own gorgeous, undeveloped beachfront. The road fizzles out at the Masaola Peninsula, which can only be crossed on foot.

Heading southwest, RN3b connects Sambava to Andapa, an alternative base for trips to Parc National de Marojejy and a popular base for hikes in Réserve Spéciale Anjanaharibe-Sud. Andapa is the main hub for rice production in the north, and the floodplain outside town is a sea of whispering rice fields.

Coming with a 4WD and driver is the best way to explore; you can get here by *taxi-brousse*, but the reserves are hidden away at the end of atrocious dirt tracks.

Loky Manambato
Protected Area
Ambilobe
Vohémar
Sambava
Réserve National
d'Antanetiambo   Manantenina
Andapa
Réserve Spéciale   Antalaha
Anjanaharibe-Sud

TOP TIP

Visiting Réserve Spéciale Anjanaharibe-Sud independently is challenging; it's better to make arrangements for a multiday tour through an agency.

Near Vohémar

PIERRE-YVES BABELON/SHUTTERSTOCK ©

Vanilla tree plantation

Take a Beach Break at Vohémar

SLEEPY SANDS AND WILDLIFE TRIPS

Running east from Ambilobe through gold-panning country, the RN5a hits the east coast at the small town of **Vohémar** (Iharana), flanked by beautiful, if wild, beaches. This is the beginning of vanilla country, but most people use the town as a base to visit the lovely Loky Manambato Protected Area at Ampanombohana, around 56km northwest. For a comfortable overnight stop, the appealing Baie d'Iharana Hôtel hugs a gleaming strip of golden beachfront north of the main road. Cheaper bungalows are available west of the centre at cosy Bungalow Beach, set on a windy beach behind the Savan Vanilla plant.

Seek Tatersalli Sifakas at Loky Manambato

RARE LEMURS, EASILY SPOTTED

Founded by the Malagasy NGO Fanamby, with offices in Diego Suarez, the **Loky Manambato Protected Area** preserves 2484 sq km of dry forest, providing a home for around 1000 critically endangered Tattersalli *sifakas*, as well as

THE GIFTED INDRI

The black *indri* (*Indri indri*) is one of Madagascar's most enigmatic inhabitants. One of the largest lemurs, the *indri* is known to Malagasy people as *babakoto*, the 'ancestor of man', a reference to the local legend that the first *indri* were human beings transformed into forest animals.

Despite being a tree-dweller, the *indri* has only a rudimentary tail, and its distinctive whooping call can be heard echoing through the forests of Réserve Spéciale Anjanaharibe-Sud.

Amongst other unique features, the *indri* is the only animal apart from human beings to have a sense of rhythm – scientific studies have shown that *indri* calls display 'categorical rhythm', a characteristic pattern of beats and pauses that was once thought to be unique to human music.

🛏️ **WHERE TO STAY AND EAT IN ANDAPA**

Hôtel Riziky
An acceptable cheapie set back from the noisy main bazaar, with bungalows set around a courtyard garden. **$**

Hôtel Beanana
A calm haven in the middle of Andapa, with airy, inviting bedrooms and verandas; meals available on request. **$$**

Hôtel Vatosoa
This courtyard hotel on the main bazaar has comfy rooms and the best Malagasy Chinese food in town. **$$**

MARTIN MECNAROWSKI/SHUTTERSTOCK ©

Indri

PARC NATIONAL DE MAROJEJY

The park headquarters for Réserve Spéciale Anjanaharibe-Sud at Manantenina also processes fees and arranges guides, porter and and cooks for trips to **Parc National de Marojejy** (p167), a highly rewarding stop en route from Sambava to Andapa.

RÉSERVE NATIONAL D'ANTANETIAMBO

Reached via a short but bumpy road running from Andapa to the village of Matsobe Sud (6km), **Réserve National d'Antanetiambo** protects bamboo forests and islands of mixed woodland, set amidst sprawling rice fields. The project is supported by the Lemur Conservation Foundation and northern bamboo lemurs and mouse lemurs are easily spotted in the trees, alongside birds, snakes and other wildlife. The reserve is managed by local residents Julien Bedimasy and Désiré Rabary, and guided daytime and nighttime walks through the atmospheric bamboo groves can be arranged in the village. Guides work together as a team using animal noises and mobile phones to stay in touch, to maximise the chances of wildlife encounters.

inquisitive crowned lemurs, giant scorpions and rarely spotted aye-ayes. It's a beautifully serene spot, and guides can be arranged in the village of Ampanombohana, a few kilometres north of Daraina on the Ambilobe–Vohémar highway (RN5a). The rough track leading to the reserve is impassable in the rainy season, and the park camp has fallen into disrepair, so it's best to day trip from either Vohémar or Ambilobe. Contact the Association Fanamby office in Diego Suarez (p158) for the latest information.

Meet the Elusive Black Indri at Réserve Spéciale Anjanaharibe-Sud

TOUGH TREKS TO SPOT ENDEMIC WONDERS

Rising west of Andapa, Réserve Spéciale Anjanaharibe-Sud – meaning 'Place of the Great God' – is a rarely visited jewel of a reserve, covering 172 sq km of pristine, old-growth montane forest. It's a vital hub for biodiversity, and the streams draining off its slopes feed the sprawling rice fields around Andapa. This is one of the best places to spot the critically endangered black *indri*, believed to be the only animal apart from humans to have a sense of rhythm.

Most visitors come on four-day trips from **Andapa**, stopping overnight at Camp Indri (900m) – a simple collection of tent shelters with toilets and a camp kitchen. From here, hikers spend several days visiting hot springs, exploring the forest in search of black *indris*, silky *sifakas* and other lemurs and the distinctive red flowers of *Takhtajania perrieri*, a primitive plant that has survived unchanged since the Cretaceous period.

To visit, you'll first have to stop at the national park headquarters at **Manantenina** (between Sambava and Andapa on RN3b) to pay fees and arrange guides, porters and cooks. The road is surfaced as far as Andapa, but you'll then face a long, uncomfortable drive on an unspeakable dirt track to either Andasibe-Mahaverika or Befingotra, where the hike begins. In practice, almost everyone comes on a trek organised through a tour agency.

Follow the Coast Road to Antalaha

WILD BEACHES AT WORLD'S END

For more beach action, follow RN5a south from Sambava to sleepy **Antalaha**, a little-visited vanilla town with some fine beaches and a shipyard producing traditional Sakalava dhows. The appealing Hôtel Océan Momo has comfortable white bungalows set in a tidy beachside garden near the football stadium.

Before you leave, take a hike or pirogue ride through the Macolline wildlife reserve, an area of riverside forest 3km north of town, where you can spot frogs, chameleons, butterflies and lots of super-sized bugs. Entry fees help to support local conservation and community projects.

RÉSERVE SPÉCIALE ANJANAHARIBE-SUD

The Marojejy park headquarters at Manantenina also oversees arrangements for visitors to **Réserve Spéciale Anjanaharibe-Sud** (p172) to the west of Andapa.

Shipyard, Antalaha

PIERRE-YVES BABELON/SHUTTERSTOCK ©

GETTING AROUND

Andapa and Antalaha can be reached easily from Sambava by *taxi-brousse*, but getting to the nearby reserves can be tricky without a hired 4WD and driver because of the dire condition of the roads.

Vehicles and drivers can be arranged through the Sava tourist office at Mimi Hôtel in Sambava, or you may be able to make arrangements through Hôtel Beanana in Andapa. Alternatively, you can limp slowly to the reserves using local *taxis-brousses*, moto-taxis and walking.

When leaving the Sava region by road, you'll have to leave as you arrived, via RN5a. It's best to break the journey for a night in **Ambilobe**, before pushing on to the north or centre of the country.

EASTERN MADAGASCAR

WELCOME TO THE WILD EAST

Eastern Madagascar is travel the way it used to be: remote and wild, and the forests are filled with lemurs.

Exploring eastern Madagascar means falling off the map for a while and going on an adventure. The further you travel from Tana, the more the traveller crowds and tourism infrastructure fall away.

In the isolated backwaters of the Pangalanes Lakes, you'll get a taste for this quieter form of travel, as you encounter lakeside villages, biodiverse Vohibola Forest, and empty white-sand beaches. But travel further north along the infamous RN5 and you'll discover forested national parks where aye-ayes, *indri* and other sought-after species live. Out here, you'll have to hike just to get to the start of a trailhead. At times, pirogues (dugout canoes) are the only option, but it means you get to watch dugongs and sharks in pristine waters. Baie d'Antongil and the Masoala Peninsula in particular are largely cut off from the rest of the country, and from each other, by awful roads. But this inaccessibility protects isolated communities and promises for the traveller a constant sense of discovery.

Like bookends to such adventurous expeditions, Parc National Andasibe Mantadia and Île Sainte Marie rank among Madagascar's most popular attractions, and deservedly so. The former is one of the best and most varied places in Madagascar to see lemurs. Sainte Marie, on the other hand, has everything from perfect beaches and hideaway seafood restaurants to whale watching from the beach on special Île aux Nattes (Nosy Nato).

ARI KUSH/SHUTTERSTOCK ©

THE MAIN AREAS

PARC NATIONAL ANDASIBE MANTADIA	**PANGALANES LAKES**	**THE TAMATAVE (TOAMASINA) COAST**	**ÎLE SAINTE MARIE**	**BAIE D'ANTONGIL & MASOALA**
Lemurs in the forest. p180	Remote lakes and canals. p187	The east's wild shore. p191	Beautiful tropical isle. p196	Isolated parks and aye-ayes. p201

Above: Île Sainte Marie (p196); left: Maroantsetra (p208)

Find Your Way

Travelling in eastern Madagascar is often a case of 'whatever works'. Stay long enough and you may require a combination of plane, car, 4WD, motorbike, scooter, pirogue (dugout canoe), ferry, cargo boat, *taxi-brousse* (bush taxi) and motorboat.

RN2 & RN5

Almost all land access to eastern Madagascar is via a single road, the RN2 from Antananarivo.

Then there's the RN5: between Tamatave and Soanierana-Ivongo it's fine, but it's spectacularly bad between Soanierana-Ivongo and Maroantsetra.

INDIAN OCEAN

0 ——— 50 km
0 ——— 25 miles

Cap Est

Antalaha

Antohitralanana

Andapa

Parc National Marojejy

Parc National Masoala-Nosy Mangabe

Masoala Peninsula

Ampanavoana

Fampotabe

Mahalevona

Marojejy Massif

Maroantsetra

Ambanizana

Baie d'Antongil

Rantabe

Manambolosy

Mananara

Fahambahy

Seranambe

Antanambe

Manompana

Parc National Mananara-Nord

Mandritsara

Soanierana-Ivongo

Île aux Nattes

Lonkintsy

Nosy

Ampasimbe

Antaniménabaka

Andilamena

Ambalanjanakomby

Maevatanana

Baie d'Antongil & Masoala, p201

This remote corner of the country has pristine waters filled with marine life, and dense, hikeable forests that shelter lemurs.

Île Sainte Marie, p196

Eastern Madagascar's tropical isle has fabulous beaches and quieter treasures like Baie d'Ampaniny, Île aux Nattes and even a Pirate Cemetery.

The Tamatave (Toamasina) Coast, p191

The easiest-to-reach region of east coast Madagascar has beach gems like Foulpointe (Mahavelona) and Mahambo, and the fine Parc Zoologique Ivoloina.

Pangalanes Lakes, p187

The quiet canals and byways are perfect for watery meanders through untouristy villages, with Vohibola Forest and Ambila-Lemaitso as further prizes.

PLANE

Despite eastern Madagascar covering a large area, the only internal flights within the region are those between Tamatave (Toamasina) and Île Sainte Marie. There is also an airport at Maroantsetra, but it only has semi-regular flights to/from Tana.

BOAT

Ferries and catamarans connect Île Sainte Marie and Soanierana-Ivongo or Mahambo on the mainland. Smaller cargo boats, fishing boats and pirogues ply the Pangalanes Lakes, Canal des Pangalanes and Baie d'Antongil.

Parc National Andasibe Mantadia, p180

Accessible from Tana and gateway to Madagascar's east coast, the parks and lakes here are great for hiking in search of lemurs.

177

Plan Your Time

Eastern Madagascar is a series of adventures that can take you as far off the beaten track as you have the time and inclination to go.

Pousse-pousse, Tamatave (p191)

If You Only Do One Thing

● Take a drive east of Antananarivo and stop to see the lemurs and chameleons of **Réserve Peyrieras** (p186) and for a picnic lunch at **Lac Mantasoa** (p184).

● After overnighting in **Andasibe** (p180), spend a couple of days exploring the **Parc National Analamazaotra** (p181) with its wonderful lemur encounters, including with the iconic *indri*. While you're here, make sure you go looking for nocturnal lemurs on a night walk in **Parc Mitsinjo** (p183).

● If you can spare one more day, go for a longer hike through **Parc National Mantadia** (p184), before driving back to Antananarivo on your final day.

Seasonal Highlights

If you avoid the rainy season when roads are at their worst, and the months when cyclones can really spoil your trip, conditions out east are almost always ideal.

JANUARY

Cyclone season begins, and runs until March. With the Christmas–New Year high season and possible heavy rain, January's best avoided.

FEBRUARY/MARCH

The height of the **rainy season** turns east-coast roads to quagmires and the RN5 into an unmitigated mess.

APRIL

The skies clear (some roads may still be impassable), everyone's smiling, and the real travel season begins.

An Island Week

● Whether you fly or drive to **Île Sainte Marie** (p196), plan on staying a week on this magical island. A couple of those days should be spent on the beach, with a day's excursion to explore and eat seafood by the waters of **Baie d'Ampanihy** (p197), and another up north around the **Piscines Naturelles d'Ambodiatafana** (p196).

● Don't miss the **Pirate Cemetery** (p199) and the former pirate stronghold of Libertalia. But reserve at least three days for the quieter charms of **Île aux Nattes** (Nosy Nato; p200) where you might spot whales from the beach and generally never want to leave.

Leave the Crowds Behind

● Start your two-week exploration of Madagascar's remote east coast in the **Pangalanes Lakes** (p187), where you can cruise the byways and backwaters of this forgotten Malagasy world.

● Make sure you visit **Ambila-Lemaitso** (p189) and **Lac Ampitabe** (p189). Track north through **Tamatave** (p191), stopping off in the **Parc Zoologique Ivoloina** (p195), **Foulpointe** (p194) and **Mahambo** (p192) on your way to **Parc National Mananara Nord** (p206) and **Aye-Aye Island** (p203).

● Then drop off the map for a week exploring the shark-rich waters and forgotten shoreline of the **Baie d'Antongil** (p201) and lemur-rich parks of the **Masoala Peninsula** (p205).

JULY

Humpback whales pass by the east coast, Ambodifotatra has a whale festival, most roads are open and the weather is gorgeous.

AUGUST

High season, so things are busy, but the air smells of vanilla, and ocean conditions are perfect for water-based activities.

SEPTEMBER

The crowds have ebbed, whales are still swimming past and the weather is magnificent.

NOVEMBER

The last of the crowds have gone, eastern roads are at their best and it's a lovely time to explore the east.

PARC NATIONAL
ANDASIBE MANTADIA

Parc National
Andasibe-
Mantadia
& Around

ANTANANARIVO

Everybody wants to see the wailing, charismatic *indri,* the largest of all lemur species and an icon of the Malagasy wild. And there's no better place to do this than in and around Parc National Andasibe Mantadia. But there's more. Where else in Madagascar can you see both *indri* and aye-aye in the same forest? Or hike through primary rainforest so dense that the sun barely penetrates the canopy, all the while looking for endangered birdlife, abundant chameleons and other forest species? Best of all, in these humid forests, the wildlife long ago became used to the human presence, making for some incredible, up-close encounters.

A visit here requires careful planning. In addition to the two parts of the national park – Analamazaotra and Mantadia – numerous private reserves of astonishing biodiversity lie scattered across the nearby hills, and there are night walks, village visits and even tree-planting to add to your *indri*-spotting expeditions.

TOP TIP

Most visitors only stay in the Andasibe area for two nights (ie one full day). Plan instead on spending two full days. By doing so, you increase your chances of seeing all 12 lemur species. You'll also have time to do the many activities on offer.

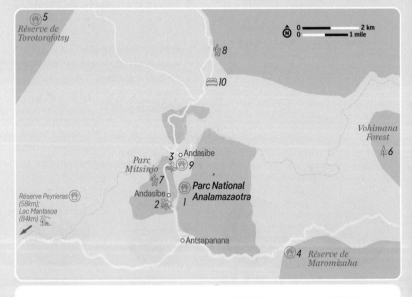

HIGHLIGHTS
1 Parc National Analamazaotra

SIGHTS
2 Andasibe
3 Parc des Orchidées

4 Réserve de Maromizaha
5 Réserve de Torotorofotsy
6 Vohimana Forest

ACTIVITIES
7 Parc Mitsinjo
8 Parc National Mantadia
9 Parc Villageois (VOIMMA)

SLEEPING
10 Vakôna Forest Lodge

Indri, Parc National Mantadia (p184)

Look for the Indri in Parc National Analamazaotra

ONE OF MADAGASCAR'S BEST LEMUR PARKS

If you only visit one park in the Andasibe area, make it Parc National Analamazaotra (which is the westernmost part of the Parc National Andasibe Mantadia). Yes, it's the busiest of the parks in the area but that's with good reason: the trails are accessible and the lemur sightings here can be exceptional. It's also among the best parks in Madagascar to see the fabled *indri*. Other highlights include the charismatic Diademed *sifaka*, and birdlife (over 100 species) that might include the crested ibis scurrying along forest paths, the paradise flycatcher and the Madagascar blue coua that preys on chameleons. Analamazaotra is also home to the endemic palm tree *Ravenea louvelii*, which is found nowhere else in Madagascar.

The park has four main circuits, and we recommend walking as much of this forest as you can. Almost as soon as you leave park headquarters and set out on the trail, dense rainforest envelops you in sights and smells and sounds. If you're lucky, the haunting wails of a family of *indris* will call you deeper into the dense, dark forest.

LEMURS OF ANDASIBE

Most of the parks in the Andasibe area share the same 12 lemur species, six of which can be seen by day, and six of which are nocturnal. In descending order of size, the six daytime species are the *indri*, Diademed sifaka, red-bellied (or red-fronted) lemur, black-and-white ruffed lemur, common brown lemur, and the grey bamboo lemur. The six nocturnal species are the aye-aye, eastern woolly lemur, sportive lemur, dwarf lemur, rufous mouse lemur, and the Goodman's mouse lemur; the latter was only discovered in 2005.

 WHERE TO STAY IN ANDASIBE

MNP Campsite
You can camp for free behind the entrance to Parc National Analamazaotra, but you'll need your own equipment. **$**

Vohitsara Guest House
Family-run operation near the old station; budget rooms with external showers and Malagasy food on request. **$**

Hôtel Les Orchidées
Combines very basic rooms with an on-site village nursery, so expect to be surrounded by lots of children. **$**

IF YOU ONLY HAVE ONE DAY AROUND ANDASIBE

Sitraka Jean Fredy Andriamihaja, local guide in the parks around Andasibe for 12 years, shares his recommendations.

Parc Villageois (VOIMMA)
Start early morning in Parc Villageois (VOIMMA) where you're sure to see the *indri*. The *indri* is the easiest to spot here, but other lemurs can be more difficult, so now you can focus on other species elsewhere in the Andasibe area.

Parc National Analamazaotra
Follow up with a visit to Parc National Analamazaotra: by 9am or 10am, all of the other lemur species should be active and easier to see, so plan on hiking here for a further three to four hours.

Parc Mitsinjo
In the afternoon, head for Parc Mitsinjo to see lemurs along pretty forest trails. In the evening go on a night walk to see nocturnal species, either here or in Parc Villageois (VOIMMA).

Lac Vert

If you're travelling with a small family, consider the Palmier Circuit (2km, one to two hours); an easy forest walk overflowing with botanical interest (palms and orchids, the latter from October to December) as well as *indri* possibilities.

If your time or mobility is limited, take the two-hour Circuit Indri 1. The trail takes you past the park's two small lakes: Lac Vert (Green Lake) and Lac Rouge (Red Lake). It also passes through the territory of at least one family group of *indris*, and we've had luck with other lemur species along the way. The trail is enough to give you a taste of the lush vegetation, as well as some of the smaller species, such as the park's nine species of chameleon, leaf-tailed geckos and more.

The three-hour Circuit Indri 2 is similar, if slightly more strenuous: it takes in the two lakes and increases your chances of seeing *indris* as you pass through more family territories. Circuit Aventure (four to six hours, 8km) combines the two Indri circuits and adds some quite steep hill walking through the forest; watch your step carefully: smaller forest species hide in the leaf litter, and some sections of trail can be slippery in this perennially humid forest.

 WHERE TO STAY IN ANDASIBE

Hôtel Mikalo
An excellent roadside restaurant, a fragrant garden and bungalows in a range of sizes and styles. **$$**

Hôtel Feon'ny Ala
'Song of the Forest' is so close to the forest that you can hear the *indris*. It has 60 closely spaced bungalows. **$$**

Andasibe Lemurs Lodge
Resort-like hotel with a swimming pool, huge, comfy bungalows and a restaurant in a forest location. **$$$**

Hike the Rainforest with Indris

COMMUNITY-RUN *INDRI* SANCTUARY

A fine little complement to the Parc National Analamazaotra, the contiguous and community-run **Parc Villageois (VOIM-MA)** has dense rainforest cover and the sun barely penetrates the canopy here – there's a real sense of entering a different world as you set out on one of the two- and three-hour trails that run through the 42-hectare park.

This community reserve, which opened in 2009, has all of the same lemur species as the national park (except for the black-and-white ruffed lemur). It has two main reasons to visit, apart from being quieter than the national park. Firstly, you're almost guaranteed to see *indri*: the community employs spotters to help track down *indris* every morning.

Secondly, you can go on night walks here, which brings into play the region's six nocturnal lemur species in a way that's not possible in the national park. And yes, that also means that this is one of few places in Madagascar where you can see both the *indri* and the aye-aye.

Hike the High Trails of Mitsinjo

INDRIS, HIKING AND COMMUNITY CONSERVATION

Just a few hundred yards south of the entrance to Parc National Analamazaotra, Parc Mitsinjo is a private reserve run by Association Mitsinjo. The reserve was set up by guides to promote conservation and community tourism, and it nicely complements the other parks in the area. The focus here is less on lemurs (although you can see the *indri* here), and more on the other activities and hiking trails: they're a good way to fill an afternoon when most lemurs are more difficult to see.

The four hiking circuits range from one to five hours in length; the Grand Circuit and Circuit Aventure involve some steep hiking through dense forest. Apart from hiking, take your pick of the many activities on offer. These range from night hikes, village tours of Andasibe (p180), a five-hour excursion to Réserve de Torotorofotsy (p184), an encounter with a nearby sacred tree, a visit to Mitsinjo's on-site frog terrarium, and tree-planting in an area set aside for reforestation.

Our only complaint? They allow you to feed the *indris* here, an activity which has no conservation value and, conservationists argue, creates a dependency on humans among otherwise wild creatures.

INDRIS

The *indri* has been described as looking like 'a four-year-old child in a panda suit'. The *indri*'s wail-cry is an iconic sound of the Malagasy forest and can be heard up to 3km away; its repertoire includes distinctive territorial, mating and alarm calls. The best time to see them is in the morning: they become active around an hour after daybreak and spend most of their day in the forest canopy. With their strong hind legs, they can leap 7m in one go from tree to tree.

Indris are very sensitive to any change in environment, which is, of course, why they're endangered. No *indri* has ever survived in captivity, as they simply stop eating and die.

FOR MORE AYE-AYES

The Parc Villageois (VOIMMA) close to Andasibe village is one place to see the aye-aye. Others in the country's east include **Aye-Aye Island** (p203), **Parc National Mananara Nord** (p206) and **Parc National Masoala-Nosy Mangabe** (p205).

 WHERE TO STAY IN ANDASIBE

Mantadia Lodge	**Andasibe Hotel**	**Vakôna Forest Lodge**
Spectacular lodge with 28 sharply decorated bungalows, a fusion restaurant, spa and swimming pool. **$$$**	Huge rooms, with bold Asian styling, knockout views across a verdant rice paddy, a good restaurant and pool. **$$$**	Resort 7km north of Andasibe, with an island full of lemurs, crocodile park, equestrian centre, spa and golf. **$$$**

Escape the Crowds at Parc National Mantadia

TAKE A DAY TRIP TO MANTADIA

For primary rainforest without feeling like every lemur you see has its own pack of pursuing paparazzi, head for the Parc National Mantadia, which is 17km north of Andasibe.

There are lots of reasons to come here, among them another chance to see *indri*. This is also the best place of all to see the cute-as-hell black-and-white ruffed lemur and red-bellied lemur; although present in Parc National Analamazaotra and other private reserves, both species are commonly seen here but rarely seen elsewhere. The birdlife, too, is incredible, with birders looking in particular for the crested ibis and the vividly coloured *tsakoka*. But it's also about the landscapes up here in Mantadia, with stunning waterfalls accessible along the steep trails through the rainforest. Plan on spending the best part of a day here.

Take a guide with you from Analamazaotra, and choose between a number of different routes through the forest. The easiest Mantadia trail is the 1km, one-hour Circuit Rianasoa which packs a lot into a small distance, with *indri* sightings, orchids (which bloom from October to December) and a natural forest pool where you can swim. Rianasoa surely won't be enough, so combine it with the Sacred Waterfall Trail to make a 2km, two-hour overall walk; expect a couple of steep slopes along the way.

For something a little more challenging, try the three-hour Circuit Tsakoka, which is especially known for its proliferation of frogs, birds and plants, although what you see depends on a mixture of luck and the experience of your guide. And if you're really feeling energetic, set out on the 10-hour, 15km Trekking Circuit: your reward for the steep climbs is superb scenery.

OTHER ANDASIBE PARKS

Parc des Orchidees
Comes into its own from October to December when the orchids bloom. It's also good for chameleons.

Réserve de Maromizaha
This 100-sq-km ecotourism reserve has 14 somewhat elusive lemur species and a good mix of forest and open country.

Réserve de Torotorofotsy
Wetlands, forests and small villages with greater bamboo lemurs, excellent birdwatching, and red and golden mantella frogs.

Vohimana Forest
Crucial 1.6-sq-km corridor linking the Andasibe parks with the southern forests: 20km of walking trails, lemurs, birds and the pointy-nosed *Columma gallus* chameleon (not found elsewhere).

Picnic by Lac Mantasoa

PICNIC AND BOATING WITH LOCALS

If the parks around Andasibe are all about international visitors, a visit to **Lac Mantasoa** is the necessary complement as a predominantly local tourism

Lac Mantasoa

IAKO RANDRIANARIVELO/SHUTTERSTOCK ©

 WHERE TO STAY IN MOROMANGA

Hotel Nadia
Basic, noisy budget option around the busy market, with its own cafeteria and hammock-saggy beds. **$**

Bezanozano
Large rooms overlooking a huge pool. The decent restaurant is popular with passing tourist buses. **$$**

Hôtel Restaurant Espace Diamant
A quiet garden setting and tiled rooms with big beds and a large restaurant. **$$**

Red-bellied lemur

A LAKE WITH HISTORY

Lac Mantasoa occupies a special place in Madagascar's history: it is here that Madagascar's industrial revolution started, and there are still some ghostly ruins that tell the story.

Back in 1833, Frenchman Jean Laborde built a country palace for Queen Ranavalona I. As part of the project, he established carpentry and gunsmith shops, a munitions factory, an iron forge and a foundry to supply the monarch with swords, arms and ammunition, although it grew into quite an industry. Most evidence of this period was destroyed in 1851 when slaves rebelled. Other areas were flooded when the lake was founded in 1931. But a handful of notable buildings can still be seen and visited in the village of Mantasoa.

experience. Built in the 1930s, this 20-sq-km artificial lake is an unrelentingly pretty spot with a climbing, forested shore and numerous quite corners. On weekends, it draws Antananarivo residents in great numbers. Almost universally, they're here for an extended family picnic, and then make a day, or an entire weekend, of it by taking to the water to sail, fish, laugh uproariously at the complicated steering systems of pedalo boats, and even race the occasional speedboat. Join them and you might even find yourself invited to a picnic: it could just be the highlight of your whole trip. The many hotels that front onto the lakeshore rent out boats and equipment for all of the activities.

WHERE TO STAY AROUND LAC MANTASOA

Domaine de l'Ermitage
Large hotel, set in beautiful gardens, with excellent facilities, a restaurant and lots of activities on offer. **$$$**

Mantasoa Lodge
Bungalows set in a manicured garden with a restaurant; popular with locals and international visitors. **$$$**

Le Chateau du Lac de Mantasoa
Overlooks the lake, with appealing modern rooms and stone-walled public areas. **$$$**

VLADISLAV T. JIROUSEK/SHUTTERSTOCK ©

Chameleon, Réserve Peyrieras

A trip here requires careful planning, not least to make sure you keep your spending under control. All prices are listed on a board outside each park or reserve entrance. For a start, plan on paying a guide, which can be arranged through your hotel or at the Parc National Analamazaotra entrance for around Ar150,000 per day.

You also pay entry fees for each park and private reserve. Most often, the amount depends on which hiking trails you plan on undertaking, ranging from Ar40,000 to Ar120,000 in parks, and from Ar30,000 for most private reserves. For night walks, it's Ar30,000 for a two-hour walk in Parc Villageois (VOIMMA), or Ar35,000 for the 1½-hour version in Parc Mitsinjo.

Get Close to Chameleons at Réserve Peyrieras

CHAMELEONS, LEMURS AND MORE

Around halfway between Antananarivo and Andasibe, at the base of where the RN2 drops steeply down off the high plateau near the village of Marozevo, **Réserve Peyrieras** is a fun little detour. The reserve protects 35 hectares of native forest, and short, climbing trails take you up to where your obligatory guide will help you find Coquerel's sifaka and brown lemurs.

Back down near the entrance, the covered enclosures shelter numerous snake, frog and chameleon species, most of which are being bred for release into the forest. The chameleon enclosure is the highlight with five different species clinging to the branches, but don't forget to look down in case you step on one!

 GETTING AROUND

If you made it to Andasibe, chances are you did so in your own vehicle. Hold onto it, because you'll need it to get between your accommodation and the various parks and reserves around Andasibe.

If you arrived here using public transport,

ask your guide about arranging transport between the various attractions. You could walk between the village, the Parc Villageois (VOIMMA), Parc National Analamazaotra and Parc Mitsinjo, but you'll need a vehicle to get everywhere else.

PANGALANES LAKES

Pangalanes Lakes

ANTANANARIVO

The Pangalanes Lakes system feels utterly unlike anywhere else in Madagascar. Sheltered from the tempestuous Indian Ocean coastline only by a narrow strip of sand, Pangalanes still carries with it an awareness of what lies beyond; storm clouds billow out over the ocean in the middle distance, while calm lake waters barely ripple.

But the appeal of Pangalanes is not just about the views. The lake system invites exploration, offering the experience of getting around in the long, narrow metal canal boats, which ply the waters. Fringed with lush palms and other tropical vegetation, its sandy riverbanks are home to the villages of the Betsimisaraka people. There is a timeless quality to visiting here, helped by the near-complete absence of tourist infrastructure: people cast nets, tend to the fishing weirs, paddle by in pirogues (dugout canoes), and dry eels in the sun just as they have for centuries.

TOP TIP

Slow down to the pace of local life. Throw away the itinerary. And let the unfiltered beauty of local life flood in. The best journeys here are those where you join a boat going somewhere they'd be going anyway: you'll feel less like a tourist and get to see so much more.

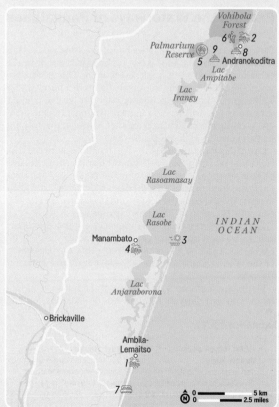

SIGHTS
1 Ambila-Lemaitso
2 Andranokoditra
3 Lac Rasoabe
4 Manambato
5 Palmarium Reserve

ACTIVITIES
6 Vohibola Forest

SLEEPING
7 Nirvana d'Ambila

TRANSPORT
8 Canal des Pangalanes
9 Lac Ampitabe
(Akanin'ny Nofy)

Canal des Pangalanes

THE CANAL DES PANGALANES

The Suez (or Panama) Canal it is not. But the **Canal des Pangalanes** is crucial for the livelihoods and economic health of Madagascar's eastern coastline. Built between 1896 and 1904 by the French colonial authorities, the canal was expanded after WWII so that 30-tonne barges could travel the 160km from Tamatave to Vatomandry. The Malagasy authorities added a new barge network during the 1980s, but the canal is in dire need of investment. The sections north of Tamatave, between Vatomandry and Mahanoro, and south of Mananjary in particular need lots of work, while the remains of the old barge network are rotting by the pier in Tamatave. These days, you can use the canal to get around, but expect some breaks in the journey due to silting and erosion.

Explore the Waterways of Pangalanes

CRUISE MADAGASCAR'S EASTERN BACKWATERS

Pangalanes is a region to explore by boat, passing villages that see very few tourists, and lakeshores lined with sandy beaches, palm trees and dense tropical vegetation. This is Malagasy travel the old way, where nothing happens in a hurry, and, if you have the time and inclination, you can have a quiet adventure as you drift past (or immerse yourself in) one priceless vignette of local life after another. Travel in this way and no two journeys will ever be the same.

Canal des Pangalanes is also a part of the experience. This collection of natural and artificial waterways stretches over 645km along the east coast from Foulpointe to Farafangana. It was built to create a safe passage for cargo boats to Tamatave; the waves on the nearby Indian Ocean or the terrible state of RN5 north of Tamatave explains why.

The canal offers a chance to pick up a bit of speed – catch a ride with a local cargo boat or a smaller trading vessel. In between, you can hire a boat to go deeper into the backwaters of the lake, or join a local as they move from one village to the next.

There are numerous starting points for visiting the lakes. One is relatively touristy Andranokoditra, on **Lac**

 WHERE TO STAY IN ANDRANOKODITRA

Chez Nolah
This simple, family-run place has six thatch huts, with meals, mosquito nets and shared facilities. **$**

Hôtel Pangalanes Jungle Nofy
Ten massive bungalows front an exquisite white-sand beach, with a bar and restaurant. **$$$**

Bush House
Bush House overlooks a sandy bay with good bungalows, meals, lots of activities and Fair Trade accreditation. **$$$**

Ampitabe (Akanin'ny Nofy). Here's where you can hire a solar-powered boat (try Chez Nolah) to explore the lakes; prices vary depending on the boat, the number of people, and how long you're travelling for. The further you go from Andranokoditra and the longer you travel, the more likely you are to find your own adventure away from the crowds. Andranokoditra also offers access to some fine ocean beaches with tempestuous seas; swim at your own risk.

Another entry point to the Pangalanes Lakes is **Manambato**, which puts you in the perfect position to visit the white-sand beach on the shore of **Lac Rasoabe**, as well as explore further.

Eyeballing Lemurs in a Primary Forest

MADAGASCAR'S SMALLEST CREATURES

If you're in the Lac Ampitabe area, Andranokoditra village is the starting point for other, non-lake adventures, including the hiking trails in Vohibola Forest. Itself under threat from logging, Vohibola is one of the last tracts of primary littoral (or coastal) forest in the country and has incredible biodiversity. Once you step beyond the outer wall of trees, let your eyes become accustomed to the dark and, in the enclosed, sometimes claustrophobic world of the forest where the dappled sunlight barely reaches the forest floor, train your eyes on the detail: the leaf litter here contains some of Madagascar's smallest and most intriguing creatures, a few of which are so new to science that they're still known by their scientific names. Vohibola has seven species of lemur, 30 species of frog, 13 different chameleons, and over 150 different tree species, all in just over 1000 hectares.

Arrange a guide through Chez Nolah (or through your accommodation) in Andranokoditra, and set out along one of three hiking trails through the wildlife-rich forest; expect to pay at least Ar15,000 for a two-hour hike.

Rest at the End of a Long Road

GO ON AN ADVENTURE, THEN RELAX

It may not look like it on the map, but just getting to **Ambila-Lemaitso** can be an adventure and it's a short classic of hardcore Malagasy travel. The turnoff for Ambila-Lemaitso is on the RN2 a few kilometres north of Brickaville and just over the bridge (look for the faded sign for Hotel Nirvana). This is where the fun starts.

From this turnoff it's a 17km track which is in an absolutely terrible state and a 4WD with high clearance is required. Allow two to three hours to cover these few short kilometres.

WILDLIFE ODDITIES OF VOHIBOLA

Calumma vohibola
A species of chameleon discovered only in 2009 and endemic to Vohibola Forest and the immediate coastal fringe.

Brookesia minima
The world's smallest chameleon lives here.

Stumpffia vohibolensis
Discovered in 2012 in Vohibola, this could be the world's smallest frog species, and is little bigger than a grain of rice.

Diademed sifaka
A handsome, critically endangered lemur with golden legs, a grey torso and white crown.

Fossa
Madagascar's largest carnivore and predator lives in the forest.

 WHERE TO STAY AROUND PANGALANES LAKES ———————

Tropicana
Very simple accommodation in Ambila-Lemaitso with a million-dollar beach setting. **$**

Nirvana d'Ambila
Sits astride the barrier beach, with clean, basic bungalows (private bathrooms and hot water) and a restaurant. **$$**

Acacias
Good-value, thatched-roof bungalows on Lac Rasobe's beach in Manambato with meals available. **$$**

WHERE TO PHOTOGRAPH LEMURS

If you've been frustrated by the quality of your lemur pics, by the dense forests that never quite allow a clear shot, it might be time to start cheating a little. Not far from Andranokoditra, **Palmarium Reserve** is one of the more popular attractions in the Pangalanes Lakes area. Best of all, the reserve has a reputation for being one of the best places to photograph lemurs. But let's be clear: this is a photo op in what looks like an extended hotel garden, rather than a wild journey of discovery. As long as you understand this, it's a chance to get up close and personal with incredibly tame lemurs from seven different species (including two cross-breeds).

ROSTASEDLACEK/SHUTTERSTOCK ©

Coast near Ambila-Lemaitso

After heavy rain, it might be impassable. Once (if!) you get to the end of the track, you still have to cross the canal by hand-operated ferry to Ambila-Lemaitso. If this vehicle ferry is out of action, as it often is, you will have to cross in a small boat. From the other side, call **Nirvana d'Ambila** (033 15 017 78) for a transfer, or walk 4km into the village.

Your reward at the end of this minor epic is the sleepy, go-slow tropical fishing village of Ambila-Lemaitso. It's the sort of place where whole days can pass by under the shade of a mango tree. The setting is also something special: on one side the calm lake beach, and on the other the ocean beach facing a tumultuous sea; barely 50m separates the two. Take a boat trip out on the lake, walk for miles along an empty beach, or simply chill under said mango tree. Either way, you'll need a few days to prepare yourself for the return journey...

GETTING AROUND

Just getting to and around Pangalanes Lakes by road can be an adventure. Most people travel to the region by road (in a tour vehicle, usually a 4WD, or a *taxi-brousse*) from Antananarivo or Tamatave. To Brickaville, it's around five to six hours from Antananarivo, three hours from Moromanga, two to three hours from Andasibe and 1½ hours from Tamatave.

Getting around by boat is much easier, but requires patience and good negotiating skills to get prices down. For example, Manambato is the main jumping-off point for Lac Ampitabe. From Manambato you have to charter a boat to your hotel; talk to the people at the beach, but they're never all that keen on negotiating... Alternatively, wait until the next tour group shows up and see if they're going your way, as a single seat will be much cheaper.

THE TAMATAVE (TOAMASINA) COAST

While everyone else flies to Île Sainte Marie and skips the long and difficult RN5, the coastal route via Tamatave is an adventure in itself. Yes, conditions can be difficult. And it certainly does take considerably longer. But this is for those looking for more than a fly-in-fly-out beach holiday. Along the way, you'll enjoy a real sense of discovery and experience a side to Madagascar that few other travellers see. Take Tamatave (Toamasina) as an example. Madagascar's most important seaport, it's a hot and dusty chaos of ad hoc markets and unrelenting vehicle and foot traffic, redeemed a little by the facades of decaying colonial buildings across the *centre ville*. This is a city with a strong Malagasy feel, one where any tourists seem almost incidental. As you travel elsewhere along the coast, you'll discover isolated beaches, quiet coastal villages, a ruined fort and even a well-run zoo rich in – you guessed it – lemurs. Best of all, you might be the only traveller there.

TOP TIP

Most visitors fly to Île Sainte Marie. And too many who drive hurry through. As with Pangalanes Lakes, slow down and make this coast your journey of discovery. If you do, you'll treasure the chance to escape tourist Madagascar.

Tamatave

191

ROUTE NATIONALE 5 (RN5) DRIVING TOUR

Setting out along the RN5, it's difficult not to ponder the road's reputation. In a country where back roads are notoriously poor, the RN5, which runs for 402km from Tamatave (Toamasina) to Maroantsera, takes things to a whole new level.

Not that you'd know it at first. From **1 Tamatave** the road is paved all the way to Soanierana-Ivongo. This means you can detour to **2 Parc Zoologique Ivoloina** (p195), reach the picturesque beach at **3 Foulpointe** (p194) and even stop by agreeable **4 Mahambo**, with its dense, tropical beachside vegetation; how long this takes all depends on how long you spend in each place. Just north of Mahambo, **5 Fenoarivo-Atsinanana** is an agricultural market town with a bank and a strong scent of cloves; locals call it 'Fenoarivo' or 'Fénérive'. The slightly chaotic riverside town of **6 Soanierana-Ivongo** is where boats head for Île Sainte Marie.

For those continuing north, the paved road ends and the adventure begins. There are plans to pave the RN5 all the way from Soanierana-Ivongo to Mananara. Until that happens, the 'road' deteriorates rapidly, but continues to hug the coast, passing small-town **7 Manompana** (p206), with its quietly beautiful beach, then skirting the lovely **8 Parc National Mananara Nord** (p206). In some places you'll end up driving along beach; in others, expect sheer rock mixed with slippery red clay and steep gradients... The RN5 eventually reaches **9 Mananara** (p205).

North of Mananara, the 108km to **10 Maroantsera** remains in terrible condition, with more than a dozen river crossings. Apart from a handful of bridges, you'll need to cross the rest using rafts or diesel-powered ferries. Expect it to take at least six hours, with some stirring glimpses of beautiful Baie d'Antongil to the west along the way.

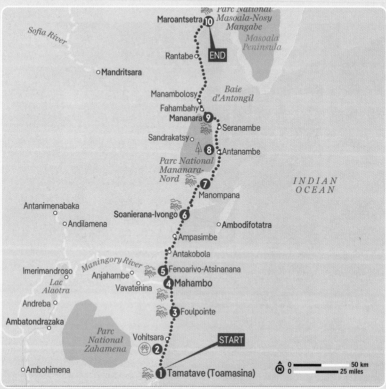

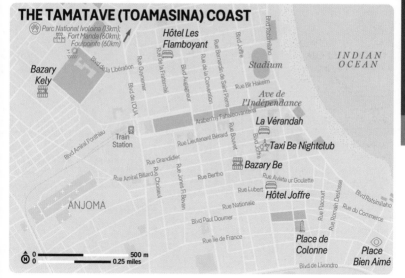

THE TAMATAVE (TOAMASINA) COAST

Parc National Ivoloina (13km);
Fort Manda (60km);
Foulpointe (60km)

Hôtel Les Flamboyant

Bazary Kely

Blvd Ratsimilaho

Blvd Joffre

Stadium

INDIAN OCEAN

Blvd de la Libération

Rue Gaymener

Rue de la Fraternité

Blvd Augereur

Rue Bernardin de Saint-Pierre

Rue de la Convention

Rue Bir Hakeim

Ave de l'Indépendance

Blvd de l'OUA

Araberny Fahateovantena

La Vérandah

Blvd Amiral Ponthiau

Train Station

Rue Lieutenant Bérard

Rue Bouvet

Taxi Be Nightclub

Rue Grandidier

Bazary Be

Rue Amiral Billard

Rue Choiseul

Rue Jones Ft Bevan

Rue Bertho

Rue Aviateur Goulette

Rue Lubert

Hôtel Joffre

ANJOMA

Rue Nationale

Rue Flacourt

Rue Romain Desfosse

Blvd Ratsimilaho

Rue du Commerce

Blvd Paul Doumer

Rue île de France

Place de Colonne

Place Bien Aimé

Blvd de Livondro

0   500 m
0   0.25 miles

Experience Malagasy City Life

MARKETS AND PUBLIC SQUARES

Tamatave (Toamasina) is one of the best places to experience life in a Malagasy town utterly free from tourist pressures. Spend at least a full day here so that you can wander its public squares and dive into its markets to get the measure of the place.

Not far from the port, and with big ships looming above the city in the middle distance, visit decaying **Place Bien Aimé**, which is both a hub of city life and emblematic of a city living off the memories of a more prosperous past. A dozen magnificent banyan trees weep before a crumbling colonial mansion and add considerable charm; do as locals do and sit on one of the benches and watch the world go by. Northwest of here, **Place de Colonne** seems to be crumbling before your very eyes, but is also popular with locals sitting and chatting, the plaza's monument honours those killed in the 1947 uprising against the French.

Head next to **Bazary Be** (Big Market). Connected like a thread to the busy commerce of the port, the market is one of the liveliest places in the city. Stalls sell fruit, vegetables, spices and beautiful bouquets of flowers; if you look hard, there's the occasional stall selling handicrafts in case a

 WHERE TO STAY IN TAMATAVE

Hôtel Les Flamboyant
Old, but well-kept concrete-box hotel, with air-con, large rooms (some with balconies) and a restaurant. **$$**

La Vérandah
Smart, spacious rooms (a few have balconies), arty touches and an excellent restaurant. **$$$**

Hôtel Joffre
Central boutique hotel with an attractive terrace cafe, excellent service, artistic flourishes and more. **$$$**

WHERE TO EAT IN TAMATAVE

Adam & Eve Snack Bar
A popular option along Blvd Joffre, with Malagasy dishes like zebu samosas and crepes. $

La Terrasse
This hopping street-side bistro with tasty pizza and grills is the go-to lunch spot for people on the move. $

La Véranda
Tamatave's finest table, classy La Véranda draws French expats to its wide-ranging menu of European and Malagasy dishes. $

Ocean 501
The freshest possible seafood right by the beach, just north of the centre. Bliss. $$

PIERRE-YVES BABELON/SHUTTERSTOCK ©

Soanierana-Ivongo (p192)

tourist wanders in. Otherwise, it's a sensory overload of unfamiliar smells and locals haggling over the price of jackfruit or vanilla essence. Away to the west (take a taxi), Bazary Kely (Little Market) sells fish and produce in a building's ruined shell; very few travellers make it here, and you'll attract no more than the occasional curious look as you wander, assailed by fishy smells.

A Beach Town Without the Crowds

DISCOVER AN INDIAN OCEAN BEACH AND FORT

You've experienced the gritty port culture of Tamatave, now you can enjoy its alter ego, **Foulpointe** (pronounced *fool-pwant*, and also called Mahavelona). You won't be the first traveller here (there's a small strip of accommodation and dining), but it will still feel like your own private slice of paradise. The beach runs along the town front like a cliché of Indian Ocean perfection: white sand, palm trees and crystalline lagoon waters, with the waves breaking on the reef out on the near horizon.

 WHERE TO STAY OUTSIDE TAMATAVE

Sahorana Lodge
Superb rustic-chic lodge in a delightful location just south of Fenoarivo-Atsinanana. Gourmet meals. $$

Le Grand Bleu
The 'Big Blue' in Foulpointe fronts onto the beach; sea breezes keep the wickerwork bungalows cool. $$

La Pirogue
This elegant reef-front resort has delightful bungalows, a stunning beach and a beautiful garden with lemurs. $$

Foulpointe has the added bonus of its very own fort, some 500m along the beach north of town. Built in the 19th century for King Radama I, the coastal **Fort Manda** has decayed just the right amount, with its shabby ruins given atmosphere by the mossy, salt-scarred facade, yet it's still intact enough to evoke the fortress' somewhat grander past. With your compulsory guide, climb the 8m-high, 6m-thick ramparts and marvel at their survival despite being built from a rather unusual mix of coral, sand and eggs. The views from the summit, with a soundtrack of lagoon waves lapping quietly on this isolated shore, are superb.

Conservation at a Zoo & Botanical Gardens

HOME TO LEMURS AND LOTS OF TREES

Off the road just north of Tamatave, the excellent **Parc Zoologique Ivoloina** (*ee-va-la-ween*) consists of a well-run zoo and botanical garden set on a lovely lake. Take a couple of hours to wander the beautiful grounds, home to more than 100 lemurs from 10 different species (some free-range, others in cages), chameleons, radiated tortoises, tree boas and tomato frogs. You'll get more satisfaction tracking lemurs in the wild, but that shouldn't stop you from enjoying this as well: it's a chance to watch lemurs up close (which isn't always possible in the wild) and see some of the species that you might otherwise miss.

Also here is a fine **botanical garden** that contains more than 75 species of native and exotic plants, and a model farm designed to demonstrate sustainable agricultural methods. Pick up the English- or French-language booklet that describes four walking trails through the gardens.

To really make the most of your visit, take one of the optional guides (they cover both the zoo and gardens) who'll greet you at the entrance; night tours are also possible if you want to steal a look at some of the zoo's nocturnal lemurs. Expect to pay Ar20,000 for a couple of hours with your guide.

Par[...] Ivoloi[...] the Mada[...] Fauna & Flor[...] (MFG; madagas[...] faunaflora.org), a global conservation association headquartered at Naples Zoo in Florida, USA. The park has breeding programmes for endangered species and a refuge for animals being reintroduced into the wild. Among its many projects, MFG are raising local awareness of wildlife and conservation issues – around 70% of the estimated 14,000 annual visitors are Malagasy – and tackling the massive problem of invasive species. The latter includes programmes to manage toxic Asian toads and a ground-breaking project, relying on surveillance by locals, to eradicate the non-native and very destructive house crow (*Corvus splendens*) from Tamatave (Toamasina) and Fort Dauphin (Taolagnaro).

 GETTING AROUND

Taxis-brousses and minibuses run along the coast between Tamatave and Soanierana-Ivongo; most stop in Foulpointe and Fenoarivo-Atsinanana; you may need to change transport (or walk 2km into town from the intersection) if you're heading into Mahambo. To reach Parc Zoologique Ivoloina, either charter a taxi in Tamatave, or take a *taxi-brousse* to Ivoloina village and walk four scenic kilometres to the park entrance.

Boats to Île Sainte Marie leave from both Soanierana-Ivongo and Mahambo. For the latter, El Condor's shuttle bus leaves from Tanambao V in Tamatave at 6am to arrive in Mahambo at 9am.

MADAGASCAR
FAUNA & FLORA
GROUP

...rc Zoologique
... is run by
...gascar
... Group
...ar

THE GUIDE

...MARIE

...vely flat tropical island of
...ter child for Indian Ocean
...and reef, and spotted with
...t the right mix of tourism
...t's yet to be swallowed up
...ast port of Ambodifotatra
is the only size...

As a general rule, the east coast, especially around Baie d'Ampanihy or Piscines Naturelles d'Ambodiatafana are the most unspoiled sections of the coast. Off the island's southern coast, Île aux Nattes (Nosy Nato) is like a smaller, quieter version of the main island. And there are enough attractions here – from whale watching to visits to a near-mythical pirate cemetery – to keep you occupied for a week or more. It all depends also, of course, on how long you spend doing nothing on the beach.

Île Sainte-Marie

ANTANANARIVO

TOP TIP

Choose your time to visit carefully. The best weather is from April to December; cyclones are possible from January to March. Whale-watching season is from June to September. High season is especially busy (and pricey) in July and August and over the Christmas–New Year period.

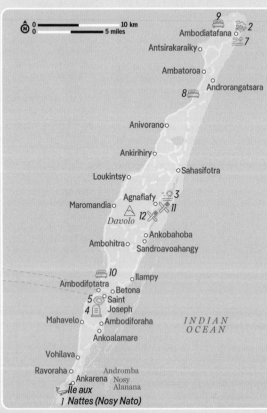

HIGHLIGHTS
1 Île aux Nattes (Nosy Nato)

SIGHTS
2 Ambodiatafana
3 Baie d'Ampanihy
4 Cimetière des Pirates
5 Île aux Forbans
6 Maison Blanche

ACTIVITIES
7 Piscines Naturelles d'Ambodiatafana

SLEEPING
8 Le Bon Endroit
9 Les Tipaniers Lodge
10 Ravoraha

EATING
11 Chez Nono
12 Chez Samson

Île Sainte Marie

Discover Île Sainte Marie's Best-Kept Secret

VISIT BAIE D'AMPANIHY

Anyone can find their way to a luxury hotel or to the popular beach: just ask around and follow the crowds. But wild and untouristy **Baie d'Ampanihy**, running along the east coast, is where you'll really fall in love with Île Sainte Marie.

Scattered along the shore of this long narrow bay are settlements where village life goes on much as it has done for centuries. To reach the bay, ask your hotel about renting a motorcycle or a quad bike, or even arrange a guided hike. Whichever way you travel, your view on arrival will be superb.

Once at Baie d'Ampanihy, one of the many quiet pleasures to experience is a fresh seafood meal right by the shore. Or take to the water in a pirogue (dugout canoe) to explore the bay. If you happen to be doing so from mid-November through December, watch for sharks, larger than your pirogue, that swim the shallow waters – they enter the bay along a narrow, deep channel – and perhaps even give birth. Attacks on pirogues are unheard of, so stay calm and resist the urge to

SEAFOOD BY THE BAY

There are two fabulous seafood restaurants along the Baie d'Ampanihy's west-central shore. Call ahead (or ask your hotel to check they're open and make the booking) to reserve a table at either place.

Chez Samson
(034 38 129 60; borahamazava@yahoo.fr)
The better option for food – think fine dining à la Madagascar, thanks to Samson, who trained as a chef in the best kitchens of the country.

Chez Nono
(020 57 901 98)
Has the edge when it comes to location: Chez Nono occupies a clearing overlooking the Baie d'Ampanihy. The fish, mangrove crabs and shrimps couldn't be any fresher.

WHERE TO STAY ON ÎLE SAINTE MARIE

Samaria
Has a natural pool, coastal views, great snorkelling, excellent bungalows and good bar-restaurant. **$$$**

Libertalia
On a private island, with a top restaurant and rooms, and hydrophones for listening to whales singing. **$$$**

Les Tipaniers Lodge
Remote, stunning Tipaniers has white-sand beach, swaying palms, turquoise water and eight pretty bungalows. **$$$**

ÎLE SAINTE MARIE ACTIVITIES

Beaches
The island's western beaches are smaller but more sheltered than those on the relatively undeveloped east coast.

Diving
Île Sainte Marie's marine fauna and flora is fantastic and there are shipwrecks, too. Recommended operators include Bora Dive & Research and Sainte-Marie Plongée.

Water Sports
Most hotels have snorkelling gear and kayaks that guests can use for free. Kitesurfing is taking off on the east coast, while water-skiing is possible in spring and summer.

Mountain Biking
You can rent mountain bikes in most hotels, but ask about a guided mountain-bike tour that will take you on scenic/challenging trails you'd struggle to discover by yourself.

Cimetière des Pirates

flee the huge dorsal fin coming your way. You can also walk along the less-protected ocean side of the peninsula, where Indian Ocean waves drive ashore on winds that began far across the sea.

Watch Whales along the East Coast

HUMPBACKS (AND A FESTIVAL)

In a migration eagerly awaited every year on Île Sainte Marie, large numbers of humpback whales pass by the island's east coast as they journey north from cooler Antarctic waters to Madagascar's Baie d'Antongil and surrounding waters. There, in the considerably warmer waters, they breed and give birth, before returning south as temperatures warm again. What this means is a fantastic chance to see these giants of the sea as they swim past Île Sainte Marie between July and mid-September. Witnessing this stirring annual spectacle up close can be can be a highlight of a visit to Madagascar.

To make this happen, join a 'whale safari' around the island; most are organised by hotels. You'll head out to sea and, if all goes according to plan, you'll see one of these extraordinary creatures breach close to the boat; it can also be amazing to see mothers and calves, or even a larger pod, swimming in

 WHERE TO STAY ON ÎLE SAINTE MARIE

Chez Nath
Classy backpacker hangout with great rooms and dorms, and a terrific restaurant-bar with live music and BBQs. **$**

Le Bon Endroit
Brilliant budget guesthouse with simple ensuite bungalows on a rugged coral beach, with a good restaurant. **$**

Ravoraha
Bungalows and a tree house, fine dining, and a commitment to sustainability and community engagement. **$$$**

JAVARMAN/SHUTTERSTOCK ©

unison. On one occasion, we even drew up alongside a sleeping humpback drifting just beneath the surface, in perfect peace: a profoundly special experience. Boats vary in size and quality: heading out in an unmechanised fishing canoe is increasingly rare these days, but you really feel close to the action if you do.

Coinciding with the humpback migration, Ambodifotatra hosts its annual Whale Festival in July. In this celebration of all things whale, it celebrates the start of humpback season with a big parade, concerts and much general merriment. It also has a serious side, by raising awareness about the species and encouraging ethical whale-watching practices.

Visit a Pirate Cemetery

X MARKS THE SPOT

Welcome to one of the world's great pirate locations; a place that swirls with myths and legends about lost treasure and utopian settlements far from the world and its governments and authorities. Back in the late 17th and 18th centuries, Île Sainte Marie was a renowned pirate centre, perhaps the largest in the world. Its sheltered harbours, lack of any government control, and proximity to maritime trade routes – to say nothing, of course, about its abundant food and female company – made it the perfect place for Libertalia, a true pirate settlement on **Île aux Forbans**, near Ambodifotatra. Even William Kidd once brought his boat here for repairs, and he liked it so much that he set up house here. At the time, almost 1000 people called it home. Today the remains of several pirate ships still lie scattered offshore, including some of the great ships of pirate history, among them Kidd's *Adventure*, and Captain Condent's famous *Fiery Dragon*.

These aren't just stories in history books. Not a lot remains of Libertalia, but you can still see the crumbling piers used for ship repairs. Best of all, the **Cimetière des Pirates** has the graves of missionaries, colonial and marine officers, and yes, more than a few pirates: the skull and crossbones on the grave of one English pirate are clearly visible.

Access to the cemetery is via an isolated foot track, which crosses several tidal creeks and slippery logs about 10 minutes south of the causeway. Organise a guide through your hotel or Ambodifotatra's tourist office to really make the most of your visit.

MORE ABOUT HUMPBACKS

Humpbacks can reach 15m in length and, despite weighing as much as 35,000kg, they are remarkably agile, capable of acrobatic moves such as dramatic breaching (launching themselves out of the water). These whales are also renowned for their singing, which may be related to mating patterns. Humpback songs can last an hour, and are among the most complex of all whale songs.

The whale-watching business around Île Sainte Marie is loosely regulated by Cétamada (cetamada.org), a local conservation organisation that promotes responsible whale watching. Participating operators agree to respect a code of approach, assure security protocols on board and have a qualified guide.

Scan this QR code to find out more about Cétamada.

 WHERE TO STAY & EAT ON ÎLE AUX NATTES

Chez Sica
An absolutely gorgeous garden location on a fringing reef, with excellent bungalows, meals and dreamy views. **$**

Les Lémuriens
This beachside boutique number in the island's south has gorgeous bungalows and outstanding food. **$$**

Sambatra
South African–owned lodge, with a beach dining room, appealing bungalows and bar, and incredible sunsets. **$$$**

BEST PLACES TO EAT IN AMBODIFOTATRA

Choco Pain
This little cafe is ideal for those catching a dawn boat to the mainland (it opens at 4.30am). Otherwise it has coffee, pastries, cooked breakfasts and good sandwiches. $

La Terrasse
Get your fill of *poisson sauce coco* (fish in coconut sauce) or fried calamari. We love the open-air setting, right by the sea. $

La Paillote
This *vazaha* (foreigner) hangout entices with its attractive open-air floor plan, street-front location and broad menu, from pizza or langouste to thick zebu fillets. $$

Idylle Beach
One of the island's best restaurants, with fusion cuisine that blends European and tropical influences to produce tuna carpaccios, zebu steak in green-pepper sauce and fine desserts. $$$

TIM DE WAARDT/SHUTTERSTOCK ©

Île aux Nattes (Nosy Nato)

Find Paradise on Nosy Nato

SMALL-ISLAND PERFECTION

Île Sainte Marie will feel like paradise until you've visited **Île aux Nattes** (**Nosy Nato**). Then you'll never want to leave.

The trip to this wonderful place begins with a brief pirogue (dugout canoe) ride from the southern tip of Île Sainte Marie. The journey is very short, but it takes you to another, altogether quieter world. In fact, if you could paint a picture of a tropical Malagasy idyll, it would look something like Île aux Nattes: perfect arcs of powder-white sand, palms leaning into the ocean breeze, azure seas and waves breaking out beyond the lagoon and reef. Walk the island's sandy pathways, wade out into the shallows to start your snorkel and, if you're here between July and September, stare out to sea to maybe spot whales breaching just off the beach. You can also go diving with the PADI-certified instructors of Sainte-Marie Plongée; the best months are from August to February. For the best views at sunset, visit the rooftop terrace of **Maison Blanche** for 360-degree views of the island, Sainte Marie and the surrounding lagoon. It's jaw-droppingly beautiful and well worth the entry fee (or even better, a drink).

GETTING AROUND

You can get to Île Sainte Marie by air from Tana, Tamatave and the French island of Réunion, or by boat from Soanierana-Ivongo (1¼ hours) and Mahambo (three hours).

A good paved road runs along the island's western side between the airport and the northern tip. The remaining roads are dirt, rock or sand. All midrange and top-end hotels offer private transfers from the port and the airport. You can rent cars, bicycles, scooters, motorcycles and just about anything with wheels from your hotel. Tuk-tuks and *taxis-brousses* are possible for shorter trips.

BAIE D'ANTONGIL & MASOALA PENINSULA

If you're seeking a place that captures eastern Madagascar's blissful isolation from crowds and feels a million miles from anywhere, look no further. Baie d'Antongil and the adjacent Masoala Peninsula may look close on the map to Île Sainte Marie. Yet they really are worlds apart. Cut off from easy road access to the south, with only occasional flights into Maroantsetra and seasonal ferries to Manana, and with nothing but hiking trails elsewhere, the Baie d'Antongil and surrounding areas are a brilliant adventure destination. The Malagasy mainland, from Mananara around Maroantsetra to Cap Masoala at the end of the Masoala Peninsula, wraps around the Baie d'Antongil. Both the bay's waters and the mountainous forests that tumble into the sea around Nosy Mangabe or Unesco World Heritage–listed Masoala are incredibly rich in wildlife. Not to mention that delicious sensation of being somewhere blissfully remote.

Baie d'Antongil & Masoala Peninsula

ANTANANARIVO ✪

TOP TIP

It's a long way to come and not see an aye-aye, so allow enough time for a couple of days on Aye-Aye Island or Nosy Mangabe to ensure you don't miss these charismatic little creatures.

Traditional village, Maroantsetra (p208)

ARTUSH/SHUTTERSTOCK ©

BAIE D'ANTONGIL & MASOALA PENINSULA

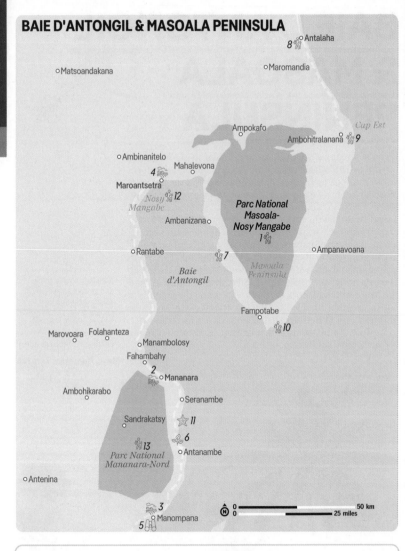

JAVARMAN/SHUTTERSTOCK ©

Aye-aye

Spot the Aye-Aye

MADAGASCAR'S STRANGEST LEMUR

Ask any traveller for the lemur species they'd most like to see and chances are they'll say the aye-aye. You'll never forget the first time you see an aye-aye, looking for all the world like a Hollywood creation. And yet, with its piercing eyes and witch-like fingers, the weirdly wonderful aye-aye can be very difficult to see. **Aye-Aye Island** solves that problem: leaving aside Mananara's remoteness, the island is the easiest place in the country to see the species.

Aye-Aye Island is a small, privately owned island in the middle of the Mananara River. It's home to between 12 and 15 aye-ayes brought here from elsewhere in Madagascar (as well as other lemur species) and they're all present within a relatively small (and contained) area. Take a pirogue (wooden canoe) out to the island and walk amid the coconut trees; the guides usually know where to find the aye-ayes. Although sightings are by no means guaranteed, your best bet is during a night tour, when aye-ayes are more likely to be active. Arrangements can be made through Chez Roger.

THE AYE-AYE

With its shaggy, grizzled coat, bright-orange eyes, leathery bat-like ears and long, dextrous fingers, the aye-aye is a strange-looking animal and the subject of much superstition. The middle digit of each forehand is elongated, and is used to probe crevices for insect larvae and other morsels.

Aye-Ayes also have rodent-like teeth that can gnaw through wood; like woodpeckers, aye-ayes tap on wood to locate the grubs before going to work with their teeth and long fingers. Although aye-ayes rarely weigh more than 2.5kg, they are the largest nocturnal primate on Earth.

They're found across a wide geographical area, along Madagascar's eastern hinterland in rainforests and dry deciduous forests. But aye-ayes are endangered due to habitat loss and can be difficult to see. Look for them at Aye-Aye Island and Nosy Mangabe.

 WHERE TO STAY AROUND MANANARA & MASOALA

Chez Roger
Basic rooms, friendly service, and a good restaurant make this the best place to stay to visit Aye-Aye Island. **$**

MNP Campsite
Idyllic campsite in Parc National Masoala-Nosy Mangabe with a kitchen, showers and flush toilets. **$**

Tampolodge
Great location on a fantastic arc of beach with basic bungalows, and an Italian manager and chef. **$$$**

AN OMNIBUS NATIONAL PARK

The **Parcs Nationaux Masoala et Nosy Mangabe** is something of a Noah's Ark for protected areas: although the bulk of the park is on the mainland peninsula, it also encompasses the small island of Nosy Mangabe off Maroantsetra and an isolated pocket around Cap Est, the country's easternmost point.

There are also three protected marine areas: **Tampolo Marine Park** on the peninsula's southwestern coast, **Cap Masoala Marine Park** at the tip of the peninsula. and **Tanjona Marine Park** on the southeastern coast. The park is famous for its rare hardwoods, bamboos, and dozens of species of fern, palm and orchid, as well as ten lemur species, several tenrec and mongoose species, 14 bat species, 60 reptile species and about 85 bird species.

ARTUSH/SHUTTERSTOCK ©

Waterfall, Parc National Masoala-Nosy Mangabe

Discover the Perfect Island

THE JEWEL OF MADAGASCAR'S EAST

Part of Parc National Masoala-Nosy Mangabe, the island of **Nosy Mangabe** is simply magnificent. Huge, soaring canarium trees with buttress roots the size of small houses rise from the forest floor. Waterfalls cascade through the forest canopy. A lonely shipwreck. Beautiful beaches, all watched over by a jungle alive with birdsong. You really will feel like Robinson Crusoe here.

Take a boat to the island, then get out and walk. One popular trail takes you to the summit of the island. Another leads to Plage des Hollandais, a beach with rocks bearing the scratched names of some 17th-century Dutch sailors. From July to September, you can see whales offshore. Yes, this really is paradise. And as you move around the island, scan the leaf litter for some of the reptiles and amphibians that thrive here thanks to the lack of predators, including the leaf-tailed gecko, one of nature's most accomplished camouflage artists. Don't forget to look up into the trees for the aye-aye, the white-fronted brown lemur, and the black-and-white ruffed lemur. If time is tight, visit Nosy Mangabe on a day trip from Maroantsetra. But stay overnight in the MNP's beachside campsite if

 WHERE TO STAY AROUND PN MASOALA ET NOSY MANGABE

Chez Maman'iMela
Four impeccable bungalows (with electricity) in Ambodifohara; book through the MNP Office. **$**

Masoala Forest Lodge
Like a high-end safari with luxury tents (and hot water) up in the trees. Fine meals and lots of activities. **$$$**

Ecolodge Chez Arol
Arol offers forest-edge thatched-hut bungalows with hot water, activities and community engagement. **$$$**

you can. Both Mada Expeditions (mada-expeditions.com) and local guide Elysée Velomasy (elyseeguide@yahoo.fr) can get you organised and equipped.

Hike & Watch Whales in Magical Masoala

MADAGASCAR'S BEST REMOTE HIKING

This one's worth crossing the country for. Masoala (pronounced 'mash-wala') is the site of the 2100-sq-km **Parc National Masoala-Nosy Mangabe** containing one of the richest primary rainforests in the country.

There's so much to do here. There are excellent opportunities for hiking, sea kayaking, snorkelling and swimming. You can go whale watching from July to September, when humpback whales visit the bay to give birth and mate: they can be seen from the coast and on boat transfers from Maroantsetra.

But above all, this is a hiker's paradise. Hikes range from the numerous short trails from **Ambodiforaha** to three long-distance trails for serious hikers. If you can only spare five days, the route from Maroantsetra to **Antalaha** passes through rice paddies and unchallenging terrain; it's the easiest of the three and offers a mix of culture and wild scenery.

For a hike dominated by the latter, take eight days in the forest to trek from Maroantsetra to **Cap Est**. A more serious undertaking, this route takes you to the spectacular Cascade (waterfall) Bevontsira and traverses tough terrain, river crossings, and mountains with plenty of leeches in attendance in the humid, tropical forest.

But the real epic involves hiking the entire rim of the peninsula, from Maroantsetra to Antalaha, via **Cap Masoala** and Cap Est. This journey takes up to 15 days. A guide costs just over Ar2 million.

Contact Mada Expeditions (mada-expeditions.com) and local guide Elysée Velomasy (elyseeguide@yahoo.fr) to organise a package including supplies, cook, porters and camping equipment. The park's headquarters are in Maroantsetra, where you can also get permits and guides. There is also a park office in Antalaha on the east coast.

When planning your trip, remember this: these are not idle strolls, but rather strenuous expeditions that require careful planning. Sometimes you'll have to wade through rivers. Some trail sections involve deep mud. And you're a very long way from anywhere. Also the entire peninsula can be exceptionally wet, particularly during June and July, when river levels are highest. October to December is somewhat drier and best for hiking.

GATEWAY TOWN: MANANARA

Mananara may have very few attractions of its own, but this small, dusty and very out-of-the-way town, which is set in a clove- and vanilla-producing area, serves as the southern gateway to Baie d'Antongil. The town (population around 50,000) has a couple of places to stay and a Bank of Africa branch (with ATM).

It's also the base for visiting Aye-Aye Island, and Parc National Mananara Nord; the park entrance is in Sahasoa, 30km south of Mananara. Unless you're travelling along the RN5 in a *taxi-brousse* or private vehicle, you'll likely arrive or depart by boat, with services from here to/from Soanierana-Ivongo (five hours) or Maroantsetra (three hours).

WHERE TO STAY IN MANOMPANA

Grez Grondin
Charming bungalows (with hot water), a friendly owner and great meals in a stunning beachside location. **$**

Chez Gonneau
French-run B&B with six bungalows and good restaurant in expansive grounds; lots of excursions. **$**

Au Bon Ancrage/ Chez Wen Ki
As basic as bungalows come, but on the beach, with running water. No meals. **$**

Hike a Remote Rainforest

FALL OFF THE MAP

If you like to hike far from other travellers, and if you like the idea of an adventure just to reach the trailhead, **Parc National Mananara Nord** is your sort of place.

This remote 240-sq-km park encompasses some of Madagascar's last remaining lowland rainforest. While hard to reach, it is, wonderfully, a very long way from anywhere, which is why, of course, the rainforest has survived until now. The park entrance and MNP office is in **Sahasoa**, about 30km south of isolated Mananara.

Known as the terrestrial circuit, the main hiking trail begins 6km south of the park office by foot. It takes four hours to get there; two to do the circuit, and another four to get back, which is why it makes sense to camp overnight in the park – you'll need to be self-sufficient with food and water, and in good shape. Although the trail is well-marked, it's a challenging hike, one that is quintessentially Malagasy: you'll hike through dense forest, always on the lookout for what lives in the trees. While lemurs are not always seen, Mananara Nord has some incredible prizes to watch for: *indris*, aye-ayes and ruffed lemurs all live here. Mananara Nord is also the only known habitat of the gloriously named hairy-eared dwarf lemur.

Get Out on the Water

LOOK FOR DUGONGS

In addition to Parc National Mananara Nord's on-land territory, an additional 10 sq km of uninhabited islets and surrounding reefs are also protected as a marine park. Once you're done with the hiking, rent a boat and head out onto the water, including a visit to the largest of the islands, **Nosy Atafana**. The islands are picturesque in themselves, but the pristine waters set against the backdrop of dense rainforests rising from the shore are one of the loveliest views in Madagascar's east. And if you can tear your eyes away from the views, watch for the gentle sea cows known as dugongs swimming like slow-motion apparitions in the clear, turquoise waters.

Explore a Biodiversity Hotspot

WATERFALLS, LEMURS AND ORCHIDS

Tucked away between Parc National Mananara Nord and Soanierana-Ivongo, small **Manompana** is another fine example of rural isolation with a fascinating forest on its doorstep. Start

TOP FIVE SPECIES AROUND BAIE D'ANTONGIL

Aye-Aye
This most sought-after of Madagascar's lemurs is best seen on Aye-Aye Island (p203) and on Nosy Mangabe (p204).

Indri
You'll hear it haunting the forest before you see it, but the *indri* is sometimes seen as well in Parc National Mananara Nord (p206).

Tomato Frog
The backyards and gardens of Maroantsetra are where you'll find this bright-red, bulbous amphibian.

Dugong
Take a boat trip out to Nosy Atafana (p206) in Parc National Mananara Nord, and watch for slow-moving dugongs in the clear waters.

Hairy-Eared Dwarf Lemur
The forests of Parc National Mananara Nord (p206) are the last refuge for this fine-looking lemur.

 WHERE TO STAY IN MAROANTSETRA

Bungalows Vanga
Beachside bungalows a fair walk from town but with gorgeous views of Nosy Mangabe; meals possible. **$**

Masoala Resort
Fine location with Nosy Mangabe views, a restaurant, and simple bungalows. **$$**

Manga Beach Hotel
Large rooms in a modern concrete building, and a bar-restaurant, with a terrace overlooking the canal. **$$$**

HAJAKELY/SHUTTERSTOCK ©

Mouse lemur

by enjoying the views from scenic **Point Tintingue**. Up close, there's the deepening shade of blue that begins at the water's edge and darkens the further you look out to sea. And on a clear day, off in the distance, you might even see Île Sainte Marie as a thin ribbon of green on the horizon.

But the real attraction here is **Ambodiriana Forest**. Step inside the forest, and you're assailed by humid, tropical smells and sounds (such as waterfalls cascading down over the rocks behind the wall of trees), all of which suggest more than they reveal. Your inner botanist and wildlife seeker will love the rare species that flourish here, including the mouse lemur, the candy cane palm (*Dypsis paludosa*) and a parasitic orchid (the formidably named *Gastrodia madagascariensis*).

Visit through the association ADAFAM (adafam.org), which manages the forest and organises day trips that take in the reserve's three waterfalls. It can be an expensive day, easily costing Ar100,000 to cover lunch, transport in a pirogue, a permit and a guide, but there's no other way to visit. And anyway, you'd miss many of the more unusual species, which hide in plain sight and can be difficult to spot without a guide.

Scan this QR code to find out more about CPALI.

✖️ WHERE TO EAT & DRINK IN MAROANTSERA

Chez Binina
Typical Malagasy bar, open-air with a BBQ at the front churning out *masikita* (small kebabs). **$**

Vivanette
Open-air restaurant-bar with beer, *mi sao* (noodle stir-fry), soups, kebabs, and a side of sea breezes. **$**

Restaurant Ravinala
Along with the usual assortment of stir-fries and grilled fish, Ravinala also serves decent pizzas. **$$**

ARTUSH/SHUTTERSTOCK ©

Maroantsetra

Take a Tour of Maroantsetra

DISCOVER A TROPICAL TOWN

Too often in Madagascar, at the end of a very long and arduous road lies a nondescript town of no discernible beauty. Languid **Maroantsetra**, where the Antainambalana River empties into the Baie d'Antongil, is a stunning exception. Use it as a base to visit Masoala by all means, but stay a few days and this place could really get under your skin.

To make the most of your time here, join a '*tour de ville*' (guided tour of town). You'll walk through coconut groves, inhale deeply as you pass among vanilla and clove plantations, and love the experience of the boatyards along the canal, all the while admiring river and ocean views. There's also an MNP interpretation centre where you can learn more about the region's parks that lie out in the great beyond (which actually begins on Maroantsetra's outskirts). You'll get to enjoy Maroantsetra's river scenery and ocean views. If you're lucky, your guide will also point out the tomato frog, a big bright-red frog found nowhere else on Earth except in Maroantsetra's back gardens. The MNP Office (032 04 627 70; parcs-madagascar.com/aire-protegee/parc-national-masoala-nosy-mangabe) and most hotels offer these tours.

There's just one catch when it comes to any visit here: be aware that Maroantsetra's climate is one of the wettest in Madagascar, particularly from May to September.

MORE COASTAL FORESTS

Forests are under threat across Madagascar, with coastal forests particularly imperilled. Like **Mananara Nord** (p206), **Parcs Nationaux Masoala et Nosy Mangabe** (p205) and **Vohibola Forest** (p189) are part of the patchwork that still remains along the east coast and similarly rich in wildlife.

Zebu herder, Baie d'Antongil

GETTING AROUND

Baie d'Antongil is hard to reach, and just as hard to get around. The main gateway is Maroantsetra, which you can fly to from Antananarivo once or twice a week. But Maroantsetra is one of the most isolated towns in Madagascar, and more flights here are cancelled than arrive.

The RN5 from Maroantsetra to Mananara is in terrible condition, with more than a dozen river crossings; there is no regular *taxi-brousse* service and the only way to drive it is by motorbike. Moto-taxis do the trip in about six hours. From September to February, ferry services link Maroantsetra with Mananara and Soaniera-Ivongo.

Manompana is on the *taxi-brousse* route between Mananara and Tamatave. These are often full but you may get lucky. To be sure of a seat between Manompana and Mananara, plan ahead by calling the *taxi-brousse* station at either end the day before and booking your seat.

Some areas of Baie d'Antongil – Parcs Nationaux Masoala et Nosy Mangabe, for example – are accessible only by boat.

TOOLKIT

The chapters in this section cover the most important topics you'll need to know about in Madagascar. They're full of nuts-and-bolts information and valuable insights to help you understand and navigate Madagascar and get the most out of your trip.

Arriving
p212

Getting Around
p213

Hiring a Vehicle & Driver
p214

Accommodation
p215

Money
p216

Health & Safe Travel
p217

Food, Drink & Nightlife
p218

Responsible Travel
p220

LGBTIQ+ Travel
p222

Accessible Travel
p223

Family Travel
p224

Nuts & Bolts
p225

✈ Arriving

Most people reach Madagascar via Ivato International Airport in the capital, Antananarivo. This is certainly the cheapest way to reach the island, and the most convenient hub for the centre and south. If you're bound for the north, you can fly directly into Nosy Be or Diego Suarez (Ansiranana), bypassing the capital completely.

Visas

Visas valid for 15, 30 or 60 days are available on arrival for most nationalities at international airports in Madagascar. The process is fairly painless, but you'll need to pay in cash in euros or US dollars.

SIM Cards

Madagascar's mobile phone operators – Orange, Telma and Airtel – have booths at Antananarivo's airport selling prepaid SIM packages with good data coverage. If you arrive elsewhere, find a phone shop when you reach town.

Changing Money

Foreign exchange facilities are available in the airport at Antananarivo. At other airports, arrivals staff may be willing to change euros and dollars to ariary at poor exchange rates – just change enough to get to town.

Wi-Fi

Wi-fi is available at better hotels and tourist-oriented restaurants, but connections are unreliable. Make sure you have a data SIM package for your mobile as a back-up, and for secure communications such as online banking.

Taxis from Madagascar's Airports

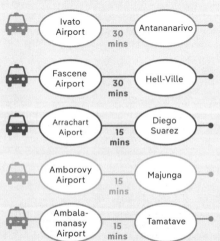

Ivato Airport	30 mins	Antananarivo
Fascene Airport	30 mins	Hell-Ville
Arrachart Aiport	15 mins	Diego Suarez
Amborovy Airport	15 mins	Majunga
Ambalamanasy Airport	15 mins	Tamatave

ARRIVING IN MADAGASCAR'S SMALLER AIRPORTS

If you bypass Antananarivo and fly directly to one of Madagascar's smaller airports, don't expect much in the way of arrival facilities. There'll be a customs and immigration desk and an officer processing on-arrival visas, but not much else. You may be able to find an ATM or change money informally (at a poor rate) – if not, keep some small euro bills handy for a taxi into town. You may need to bargain to get a fair price; if you have a hotel booked, they may be able to send a taxi to meet you for a fixed price.

Getting Around

Travellers have three main choices for getting around Madagascar – the cheap (taxis-brousses), the fast (domestic flights) and the practical (renting a 4WD with a driver plus boats connecting to islands offshore).

TRAVEL COSTS

Rental
From Ar150,000 (€30)/day

Motorcycle/scooter rental
From Ar50,000 (€10)/day

Petrol
Approx Ar5900 (€1.25)/litre

Taxi -brousse from Antananarivo to Diego Suarez
Ar120,000 (€35)/hour

Taxis-Brousses

Known collectively as *taxis-brousses*, shared vans and minibuses (and sometimes cars) provide the local bus service in Madagascar. They carry multiple passengers and leave when full. They're frequent and cheap, but slow and uncomfortable, and luggage goes up on top, regardless of weather conditions.

Local Taxis

Taxis-brousses can often be hired for 'special' trips, with you as the only passenger, for a fare matching what the driver would make if the vehicle was full of passengers. Large towns also have ordinary taxis – often ageing Renault 4s – that can be hired for trips around or out of town.

TAXI-BROUSSE 101

Despite the appearance of anarchy, *taxis-brousses* are generally well organised. Taxi *coopératives* maintain a booth or agent at the *gare routière* or *parcage* (taxi station) where you can book tickets. Journeys can be slow and cramped, but there are regular stops for toilet breaks and meals at *hotelys* (roadhouses). *Ligne nationale* services run direct, while *ligne régionale* services drop off and pick up along the route. For more comfort, **Cotisse Transport**, **Gasy'Car VIP** and **Malagasy Car** offer premium services between Antananarivo and major cities.

TIP

When travelling by boat, book the trip yourself at the official ticket desk – if you go through a tout, you'll pay extra.

Tuk-Tuks

Bajaj and Piaggio autorickshaws provide the local taxi service in many areas. They operate on a shared basis along the main streets in town, charging a fixed fare for short trips, but can also be hired for longer journeys for a negotiable fare. On short trips, you'll share the ride with other passengers.

Island Transfers

Alongside pricier vehicle ferries, motorboats and pirogues (outrigger boats) provide transfers from the mainland to offshore islands. Boats usually operate on a shared basis and leave when full, but services wind down in the afternoons when crossings are rougher. You can also charter a 'special' journey for a much higher fare.

Domestic Flights

Domestic routes are covered by Tsaradia, a subsidiary of Air Madagascar, and longer routes often involve a stop in Antananarivo. Demand is heavy for domestic flights so book ahead for peak season. If you're heading to Nosy Be, Diego Suarez, Tamatave or Majunga, you can fly in via neighbouring Réunion or Comoros.

DRIVING ESSENTIALS

Drive on the right

50

Urban speed limit is 50/80km/h

.08

Blood alcohol limit is 0.08%

Hiring a Vehicle & Driver

The easiest way to explore Madagascar is with a chartered vehicle and driver. While you can hire self-drive vehicles, driving conditions are challenging and you'll be safer in the hands of an experienced local.

ROAD HAZARDS IN MADAGASCAR

Road travel in Madagascar can be alarming for first-time visitors. Vehicles veer all over the road in search of a smooth surface, approaching other vehicles head-on before one driver gives way at the very last moment. Drivers slow down to avoid zebu and navigate potholes, but dogs and pedestrians are expected to jump out of the way of speeding vehicles. On the plus side, drivers have a remarkable ability to read the road, knowing exactly which potholes can be driven over at speed, and which require slowing to a crawl.

LANGUAGE SKILLS

Smaller agencies usually only have French-speaking drivers; for English-speaking drivers, it's best to go with a nationwide agency, even if this means paying more to return the vehicle to Antananarivo. Ramartour (ramartour.com) has quality vehicles and drivers with good language skills.

Where to Find a Driver

It's easy to arrange a car and driver through tour agencies and larger hotels in Madagascar, typically for around €40 to €65 per day. This includes the driver's meals and accommodation, but not fuel, which you'll have to pay for as you go. Drivers can meet you at your accommodation, or at a convenient airport or ferry port.

What Kind of Vehicle?

With the exception of the RN7 linking Antananarivo and Tuléar (Toliara), you'll need a 4WD to safely navigate most roads in Madagascar. Even surfaced roads are riddled with potholes and getting to national parks almost always involves dirt-road driving. During and just after the rainy season, a 4WD is essential everywhere.

Choosing a Company

For experienced drivers and well-maintained vehicles, go through a nationwide tour agency such as Ramartours, Evasion Sans Frontière, Sobeha Tours or Tany Mena Tours, or an agency in a well-established tourist hub; Madabest in Diego Suarez is a trusted operator. Most national agencies are based near Antananarivo, but will pick up elsewhere (with a surcharge to get the vehicle and driver to your location).

Additional Costs

On top of fuel, some agencies charge higher fees for unsurfaced roads. You'll also be responsible for the cost of getting the vehicle back to where it started if you end your journey in a different location. A tip of around 10% (or Ar10,000) per day is appropriate for your driver.

Accommodation

Local Hotels

Most towns have a mixture of pricier hotels targeting tourists and inexpensive hotels used mainly by locals. Local hotels can be fine for a night and they usually have mosquito nets on the coast, but staff often speak only Malagasy and French, hot water and air-con are rare, and there can be a risk of theft and prostitution.

Tourist Hotels

In cities and tourist hubs, you'll find upmarket hotels with reliable hot water, air-con, wi-fi, a decent restaurant and sometimes a pool. Many offer a mix of hotel rooms and 'bungalows' – a term that covers a wide variety of cabins, A-frames and villas in the garden. Prices are higher compared to local hotels, but staff are adept at helping tourists find tours and public transport.

Resorts

Resorts in Madagascar tend to be bungalows set in a tropical garden around a central restaurant, and some are truly delightful, making full use of local construction techniques. Many resorts are by the beach, but others are on raised hillsides with excellent views, or on the edge of national parks. You'll often get a pool, and usually a touch of Robinson Crusoe charm.

Homestays

Many of Madagascar's homestay projects went into hibernation during the pandemic, but tour agencies are attempting to restart stays in village homes. Accommodation is simple but you'll get a deep immersion into Malagasy life. You may be able to arrange an informal homestay by asking in villages; pay what you'd pay for a local hotel, and bring a gift of rice for the kitchen.

HOW MUCH FOR A NIGHT IN...

A local hotel
from Ar20,000

A tourist hotel
from Ar60,000

A beach resort
from €45

Camping

Most camping sites are set within national parks, consisting of a toilet block plus spaces for tents, and posher spaces for tents under thatched canopies. Some parks rent out camping equipment, but most travellers arrange camping trips through a tour agency, with camping gear, porters and guides included in the package. Some parks also provide simple bungalows for hikers, usually sharing the campsite toilets.

AVOIDING SEX TOURISM

Some hotels in Madagascar double as hubs for prostitution, and you'll notice a disproportionately high number of older European men arriving into locations such as Nosy Be, Sainte-Marie and Diego Suarez. The sex trade is less blatant here than in destinations such as Thailand, but some resorts and hotels are taking a stand against sex tourism and prominently displaying posters indicating that they disapprove of patrons bringing prostitutes into their rooms.

Money

CURRENCY: **ARIARY (Ar)**

Credit & Debit Cards

Many banks have ATMs that accept Visa and/or Mastercard. Visa cards (and occasionally Mastercard) can be used in some upmarket hotels, restaurants and shops, and at airline offices.

Carrying Cash

Changing money may only be possible in larger towns, and banks close at lunchtimes and weekends. Get into the habit of changing larger amounts less often.

Changing Money

In tourist towns and cities, you'll find private forex offices, offering slightly lower rates than banks but open at weekends. Elsewhere, The Société Générale Madagasikara (SGM) and BMOI banks can usually change euros and dollars if you have your passport. SGM also changes UK pounds, Japanese yen, Canadian dollars and some other currencies.

Tipping

Taxis and local restaurants and bars Not required.

Upmarket restaurants 5% of bill; optional but appreciated.

Bag carriers From Ar1000, but expect demands for more.

National park guides and porters Around 10% of the daily fee.

Drivers Ar10,000 to Ar20,000 per day.

HOW MUCH FOR...

A local tuk-tuk ride
Ar1000–20,000

Dinner at a tourist restaurant
from Ar20,000

A hotel room with bathroom
from Ar60,000

National park entry fee
Ar45,000–65,000

HOW TO... Manage your Ariary

The highest denomination ariary bill is Ar20,000, so you'll usually end up with a big wedge of twenties when you exchange money. Unfortunately, some local restaurants and tuk-tuk drivers have trouble breaking bills that large. Try to build up a stash of Ar10,000, Ar5000 and smaller bills by paying for hotels, taxis-brousses and posher meals using Ar20,000 notes.

LOCAL TIP

Keep a stash of small denomination euro bills handy for emergencies; many tourist-oriented businesses will take euro payments, though at a poor rate of exchange.

PAYMENT PRACTICALITIES

Madagascar exists at the periphery of the international banking system, and the majority of local businesses operate on a cash basis. The ariary came into existence in 2002, replacing the Malagasy franc (MGF), but some locals still quote prices in francs, at a conversion rate of 5 MGF to 1 ariary. If you get stuck without ariary, many locals will accept euros (and sometimes dollars), though usually at below bank rates. Other currencies are not widely accepted, though some banks exchange UK pounds, Canadian dollars and Japanese yen.

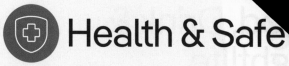# Health & Safe...

COMMON ILLNESSES

Reduce the chances of catching travellers' diarrhoea by practising good hygiene, including regularly washing hands (or using antibacterial gel). Avoid undercooked meat, fish and dairy, tap water, ice and ice cream (unless you're sure they're safe), and salads (which may have been washed in dirty water). In crowds, consider wearing a medical mask to reduce the risk of Covid and other respiratory illnesses.

Recommended Vaccinations

Your doctor can recommend the appropriate vaccinations for your trip, but many jabs take a few weeks to become effective, so arrange an appointment a month before you travel. Recommended vaccinations include Covid, hepatitis A and typhoid, plus yellow fever if travelling from an infected area. Ensure you're up to date on childhood vaccinations for tetanus, diphtheria, poliomyelitis, and measles, mumps and rubella.

Be Animal Safe

Mammals in Madagascar can carry rabies – including dogs and cats – so consider vaccination. If you get licked or bitten, seek medical attention and immediately begin anti-rabies treatment. Flukes carried by freshwater snails can transmit schistosomiasis (bilharzia) – saltwater is safer for swimming than lakes and rivers. Madagascar has scorpions and several poisonous spider species – check your shoes in the morning and be careful in undergrowth.

CRIME

Armed robbers, muggers and pickpockets are a risk, particularly in the capital and the southwest. Avoid walking alone in remote areas and at night, and stay off the roads after dark.

NATURAL HAZARDS

Bugs
Poisonous spiders, scorpions and leeches

Swimming
Strong currents on the east coast; sharks present in some areas

Temperature
Risk of heatstroke and heat exhaustion

Weather
Cyclones from December to March

Malaria & Dengue Fever

Malaria and dengue fever are present in Madagascar, and both are spread by mosquitos, which can bite during the day and at night. Visit your doctor or pharmacy for antimalarial tablets before you travel. Use mosquito nets, wear light-coloured clothing and carry plenty of repellent with a high concentration of Diethyltoluamide (DEET) – remember, there is no preventative medication for dengue.

HEALTHCARE

Healthcare standards are pretty good in Antananarivo but patchy outside the capital and inadequate in remote areas, where the only option may be the local pharmacy. Major cities and touristy areas such as Nosy Be have good private medical facilities; for serious illness, your best option may be evacuation to Réunion, where hospitals are on a par with mainland France.

Drink & Life

...dough... ...s) and
fried bananas.

Lunch (noon–2.30pm) Local restaurants serve Malagasy staples while tourist restaurants prioritise steaks, fish, pasta and pizzas; grilled seafood is common on the coast.

Dinner (from 6.30pm) The time for sit-down restaurant meals, often with dessert; few places serve after 10pm.

Malagasy Condiments

To keep things interesting, Malagasies have developed an arsenal of aromatic condiments, such as *pimente verde* (a fiery green chilli paste) and *sakay* (a red-hot pepper paste with ginger and garlic). In some areas, *sakay* can be as simple as chopped *pilipili* chillis, salt and vinegar. Dishes are also livened up by *achards* (spicy pickled frui;, usually tomato, lemon, carrot or mango, used as a relish). Every village has its own recipe, and you'll see bottles of the stuff sold by the roadside.

MENU DECODER

Achards Local pickles with chilli.

Bonbon voanjo Peanut brittle.

Brêdes mafana A green leaf that causes tingling in the mouth.

Kida amin'ny voanio Bananas in coconut milk.

Koba Rice and nut cake, cooked in banana leaves.

Laoka Dishes to go with rice.

Masikita/brochettes Small meat kebabs.

Mofo baolina Fried bread balls.

Mofo gasy Pancake-like balls.

Mofo menakely Beignet-like doughnuts.

Pimente verde Green chilli sauce.

Ramanonaka A savoury version of *mofo gasy*.

Ravimbomanga sy patsa mena Sweet potato leaves with shrimp.

Ravitoto Cassava (manioc) leaf stew.

Romazava Stew with tomatoes, beef and brêdes mafana.

Sakay Hot red chilli sauce.

Sambos Madagascan beef samosas.

Soupe chinoise 'Chinese soup' with noodles and wontons.

Vary Rice.

Vary amin'anana Rice and ginger stew.

Varenga Crispy shredded beef.

Zebu Meat from the zebu cow.

HOW TO...

Drink like a Malagasy

Hot, dusty days in Madagascar often finish with an ice-cold bottle of Three Horses Beer (THB) Pilsener (5.4%). Other THB brews include the strong Special (6.2%) and shandy-like Fresh (1%). Rivals include Star Breweries' Beaufort Lager (5%) and harder-to-find craft beers from Red Island Brewing Company and Nouvelle Brasserie de Madagascar.

For something stronger, try wines from the highlands around Fianarantsoa, or ask for *rhum arrangé* (cane rum flavoured with fruit and spices) or premium Dzama rum from Nosy Be. In coastal regions, look out for local trembo (palm wine) and blow-your-head-off *toaka gasy* (the local moonshine).

Eau Vive mineral water and fizzy drinks such as lemony Youzou, Caprice Orange, pomegranate-flavoured Grenadine and the undefinable Bonbon Anglais are sold everywhere. Alongside the popular *ranon'ampango* (hot rice water), you'll find (slightly insipid) Madagascan tea and excellent locally produced coffee and cocoa.

HOW TO... Eat like a Malagasy

At tourist-oriented restaurants, French and Italian flavours dominate, but at *hotelys* (roadhouses) and *gargotes* (local restaurants), it's Malagasy all the way. *Vary* (rice) is the default starch – indeed, the Malagasy verb, *mihinam-vary* ('to eat'), literally means 'to eat rice'. It's typically served with a meat, chicken, fish or vegetable-based side (*laoka*) – often whatever the chef is cooking that day, marked on a chalkboard that is brought to the table in place of a menu.

While fish, poultry and zebu meat are popular with rice, most dishes come with a 'sauce'. This sauce might be a stew of garlic, onions, tomatoes and spices, or a white sauce made with ginger or coconut. When ordering meat, you may be asked if you want it with or without sauce.

Along the coast, grilled or fried fish, octopus, prawns, crabs and lobsters are served at beachside shacks. Zebu steaks crop up everywhere, as do *brochettes* – grilled zebu-meat skewers, also known as *masikita*. However, meat can be tough and toothpicks are vital.

At Malagasy restaurants with proper menus, seek out Malagasy specialities such as *ravitoto* (fried beef or pork with cassava leaves), *hen'omby ritra* (oily braised beef, often flavoured with ginger), and *romazava* – a beef stew with tomatoes and *brêdes mafana*, a green leaf that will make your tongue and lips tingle thanks to its anaesthetic properties!

Did You Know?

In Madagascar, beef invariably comes from the zebu, a small cow breed that came to Africa via India. Zebu are characterised by a large fatty hump and dangling dewlap, both adaptions to arid and tropical conditions.

MADAGASCAR'S IMPORTED FLAVOURS

Madagascar's cuisine has been strongly influenced by French colonists and Italian expats, and tourist-oriented restaurants serve up tried-and-tested menus of pizzas, pasta dishes and grilled fish and steaks. At its best – in expat hangouts such as Nosy Bay and Diego Suarez (Antsiranana) – this imported cuisine can be excellent; elsewhere, it can be hit or miss.

Some of the island's best cooks have created a unique style of haute cuisine that blends Malagasy and French influences, served in elegant dining rooms set in historic colonial-era mansions. At restaurants such as Antananarivo's La Varangue and Hell-Ville's Papillon, the menus can be simply fabulous, taking diners on a culinary tour of the island and its cultural influences.

Many upmarket restaurants in Madagascar make a big deal of their desserts, which range from chocolate cakes and vanilla custard to tropical fruit flambéed with local rhum, crêpes with Madagascan confiture (jam), and a wonderful range of sorbets and ice creams made with local fruit such as tamarind, guavas and passion fruit. Many meals culminate with a shot of the house *rhum arrangé* (flavoured rum).

Madagascar's cuisine also shows the influence of other seafaring cultures who came here to trade spices. Along the coast, many cities have sizeable Indian populations, descendants of 19th-century traders from Gujarat, lending a subtle Indian flavour to local dishes. Chinese settlers left their mark on menus in the northeast, which feature dishes such as *mine sao* (fried noodles), 'Chinese soup' (noodle soup with wantons) and fish in *sauce aigre doux* (sweet and sour sauce).

Responsible Travel

Climate Change & Travel

It's impossible to ignore the impact we have when travelling, and the importance of making changes where we can. Lonely Planet urges all travellers to engage with their travel carbon footprint. There are many carbon calculators online that allow travellers to estimate the carbon emissions generated by their journey; try resurgence.org/resources/carbon-calculator. html. Many airlines and booking sites offer travellers the option of offsetting the impact of greenhouse gas emissions by contributing to climate-friendly initiatives around the world. We continue to offset the carbon footprint of all Lonely Planet staff travel, while recognising this is a mitigation more than a solution.

Responsible Lemur Interactions

In some reserves and animal parks, guides encourage visitors to use snacks to lure lemurs for photo opportunities – avoid doing this as it makes the animals dependent on humans and affects the balance of their diet.

Marine Animals

When snorkelling or diving, avoid crowding marine life and give turtles space – being chased or grabbed can cause stress for these air-breathing reptiles. Encourage boat operators to maintain a respectful distance from cetaceans on whale-watching trips.

Rubbish

Madagascar is remarkably clean, so be conscientious about disposing of rubbish responsibly. Use waste bins (in your hotel, if you can't find one anywhere else) and pick up any rubbish you spot in national parks.

Stay Responsibly

Always seek out accommodation with sound environmental policies. Many resorts and lodges use natural building materials, solar power and water recycling to minimise their impact, including respected Eden Lodge near Ankify, the world's first 100% solar-powered resort.

Respect Malagasy Culture

Malagasy culture revolves around respect for the ancestors (*razana*), alongside beliefs from Christianity and other religions. In many sacred locations, specific behaviour – such as urinating or swimming – is *fady* (taboo). Seek local guidance on appropriate behaviour.

ENERGY USE

Many hotels and resorts in Madagascar use solar power, but others rely on diesel-powered generators or overloaded mains supplies. Limit your energy footprint by turning off lights, fans and air-con when you leave your room.

WATER USE

Don't waste water – it can be in short supply. Reuse towels rather than asking hotels to wash towels every day. Consider purifying your own drinking water, rather than relying on Eau Vive mineral water in plastic bottles.

Support Community Projects

Madagascar has high levels of poverty, causing conflict between humans and wildlife. Wherever you can, hire local guides and support community-based tourism projects that provide local people with an alternative revenue stream to hunting or harvesting from nature.

Endangered Timber

Madagascar was once a major exporter of ebony and rosewood, leading to widespread deforestation. Logging both is now banned under the CITES treaty – if you buy wooden souvenirs, make sure they are not made from either timber.

Lemur Conservation Network

The pioneering Lemur Conservation Network supports projects to conserve lemur habitats and provide protection for lemurs all over Madagascar, working with dozens of ecolodges, reserves and conservation organisations around the island.

Association Fanamby

With offices in Antananarivo and Diego Suarez (Antsiranana), Association Fanamby has been promoting and supporting new conservation areas since 1997, including the Allée des Baobabs and the Loky Manambato and Camp Andrafiamena Andavakoera protected areas in Northern Madagascar.

Endangered Lemurs

Madagascar is home to more than 110 lemur species, but a third of its lemurs are now critically endangered, including the rare northern sportive lemur – just 50 individuals are thought to survive in the north of the country.

Fihavanana

Malagasy people follow a culture of *fihavanana* ('conciliation'), so avoid getting angry or using confrontational language.

Animal Products

Avoid buying souvenirs made using parts from wild animals, including seashells, coral and feathers.

RESOURCES

association-fanamby.org
Supports conservation areas across Madagascar.

lemurconservationnetwork.org
Brings together dozens of lemur conservation organisations.

lemurreserve.org
Works in the Sava region to protect rare lemur species.

LGBTIQ+ Travellers

While same-sex relationships are legal in Madagascar for people aged 21 and over, the reality is that LGBTIQ+ people face systemic discrimination and prejudice in Malagasy society, with limited legal protection. LGBTIQ+ visitors are unlikely to be targeted specifically, but it pays to be discrete while exploring the country, particularly when travelling off the tourist trail.

Gay-Friendly Locales

Madagascar doesn't have a publicly visible gay scene, and most local LGBTIQ+ people keep their relationships hidden from their community. Nevertheless, Antananarivo has a handful of venues that have become (very) low-key hangouts for the LGBTIQ+ community, including the Hotel Carlton Madagascar, the Mojo Club and Le Manson Chez Marco. Elsewhere, beach hubs such as Nosy Be, Diego Suarez and Île Sainte Marie tend to be quite accepting of same-sex couples, particularly if you stay in one of the more upscale beach resorts.

THE LAW IN MADAGASCAR

Article 331 of Madagascar's penal code stipulates that 'anyone who has committed an indecent or unnatural act with a minor of their own sex, less than 21 years old' can face a prison sentence of up to five years. Same-sex marriage and civil unions are not permitted for people of any age, and there are no laws prohibiting discrimination on the grounds of sexual orientation or gender identity.

Gay-Friendly Tours

Several international tour operators run trips to Madagascar specifically oriented towards LGBTIQ+ travellers, including Mr Hudson (mrhudsonexplores.com) and Out 2 Africa (out2africa.com). Small-group tour operators such as Explore (explore.co.uk), G Adventures (gadventures.com) and Intrepid (intrepidtravel.com) are also experienced in catering to LGBTIQ+ clients.

PERSECUTION OF LGBTIQ+ PEOPLE

Madagascar's LGBTIQ+ laws are rarely tested in court, but in 2020, a gay woman named Domoina Ranabosoa was arrested for 'corruption of a minor' over a relationship with a woman aged under 21. At the time of writing, there was little public support for reforms to provide equal rights for LGBTIQ+ people.

Advice for LGBTIQ+ Travellers

While LGBTIQ+ tourists are unlikely to face problems, be aware that same-sex couples are largely invisible in Madagascar. Public displays of affection are rare for heterosexual couples and almost unheard of for same-sex couples. You're unlikely to have issues at beach resorts in destinations such as Nosy Be, but elsewhere, being discrete is the best approach for a hassle-free trip.

LGBTIQ+ ORGANISATIONS

While a number of organisations support LGBTIQ+ people with sexual-health issues, there are few organisations actively campaigning for wider gay rights. Established by Balou Chabart Rasoana, the first person in Madagascar to publicly come out as transgender, Solidarité des MSM Madagascar is a notable exception; find them on Facebook.

Accessible Travel

Madagascar has few facilities for travellers with disabilities. This, combined with poor infrastructure in many areas of the country, can make travel here difficult for travellers with additional needs. Locals are very helpful, but you'll have a much easier time if you travel with a companion from home.

Madagascar at Street Level

Wheelchair users and the vision impaired will struggle with the condition of pavements. Where they are present, pavements are often rough and uneven; the road may be smoother but pedestrians are expected to leap out of the way when vehicles approach.

Airport

Madagascar's airports can provide wheelchairs, but there is limited additional support for travellers with disabilities. However, most airports are on one level, with access via ramps (for wheelie bags), and airlines can help wheelchair users board and disembark.

Accommodation

Many upmarket hotels in Antananarivo and provincial capitals have lifts or accommodation on the ground floor. Being at ground level, bungalows are also an option, but bathrooms can be cramped and some have steps and narrow doorways.

DANGEROUS DRAINS

One hazard people with even mild visual or mobility issues should be aware of is covered drains. Many pavements in Madagascar are made by laying concrete slabs over open drains, and these are often broken, wobbly or uneven.

Bathrooms

Hotel bathrooms rarely have room for a wheelchair, except in top-end places. Rails and other special facilities for travellers with disabilities are almost non-existent so you may need the support of a travel companion.

Transport

Public transport is crowded and *taxis-brousses* can only accommodate wheelchairs folded up on the roof. Your best option is to arrange a car and driver; discuss your specific needs with the agency.

ACCESSIBLE ISLANDS

If you fly internationally into Nosy Be, and stay in an upmarket resort such as Vanila Hôtel, you may be able to enjoy the beach and perhaps even boat or rainforest trips with a chartered vehicle and some local assistance.

RESOURCES

Specialist tours to Madagascar for travellers with disabilities are limited. **Dominique Dumas** (d.dum2@wanadoo.fr) organises tours for wheelchair users, using *joelletes* (special one-wheeled chairs) to access sites along RN7, staying in accessible hotels.

For general advice on accessible travel to Madagascar, your best option is to contact an international organisation such as **Mobility International USA** (miusa.org) or the **Society for Accessible Travel & Hospitality** (sath.org).

Accessing Madagascar's natural reserves can be difficult for travellers with mobility issues. With compacted earth paths, Réserve Privée de Berenty and Allee des Baobabs may be options. Parc National Isalo's Circuit Malaso is also partly accessible.

Family Travel

On one level, Madagascar is a spectacular destination for families – beaches are stunning, national parks deliver reliable wildlife encounters, and there are some great places to stay on the coast. However, the hassles of long-distance transport can exhaust smaller travellers. With a family in tow, you're best off sticking to a small area, or even a single resort.

Sights

Madagascar has museums and historic sites, but with kids along for the ride, prioritise the beaches and national parks. Nosy Be is the perfect destination, with international inbound flights, small distances to cover, great beaches and spectacular wildlife. Elsewhere, weigh up the sights against the time it takes to get there – a national park trip that involves hours of driving and hours of hiking will only work for very committed families.

Hotels

Here's the good news: many hotels provide *chambres familiales*, or double rooms with an extra bed (single or double), specifically for families. However, you'll only find cots for babies and toddlers in some midrange and top-end hotels. Hotels and resorts with garden bungalows are a good family option – most have on-site restaurants and some have pools and play areas.

Practicalities

Disposable nappies and infant milk formula are available in Antananarivo and other large cities, and locations with large expat populations, such as Nosy Be, but are hard to find elsewhere. For meals, meat, rice and pizzas are usually your best bet.

Transport

Hiring a vehicle and driver is the least stressful way to get around; some tour agencies can provide child seats but it's safer to bring your own. To cut out long drives, consider taking internal flights and hiring a vehicle for local exploring at each stop.

KID-FRIENDLY STOPS

Nosy Be (p142)
Great beaches, comfy accommodation, easy wildlife counters and familiar restaurant menus.

Baie de Sakalava (p160)
A great beach with kitesurfing for teens and snorkelling for younger travellers.

Parc National Isalo (p92)
A natural playground, with ring-tailed lemurs, natural pools and adventure activities.

Allée des Baobabs (p125)
Bring cameras or smartphones for the kids and get the perfect Instagram shot.

Parc National Andasibe Mantadia (p180)
Walking trails lead from the highway to forests teeming with lemurs.

MADAGASCAR'S NATIONAL PARKS FOR KIDS

To get the best out of Madagascar's wildlife with kids, look for national parks and reserves that can be reached with minimum effort, such as Isalo, Andasibe Mantadia, Ranomafana, Ankarana and Nosy Be's Lokobe, or reserves that have a cooler climate, such as Montagne d'Ambre near Diego Suarez. The ideal park trip will involve a short drive to the park headquarters and just an hour or two of walking before returning to a nearby camp or lodge. Bring extra water and snacks, and equip kids with their own cameras – sightings of lemurs and chameleons are pretty much guaranteed in many reserves.

Nuts & Bolts

OPENING HOURS

Banks (Antananarivo) 8am–4pm Monday to Friday

Banks (rest of the country) 7.30–11.30am & 2–4.30pm Monday to Friday

Bars 5–11pm

Restaurants 11.30am–2.30pm & 6.30–9.30pm

Shops 9am–noon & 2.30–6pm Monday to Friday, 9am–noon Saturday

Toilets

Western-style flush toilets are common in hotels and restaurants, but paper should be placed in the bin. Elsewhere, squat toilets are the norm. Carry some soap – and antibacterial hand gel in case there's nowhere to wash your hands.

GOOD TO KNOW

Time zone
GMT+3

Country code
261

Emergency number
117

Population
28.81 million

Weights & Measures

Madagascar uses the metric system, but fruit is often sold by the piece or bunch.

Internet Access

Many tourist-oriented hotels and restaurants offer free Wi-Fi; you'll also find internet cafes in many towns.

Electricity 220V/50Hz

Type C
220V/50Hz

Type E
220V/50Hz

PUBLIC HOLIDAYS

As well as local closures for cultural festivals, government offices and private companies close on the following public holidays (banks also close the afternoon before).

New Year's Day 1 January

Martyr's (Insurrection) Day 29 March (celebrates the rebellion against the French in 1947)

Easter Monday March/April

Labour Day 1 May

Ascension Thursday May/June; occurs 40 days after Easter

Pentecost Monday May/June; occurs 51 days after Easter

National (Independence) Day 26 June

Assumption 15 August

All Saints' Day 1 November

Christmas Day 25 December

Language

Madagascar has two official languages: Malagasy and French. Malagasy is the everyday spoken language while French is often used for business and administrative purposes, and in the more upmarket sectors of the tourism industry.

FRENCH

Basics

Hello Bonjour. *bon·zhoor*
Goodbye Au revoir. *o·rer·vwa*
Yes Oui. *wee*
No Non. *non*
Please S'il vous plaît. *seel voo play*
Thank you Merci. *mair·see*
Excuse me Excusez-moi. *ek·skew·zay·mwa*
Sorry Pardon. *par·don*
What's your name? Comment vous appelez-vous? *ko·mon voo·za·play voo*
My name is ... Je m'appelle .... *zher ma·pel ...*
Do you speak English? Parlez-vous anglais? *par·lay·voo ong·glay*
I don't understand Je ne comprends pas. *zher ner kom·pron pa*

Directions

Where's...?
Où est ...?. *oo ay...*
What's the address?
Quelle est l'adresse? *kel ay la·dres*
Can you show me (on the map)?
Pouvez-vous m'indiquer (sur la carte)? *poo·vay·voo mun·dee·kay (sewr la kart)*

Signs

Entrée Entrance
Femmes Femmes
Fermé Closed
Hommes Men
Interdit Prohibited
Renseignements Information
Sortie Exit

Time

What time is it? Quelle heure est-il? *kel er ay til*
It's (8) o'clock. Il est (huit) heures. *il ay (weet) er*
morning Matin. *ma·tun*
afternoon Après-midi. *a·pray·mee·dee*
evening Soir. *swar*
yesterday Hier. *yair*
today Aujourd'hui. *o·zhoor·dwee*
tomorrow Demain. *der·mun*

Emergencies

Help! Au secours! *o skoor*
Go away! Fichez-moi la paix!. *fee·shay·mwa la pay*
I'm ill. Je suis malade. *zher swee ma·lad*
Call a doctor Appelez un médecin. *a·play un mayd·sun*
the police la police. *la po·lees*

Eating & drinking

What would you recommend?
Qu'est-ce que vous conseillez? *kes·ker voo kon·say·yay*
I'm a vegetarian.
I'm a vegetarian/végétarienne. *zher swee vay·zhay·ta·ryun/ vay·zhay·ta·ryen* (m/f)

NUMBERS

1
un *un*

2
deux *der*

3
trois *trwa*

4
quatre *ka·trer*

5
cinq *sungk*

6
six *sees*

7
sept *set*

8
huit *weet*

9
neuf *nerf*

10
dix *dees*

NUMBERS

1	**isa/iray** *i-saa/i-rai*
2	**roa** *ru*
3	**telo** *tel*
4	**efatra** *e-faatr*
5	**dimy** *dim*
6	**enine** *e-nin*
7	**fito** *fit*
8	**valo** *vaal*
9	**sivy** *siv*
10	**folo** *ful*

MALAGASY

Basics

Hello Manao ahoana. maa·*now* aa·hon

Goodbye. Veloma. ve·*lum*

Yes. Eny. *e*·ni

No Tsia. *tsi*·aa

Please Azafady. aa·*zaa*·faad

Thank you Misaotra. mi·*sotr*

Sorry Miala tsiny. mi·*aa*·laa tsin

What's your name? Iza no anaranao? *i*·zaa nu aa·*naa*·raa·now

My name is ... ... no anarako ...nu aa·*naa*·raa·ku

Do you speak English? Miteny angilisy ve ianao? mi·*ten* aan·gi·*lis* ve i·aa·now

I don't understand Tsy azoko. tsi *aa*·zuk

Directions

Where's...? Aiza ...? ai·*zaa*...

What's the address? Inona ny adiresy? *i*·nu·naa ni aa·di·*res*

Can you show me (on the map)? Afaka asehonao ahy (eoamin'ny sarintany) ve? aa·*faak* aa·se·u·*now* waa (e·uaa·min·*ni* saa·rin·*taan*) ve

Time

What time is it? Amin'ny firy izao? aa·min·ni·fi *ri*·zow

It's (2) o'clock. Amin'ny (roa) izao. aa·min·*ni* (ru) i·*zow*

yesterday Omaly. *u*·maal

today Androany. aan·*dru*·aan

tomorrow Rahampitso. raa·haam·*pits*

Emergencies

Help! Vonjeo! vun·*dze*·u

It hurts here Marary eto. maa·*raa*·ri e

Call a doctor Antsoy ny dokotera. aant·*su*·i ni duk·*ter*

the police polisy. po·*lis*

Eating & drinking

Can you recommend a...? Afaka manoro ahy... tsara ve ianao? aa·faa·kaa maa·*nur* waa ... tsaar ve i·*aa*·now

I'm a vegetarian. Manana sakafo tsy misy hena ve ianareo? *maa*·naa·naa *saa*·kaaf tsi mis *he*·naa ve i·aa·naa·*re*·u

---

MALAGASY

Malagasy has around 18 million speakers. It belongs to the Malayo-Polynesian branch of the Austronesian language family and is unrelated to other African languages – its closest relative is a language from southern Borneo. Over the centuries Malagasy has incorporated influences from Bantu (particularly in some of the west coast dialects) and Arabic. It has also been influenced by English and French – first in the 19th century by British and French missionaries, and later as a result of colonisation by the French in the fi rst half of the 20th century. Malagasy was first written using a form of Arabic script. Its modern Latin-based alphabet was developed in the early 19th century.

The pronunciation of Malagasy words is not always obvious from their written form. Unstressed syllables can be dropped and words pronounced in different ways depending on where they fall in a sentence. If you read our pronunciation guides as if they were English, you'll be understood. Note that **dz** is pronounced as the 'ds' in 'adds'. The stressed syllables are indicated with italics.

DIALECTS

Despite the linguistic unity of Malagasy, regional differences do exist, and in some coastal areas, you'll hear little standard Malagasy.

STORYBOOK

Our writers delve deep into different aspects of Madagascar life.

Fianarantsoa (p74)
PIERRE YVES BABELON/SHUTTERSTOCK ©

A HISTORY OF MADAGASCAR IN

15 PLACES

Madagascar separated from mainland Africa around 160 million years ago, but humans set foot on the island relatively recently, arriving from East Africa, Asia and the Middle East from the 8th millennium BCE. Madagascar's modern history, however, has been shaped by invasion and the struggle to shake off the long shadow of colonialism. By Joe Bindloss

BOTH CULTURALLY AND PHYSICALLY, Madagascar has been pulled in different directions by Africa and Asia. As plate tectonics yanked apart the Pangaea landmass, the island moved east towards India, then west towards Africa, its isolation preserving species today found nowhere else on earth.

Humans arrived in waves from around 8000 BCE, but the most important arrivals came by sea from Borneo in the 8th century, bringing rice cultivation, the roots of the Malagasy language, and the construction of outrigger canoes. The island saw subsequent waves of African, Indian and Arabic settlers, before Portuguese and French explorers arrived in the 16th century.

Against a backdrop of growing European influence, the eastern Betsimisaraka people jostled for power with the Menabe (Sakalava) of the west, the Betsileo of the south, the central Tsimihety, the Antakàrana of the north and the Merina of the central highlands. Eventually, highlanders gained the upper hand, only for the French to seize control in 1896.

Resistance to French rule was already on the rise when the island was briefly captured by the British during WWII, and Philibert Tsiranana became the first president of independent Madagascar in 1960. Since then, the island has struggled with lingering poverty, political instability, and the headwinds of global trade, which have brought prosperity and hardship with fluctuations in the prices of vanilla and other commodities.

1. Parc National Tsimanampesotse
NATURE AND LEGEND

Historians have linked the legendary travels of Sinbad the Sailor in *One Thousand and One Nights* to the Yemeni island of Socotra, but the Arabic writers of these famous fables almost certainly took inspiration for the monstrous bird known as the Roc from Madagascar. Found across southern Madagascar until the 13th century, the elephant bird Aepyornis could reach 3m in height, weighing up to one tonne. It flourished in the area now protected as Parc National Tsimanampesotse – in flooded caverns, archaeologists have found hundreds of bones and eggshells from this avian behemoth, alongside the remains of gorilla-sized giant lemurs.

For more on Parc National Tsimanampesotse, see page 105.

2. Belo-sur-Mer
AN ARABIC LEGACY

On the coast and islands, Indonesian-inspired pirogues (outrigger canoes) are the default form of passenger transport, but freight is carried by boutres – slanted wooden sailing boats inspired by ancient Arabic dhows. The ancestors of these characterful vessels first sailed into the Mozambique Channel from Oman in the 7th century, trading spices, textiles and later slaves. Many coastal tribes can trace their origins to the movement of people along medieval trade routes between the Persian Gulf, East Africa and South Asia, including the Sakalava, who still assemble boutres by hand on the beach in the sleepy west-coast village of Belo-sur-Mer.

For more on Belo-sur-Mer, see page 130

3. Marodoka, Nosy Be
A GLIMPSE OF MUSLIM MADAGASCAR

East of Hell-Ville, Nosy Be's French-built capital, the ruins of Marodoka lie dotted around a Malagasy fishing village – a relic of centuries of settlement by Muslim traders. Amongst the time-worn structures are crumbling mansions with Swahili-style carved stucco and the oldest mosque in Madagascar, built in around 1700. The first residents of Marodoka were Arab and Swahili traders, who arrived seeking gold, spices, turtle shells and slaves, but later settlers hailed from Gujarat in India, filling the Cimetières des Indiens inland from the coast road. Many Indians later abandoned Madagascar when President Didier Ratsiraka forcibly nationalised private businesses in the 1970s.

For more on Marodoka, see page 146

Cathédrale de l'Immaculée Conception (p55)

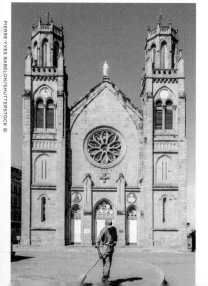

PIERRE-YVES BABELON/SHUTTERSTOCK ©

4. Ambohimanga
MADAGASCAR'S ROYAL CAPITAL

A Unesco World Heritage Site, Ambohimanga (meaning 'Blue Hill' or 'Beautiful Hill') was the capital of the Merina royal family, who ruled Madagascar for more than 300 years. The seat of government shifted to Antananarivo in 1794, but Ambohimanga continued to be revered as a sacred site – off-limits to foreigners until 1897, when the French stripped the site of royal relics to undermine its symbolism for Malagasy people. The sacred hill is dominated by the Rova, a fortress containing the wooden palace of King Andrianampoinimerina and the European-style summer palace of Queen Ranavalona I – two potent symbols of Madagascar's most powerful dynasty.

For more on Ambohimanga, see page 60

5. Cathédrale de l'Immaculée Conception
ANTANANARIVO'S MOTHER CHURCH

Christianity arrived in Madagascar in the 17th century with French and Portuguese explorers, and the kidnapped Antanosy prince Andriandramaka became the first Malagasy to be formally baptised in 1613. However, the new religion faced a long struggle for acceptance. Antananarivo's handsome Cathédrale de l'Immaculée Conception marks the spot where the Merina Queen Ranavalona I – sometimes described as the 'Mad Monarch' – had Christian leaders thrown from the cliffs to their deaths. The brutal crackdown was ineffective; today, 41% of Malagasies are Protestant or Catholic, though many Christians still follow traditional tribal customs such as ancestor worship.

For more on the Cathédrale de l'Immaculée Conception, see page 55

6. Réserve Spéciale Ankarana
A NATURAL BATTLEGROUND

Today, the nature reserve at Ankarana is famous for its wildlife and dramatic rock formations, but this was one of the front lines in the 19th-century tribal wars between the Antakàrana people and the expanding Merina kingdom. As Merina raids pushed deeper and deeper into their homeland, the Antakàrana fled across this impenetrable landscape of sharp, karst spikes – reputedly on their tiptoes, giving the rock formations their local name, *tsingy*. Eventually

231

the tribe was driven from the mainland, taking refuge on Nosy Mitsio and surrounding islands before returning to their ancestral territories after forging an alliance with the French.

For more on Réserve Spéciale Ankarana, see page 163

7. Fort Manda, Foulpointe
THE LAST MERINA FORTRESS

It's the Indian Ocean views that draw people to the ruins of Fort Manda today, but this towering fortification was once a symbol of the military might of the Merina kingdom. The 19th-century king Radama I ordered the construction of this imposing fortress from coral, sand and eggs (as a binding agent) to guard his kingdom from seafaring raiders. Eventually, Fort Manda fell to the French, but its Malagasy commanders slipped away via an underground tunnel. Evidence of British involvement in Madagascar can be seen on canons dotted around the grounds, marked with the symbol GR, cypher of King George V (Georgius Rex).

For more on Fort Manda, see page 195

8. Arbre Sacrée, Nosy Be
A REGAL BANYAN

Set at the tip of a forested peninsula near Hell-Ville, the sacred tree of Nosy Be is a lingering relic of tribal rule. A tangled knot of aerial roots, this mighty banyan tree was planted in 1836 by the Sakalava queen Tsiomeko, who took refuge on Nosy Be after her kingdom, Boina, fell to invading Merina armies from the highlands. Here, she formed an alliance with the French governor, Admiral de Hell, but her mainland territories were subsumed into the expanding Imerina kingdom in 1840. The current queen of Nosy Be still makes an annual sacrifice at the Arbre Sacrée to honour her tribal ancestors.

For more on Arbre Sacrée, see page 147

9. Cimetière des Pirates, Île Sainte Marie
THE REAL PIRATE BAY

Île Sainte Marie – Nosy Boraha to locals – has a long and colourful history as a hangout for pirates, who used Madagascar as a base for raids on merchant shipping in the Indian Ocean in the 17th and 18th centuries. Some of these seafaring brigands now reside in the Cimetière des Pirates, overlooking Baie de Forbans and shaded by tall traveller's palms. Look out for the skull and crossbones on old graves, and the ruined piers used to repair pirate ships, as well as the island of Île aux Forbans out in the bay, where many pirates built homes using their ill-gotten gains.

For more on Cimetière des Pirates, Île Sainte Marie, see page 199

10. Rova, Antananarivo
MADAGASCAR'S PREMIER PALACE

Once the most important royal site in the country – and nominated for Unesco World Heritage Site status before it was gutted by fire in 1995 – the fortified palace known as Manjakamiadana ('A Fine Place to Rule') crowns the capital's biggest hill. The former seat of the kings and queens of Imerina, the palace remains under restoration but you can view traces of the original palace buildings designed for Queen Ranavalona I by French engineer Jean Laborde in 1839, and the imposing stone palace added in 1867 for Queen Ranavalona II by Scottish missionary James Cameron.

For more on Rova, see page 49

11. Gare Soarano, Antananarivo
FRENCH FANCY IN THE INDIAN OCEAN

The scale of French ambitions for Madagascar isn't always obvious, but at Antananarivo's underused main railway station, you'll get a hint of what they had in mind. Constructed in 1908, this was once the hub of an expanding train network, allowing easy transport of goods to the coast. Today, the *chemins de fer* (railway lines) are slowly rusting under the tropical sun. Locals don't miss their French colonial overlords, but old-timers still remember the trains that once trundled around the island – reduced today to a handful of freight services and the Fianarantsoa-Côte Est passenger line connecting Fianarantsoa to Manakara.

For more on Gare Soarano, see page 58

12. Haute-Ville, Fianarantsoa
AN ARCHITECTURAL TREASURE TROVE

The historic heart of Fianarantsoa, Haute-Ville – Tanana Ambony to locals – offers a

PIERRE-YVES BABELON/SHUTTERSTOCK ©

Fort Manda (p195)

glimpse of the comfortable life offered by Malagasy cities in the late 19th century. More than 500 brick homes and churches dot the hillside, from the eye-catching Ambozontany Cathedral to gently fading family homes, constructed between 1870 and 1900, when Fianarantsoa became an administrative capital for territories seized from the Betsileo tribe by the Merina kingdom. Many of these stately buildings are still occupied by the descendants of the people who built them – local and international NGOs are working with locals to help preserve Haute-Ville's rich architectural heritage.

For more on Haute-Ville, see page 48

13. Presidential Palace (Ambohitsorohitra), Antananarivo

A SYMBOL OF POWER

Most people stroll right past Antananarivo's Ambohitsorohitra (Presidential Palace), noting its handsome lines without thinking about its political significance. This striking, cherry-red rococo palace was constructed in the classic French style between 1890 and 1892 for the French Resident-General, Maurice Bompard, becoming a resented symbol of French colonial rule. After Independence, the building was adopted as the presidential palace, but national politics shifted to the left and the presidential residence was moved to the Iavoloha Palace outside the capital – constructed for free by the Communist government of North Korea and modelled on the original royal palace of Antananarivo.

For more on the Presidential Palace, see page 55

14. Oranjia, Diego Suarez (Antsiranana)

RELICS FROM OPERATION IRONCLAD

The history of European colonialism in the Indian Ocean could be viewed as a five-way tug of war between local people, the Portuguese, the Dutch, the French and the British – with the French hanging on till the bitter end. On the Oranjia peninsula, just east of Diego Suarez, gorgeous beaches are backed by the sun-bleached ruins of military camps, fixed guns and other fortifications that saw fierce fighting during WWII, as British troops seized the island from the Vichy French to prevent Axis powers gaining a foothold on the western fringes of the Indian Ocean.

For more on Oranjia, see page 155

15. Parc National Montagne d'Ambre

MADAGASCAR'S FIRST NATIONAL PARK

Considering that nearly 90% of Madagascar's forest cover has been lost in modern times, the significance of the founding of the island's first national park in 1956 should not be underestimated. Named for the deposits of copal (ancient tree resin) found on its slopes, Montagne d'Ambre spans 182 sq km of montane rainforest, preserving some of Madagascar's most precious ecosystems. Following the park's inauguration, more national parks and *réserves spéciales* were established across the country, preserving 10% of the island's marine and terrestrial landscapes. These parks are vital for conservation – more than half of Madagascar's mammal species risk extinction due to habitat loss.

For more on Parc National Montagne d'Ambre, see page 162

233

MEET THE MALAGASY

Do not rush things and be patient, and you will appreciate the true essence of Malagasy culture. Nandih Andrianarisoa introduces his people.

THE MALAGASY SEEM to be quiet on first encounter. Do not be bothered by people staring; we are just curious and like to see *vazah* (foreigners) strolling around. A welcoming speech from the elder of a community is the ticket to your Madagascar cultural immersion journey. Every time you attend a local ceremony, expect to hear a special oration called *kabary*. It is an oratorical art that emphasises the importance of any particular event.

The elders are the decision-makers, and they have a great responsibility toward their family. We expect to receive advice, pearls of wisdom, and benedictions from elders. Therefore, the main purpose of our traditional ceremony (called exhumation) is to give respect to our ancestors. Following the indigenous beliefs, the spirit of our ancestors carries on to the other world. And they still deserve respect. The ceremony consists of rewrapping the remaining body of deceased beloved relatives in new silk. Then, dance with them in a sacred ritual around the family grave. It takes place every five or seven years. The family astrologer decides the optimal date and time to start the exhumation.

As an island, Madagascar is a land of cultural diversity. It covers 18 ethnic groups that are spread all over the country. We inherit our traditions and customs from Austronesians, Africans, and even Europeans. However, the official Malagasy language is the symbol of our unification. All the tribes can communicate with each other without a significant language barrier. In fact, the pillar of our culture is based on *fihavanana* (solidarity) and mutual respect.

Rice became the staple food since the arrival of Austronesian people on the island. We grow rice three times a year and eat rice three times a day. We manage to build ricefields in terraces on the mountainous terrain of the central highlands and the east. It is an efficient technique to increase rice production.

Asian cuisine has influenced the east of the country. You will easily find foods based on noodles, fresh vegetables, roasted meats, and diverse spices. On the other side, the people of the west have a close bond with zebus. They are the descendants of the Bantu people from Africa. They measure wealth by the number of zebus in possession, as they do not trust the modern bank system. They dedicate their entire life to protect and scale their assets; zebus are involved in their daily life. All rituals and traditions – weddings, funerals, and any social event – require zebu sacrifices.

Malagasy people have in common the sense of caring and welcoming. *Mora mora* (take it easy) reflects the pace of life in Madagascar. Slow down, take an easy trip and you will discover the country's hidden beauties.

Population & Demographic

Madagascar has a population of over 30 million in 2023. The Asian Pacific origins (37%) are spread on the highlands, whereas African descendants inhabit the coastal areas. There are also small groups of French, Indian, Chinese, and Comorans.

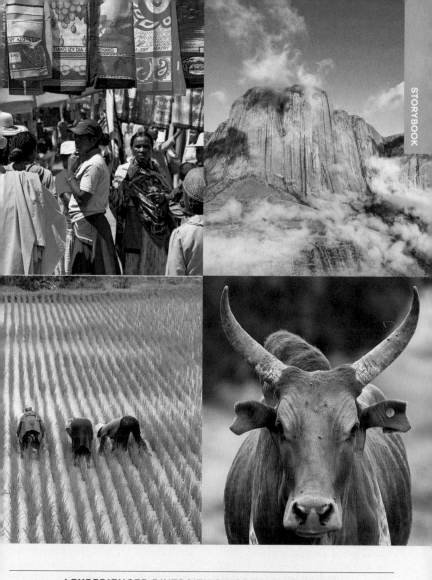

I EXPERIENCED DIVERSITY SINCE MY CHILDHOOD

I was born in Antsirabe and raised in a big family by my paternal grandparents. My parents worked at a national brewery and there we encountered diverse people from all over Madagascar. In the nineties, the brewery assigned my parents to Toliary for a year and I spent the beginning of primary school there. My parents' workmates often invited me to play with their kids at home. As a young kid, I never had difficulty learning the local dialect and getting accustomed to the people there. My parents and I spent our spare time discovering Toliary and its surroundings. For me, it was a privilege to wander in some tourist attractions of the region, such as Ifaty beach, Sarodrano, Bezaha, and get closer to the local fishing community. I started to enjoy the coastal life and was eager to discover more about other places and people of my country, and my thirst for wanderlust began to spark.

235

THE EIGHTH CONTINENT

There's nowhere on Earth quite like Madagascar; a land that has been on its own geological and evolutionary path for nearly 100 million years. The result is a magical place of all manner of landscapes, lemurs and so much more. By Anthony Ham

A Separate Evolutionary Path

Around 200 million years ago, the world as we know it was unrecognisable. The supercontinent of Gondwana took up much of the southern hemisphere and encompassed Antarctica, South America and Australasia – Madagascar was 'enclosed' within Gondwana. When the supercontinent began to break apart about 180 million years ago, Madagascar stayed connected to what we now know as East Africa. Around 160 million years ago, it began to forge its separate path, but it was not until about 88 million years ago – when the eastern half of Madagascar broke off and moved northward to eventually become India – that the country took on its present form.

So for more than 80 million years, Madagascar – its land and its wild creatures – has evolved along an entirely different evolutionary path to anywhere else on the planet. Undisturbed by outside influences and human beings (who 'only' arrived 2000 years ago), the fauna and flora followed their own interpretation of the evolution manual.

With no human hunters to contend with until relatively recently, nature was allowed to run wild. When humans finally arrived on the island, there were lemurs the size of gorillas dwarfing the *indri*, the current largest lemur species. There were 3m-tall elephant birds, giant aardvarks, hippos and tortoises. Many were wiped out: over the last 1000 years, scientists estimate that human beings have driven most of these species to extinction, including 16 species of lemur.

But for all the devastation, Madagascar remains one of the most important biodiversity hotspots in the world. Some 70% of animals and 90% of plants found in Madagascar are endemic; in other words, you find them nowhere else on Earth. And the variety is astonishing, with 5% of all known animal and plant species.

It is this scale and staggering biodiversity that has earned Madagascar the sobriquet of 'The Eighth Continent'.

A Land Like No Other

Madagascar's landscapes are more than just a backdrop to its astonishing wildlife. They form the canvas itself and are as much a part of Madagascar's story as lemurs. This is a world of rainforests and coral reefs – all but the southern tip of the country lies within the tropics – but also striking limestone formations and spiny deserts, which are as Madagascan as the aye-aye.

Let's start with the mountains. The island's highest point is 2876m Maromokotro, an extinct volcanic peak on the Tsaratanana massif, followed by the 2658m Pic Imarivolanitra (formerly known as Pic Boby) in Parc National Andringitra. A chain of mountains

runs down the eastern seaboard, forming a steep escarpment and trapping moisture that helps create the island's rainforests, which once covered the entire eastern seaboard. These rainforests are the heart and soul of Madagascar's biodiversity, sheltering a priceless portfolio of creatures found nowhere else on Earth. Here, giant forest trees are festooned with vines, orchids and bird's-nest ferns (home to tree frogs and geckos).

A world away, in the island's southwest, the sandstone substrata pushes through the surface to spectacular effect in the Parc National Isalo. But it's the island's limestone, especially in the north and west of the country, that really gets people talking and travelling large distances to see. In particular, the limestone karst formations – jagged, eroded rocks that contain caves, potholes, underground rivers and forested canyons rich in wildlife such as crocodiles, lemurs, birds and bats – are quintessentially Madagascar, where they're known as *tsingy*: look for them in the Parc National Bemaraha, as well as in the Réserve Spéciale Ankarana and Parc National Tsingy de Namoroka.

Madagascar's wildlife biodiversity is possible only because of the island's incredibly varied plant life: around 15,000 known species at last count. These include octopus trees, seven of the world's eight baobab species (of which six are endemic to the island), and a pretty flower used to treat leukaemia, among many others.

Madagascar has three main vegetation zones, each supporting unique communities of plants and animals. The hot, arid west consists of dry spiny desert or deciduous forest. The central plateau (hauts plateaux) has now been mostly deforested. And the wettest part of the country, the eastern seaboard, supports extensive tracts of rainforest.

Before we get to the abundant animal life these habitats support, remember this: there are 1000 species of orchid in Madagascar, more than in all of Africa, and more than 60 species of carnivorous pitcher plants are found in swampy parts of rainforests. Madagascar also has one-fifth of all mangroves in Africa.

In contrast, the waterless spiny desert is truly extraordinary. Dense tangles of cactus-like octopus trees festooned with needle-sharp spines are interspersed with baobabs whose bulbous trunks store rare rainwater, allowing them to survive the dry season. About 60 species of aloe occur in Madagascar, and many dot the spiny desert landscape..

Lemurs

If you always thought a lemur was just a lemur, you're in for a wonderful treat. At last count, there were a staggering 111, but this number will surely grow: such is the inaccessibility of much of Madagascar that new species are being discovered all the time.

There are five different lemur families. One of these is the beautifully marked and charismatic *sifakas*. These are grouped together with *indris* (known locally as *babakoto* and best seen in the parks of the Andasibe area; only one species of *indri* remains). *Sifakas* and *indris* are known for their agility and leaping skills, and the *indri* for its haunting wail-cry that echoes for up to 3km through the forest. *Sifakas* range from the balletic Verreaux's sifaka (which is easily seen at Parc National Isalo) and the Coquerel's *sifaka* (Parc National Ankarafantsika), to what is arguably the most beautiful of all lemur species, the large and lovely Diademed sifaka (Parc National Andasibe Mantadia).

At the other end of the lemur size scale is a family of small, nocturnal mouse lemurs. Among these are the world's smallest

Rhino chameleon, Parc National Marojejy (p167)

Radiated tortoise

primates that could fit easily into the palm of your hand. Because of their size, there are still mouse lemurs out there unknown to science (although locals tend to know of their existence long before Western scientists catch up...). For example, Goodman's mouse lemur was first 'discovered' in 2005 in the Andasibe area, with others currently under investigation.

In between these two extremes are the 'true' lemurs. These are long-tailed, monkey-like animals with cat-like faces, prominent ears and prehensile hands with separate fingers and toes. The best-known of these is the sociable ring-tailed lemur, that forages on the ground in groups of 13 to 15, searching for fruit, flowers, leaves and other vegetation in spiny and dry deciduous forest. Habituated troops live at Réserve d'Anja. The black-and-white ruffed lemur is another striking example, found in the Parc National Andasibe Mantadia

And then there's a whole cast of other lemurs, from mongoose and sportive lemurs to dwarf lemurs, and on to the utterly unforgettable aye-aye with its bizarre, long, bony middle finger. Look for the latter on Aye-Aye Island in Mananara in the country's east.

More Than Just Lemurs

Lemurs might get all of the attention, but Madagascar has a wide range of other mammals, on both land and sea.

Of the six carnivorous mammals (which include mongooses), perhaps the best-known is the puma-like fossa. This legendary creature is a solitary and elusive predator of lemurs and other animals. It is extremely agile and catlike, even descending trees head first. It is reputed to follow troops of lemurs for days, climbing trees to pick them off as they sleep at night. Fossas were the villains in the animated Disney film *Madagascar*, one of few actual Madagascan species to make the final cut. Fossas are widespread across the island, but only seen easily at western Madagascar's Réserve Forestière de Kirindy.

Of the other predators, there's the fanaloka, also known as the Malagasy or striped civet. This nocturnal, fox-like fanaloka lives in eastern and northern rainforests. During the day it sleeps in tree hollows and under logs, and can be seen – if you're really lucky – in Parc National Ranomafana.

Another charismatic group of creatures is reptiles. Found primarily in Madagascar's forests, the island has an astonishing 346 different species. These include most of the world's chameleons, ranging from the largest – Parson's chameleon, which grows to around 60cm – to the smallest, the dwarf chameleons which fit on your thumbnail! The pygmy leaf chameleon, for example, rarely grows longer than 33mm. The keen-eyed among you might also spot the king of camouflage, the leaf-tailed gecko, although realistically you'll need the expert eye of a guide to spy your first one. Other chameleon highlights include the colourful Labord's chameleon or the improbable rhinoceros chameleon.

Not one of Madagascar's snakes is poisonous to people: watch for beautiful Madagascar boa or the leaf-nosed snake. In contrast to the island's snakes, the Nile crocodile, which can grow up to five metres long, is every bit as dangerous here as it is in Africa and it kills people every year.

As if that weren't enough, Madagascar has 300 amphibian species. These include spectacularly coloured frogs such as the bizarre, bright-red tomato frog, which is restricted to northeastern Madagascar (around Maroantsetra is a good place to see them); they're endangered because of the pet trade.

Madagascar's tortoises – too beautiful for their own good – are confined to dry forests in southern Madagascar. The striking radiated tortoise, for example, is endangered due to poaching for the pet trade. It is the subject of an intensive conservation program and is being bred in captivity at Arboretum d'Antsokay.

With its distinctive and ornate shell, the ploughshare tortoise is even more threatened because of poaching (a shell can fetch US$50,000): there are fewer than 100 individuals left in the wild. In a desperate attempt to stem the illegal trade in ploughshare shells, the Durrell Wildlife Conservation Trust (which runs a captive breeding program at Parc National

BECAUSE OF THEIR SIZE, THERE ARE STILL MOUSE LEMURS OUT THERE UNKNOWN TO SCIENCE

Humpback whale, Anakao (p104)

Ankarafantsika) and the government decided in 2015 to deliberately deface all remaining animals' shells in order to make them less attractive to poachers.

And what rainforests and other dry forests are to Madagascar's land mammals, its coral reefs are to marine life: Madagascar's waters harbour dolphins, dugongs and humpback whales, among countless fish species. The island's southwest coast alone has the fifth-largest coral-reef system in the world. The reefs off Madagascar's northeast coast also have the highest coral diversity in the western Indian Ocean.

Humpback whales are the largest and easiest to see of all marine mammals, with whale-watching safaris possible in many places, from Anakao in the southwest to Île Sainte Marie in the east. Up to 16m-long, they're best seen from June (when they begin migrating north along both coasts to warmer waters where they can give birth) until September (when they return south with their young).

Other marine highlights include five of the world's seven species of marine turtle. Among these are the 1m-long Hawksbill Sea Turtle. Once abundant, it's now critically endangered because of pollution (plastic bags, which they mistake for jellyfish), loss of nesting sites,

fishing malpractice (floating nets) and hunting.

Rounding off the marine possibilities, swimming with whale sharks (the world's largest fish species) is possible off Nosy Be.

Madagascar's Birds

Last, but by no means least, Madagascar offers a unique birding experience. It has the highest proportion of endemic birds of any country: 80% of its species are found nowhere else in the world.

Among Madagascar's unique bird families are the mesites – skulking, babbler-like birds thought to be related to rails; the spectacular ground-rollers, including a roadrunner-like species unique to the spiny forests; the tiny, iridescent asities, similar to sunbirds and filling a similar niche; and the vangas, which have taken several strange twists as they evolved to fill various forest niches. There are a number of predators, including the highly endangered Madagascar serpent eagle and fish eagle, and nocturnal species as well.

Some of the best concentrations of waterbirds are in the Mahavy-Kinkony Wetland Complex on the west coast near Majunga. But the richest habitat by far for birds (and all other terrestrial life forms) is the rainforest of the eastern seaboard.

Male Schlegel's Asity, Ankarafantsika National Park (p121)

Whale shark

Red tomato frog (p241)

THE GOOD, THE BAD
& THE UGLY

Is Madagascar a paradise lost or a conservation success story?
The next few decades will decide. By Keith Drew

GREAT STRIDES HAVE been made in Madagascar since the creation of a linked-up national park system in the early 1990s. There are now 46 national parks and reserves, and over 10% of the country is protected in some form or another. But there is an awful lot to look after. Madagascar is one of the world's foremost biodiversity hotspots. Evolving in complete isolation for the last 90 million years or so, much of its flora and fauna – a staggering 95% of its amphibian and reptile species, in fact, and 90% of its mammals – are found nowhere else on Earth.

Diversity in Danger

But the habitats that harbour this incredible diversity are shrinking at an alarming rate. Research by Global Forest Watch found that between 2001 and 2021, Madagascar lost 4.36 million hectares of tree cover, nearly a quarter of which was precious humid primary forest. An estimated 80% of the country's natural areas have already been wiped out, and studies show that if the current rate of forest reduction continues, it will all be gone by 2050.

The rainforests of eastern Madagascar, including Masoala and Marojejy national parks, have been subject to severe illegal logging of precious hardwoods (ebony and rosewood in particular). The endemic spiny forests of southern Madagascar are being cut down to make charcoal; you won't get far on the region's rural roads without seeing someone cycling to market with sacks of black coal piled on the back of their bike. Charcoal production is not illegal, but the law states that if you cut down one tree, you must plant two in its place – which is, of course, impossible to police.

The main cause of deforestation, however, is the *tavy*, the practice of slash-and-burn agriculture traditionally used by subsistence farmers (some 75% to 80% of the population) to clear land. Forest is cut down, incinerated, and then the land replanted, usually with rice or – in the case of the rare dry deciduous forests of Menabe Antimena, in western Madagascar – corn, cassava and peanuts. Menabe is a protected area (it's the only home of Madame Berthe's mouse lemur, the smallest primate in the world), yet 45% of its forest has been lost in the last 20 years. Locals blame the recent acceleration on migrants from the Androy region, fleeing prolonged droughts, and deforesting in an effort to survive.

So, what good news? Well, Madagascar might be losing forest at a rapid rate, but it is also gaining it: there are dozens of successful reforestation projects across the

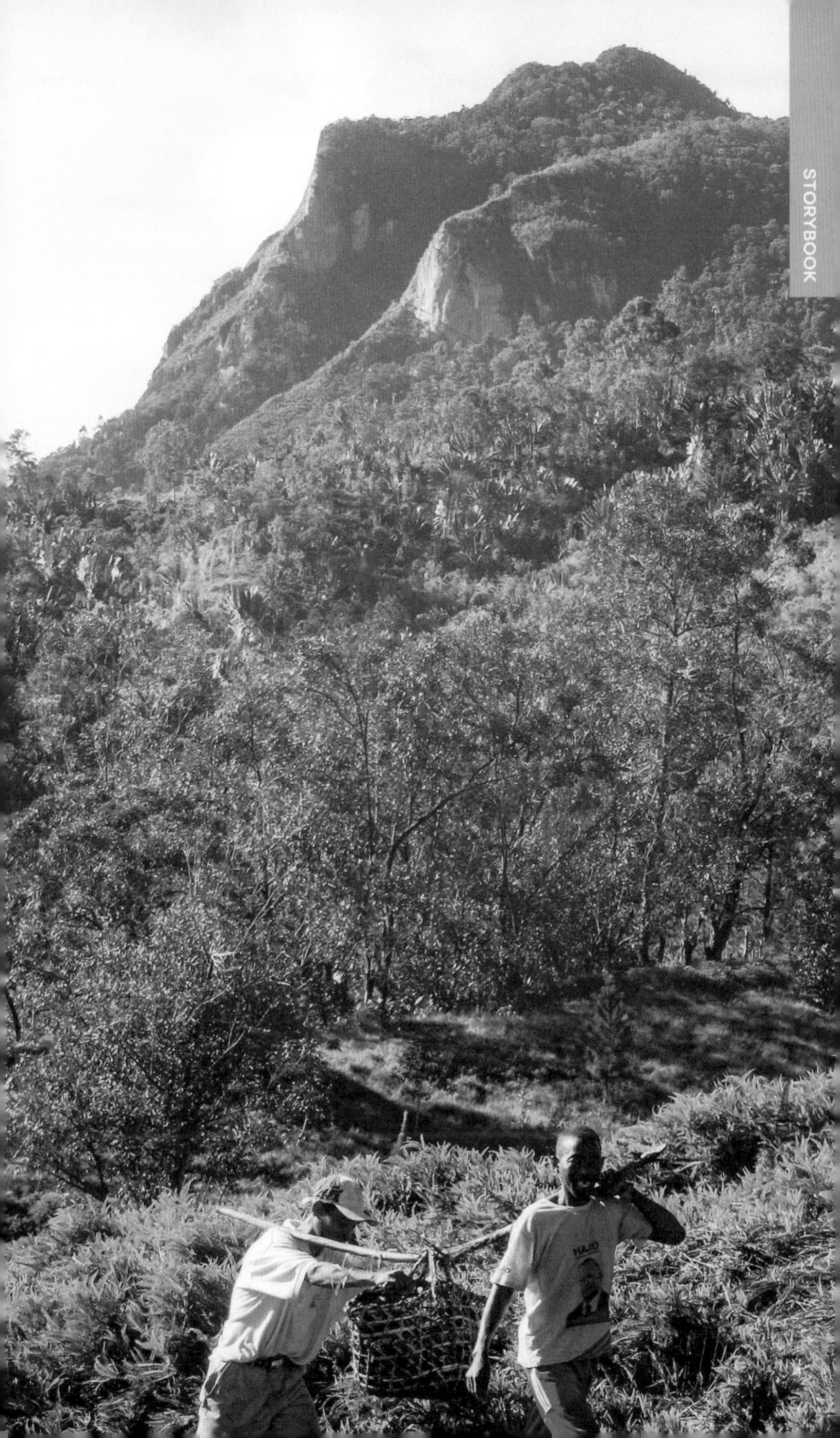

country. Since 2009, the Marat Karpeka Lemur Foundation has planted 3 million trees in Kianjavato, an area east of Parc National Ranomafana that harbours the elusive aye-aye, successfully linking up pockets of fragmented forest in the process. In Andasibe-Mantadia, Association Mitsinjo's long-term project to bridge the gap between Parc National Analamazaotra and Parc National Mantadia is nearing completion, creating a corridor that will soon allow the area's *indri* lemurs to migrate between the two.

Communities Are Key

The nature of these projects highlights two key factors of conservation in Madagascar. Firstly, that while the government manages an impressive network of national parks and reserves, a far larger area is protected by a variety of local and international NGOs, nonprofits, conservation trusts, university institutes and research centres. From the Wildlife Conservation Society (which manages Parc Naturel Makira, the largest protected area in Madagascar) to Association Fanamby and the Durrell Wildlife Conservation Trust (who are fighting together to save Menabe Antimena), the list of independent entities playing a key conservational role is long. Secondly, that working with local communities is vital for long-lasting change.

The needs of the people living in and around the parks have always been incorporated into the government's park-management plans – with money from admission fees used to rebuild schools, for example, and the use of an official park guide (always a trained local) a compulsory requirement – but the most successful examples are those where local communities are directly involved in managing the protected area. Réserve d'Anja is a case in point. Run and managed by a village association, whose members are all local residents, it attracts around 14,000 visitors a year, more than many national parks. In recent years, Managed Resource Protected Areas (MRPAs) and Communautés de Base (COBAs), where local people control the use of their own natural resources, have sprung up across Madagascar, while Locally Managed Marine Areas (LMMAs) have enabled coastal communities to rebuild their fisheries and protect their seas. The success of the Velondriake LMMA, established in Andavadoaka in southwest Madagascar in 2006 with the help of the NGO Blue Ventures, has spurred a network of over 200 LMMAs, covering about 20% of the country's coastline.

At the hub of all these lies a reason for communities to protect their local environment: partly because they have a say in what happens to it and partly because there's a vital economic incentive to do so. This is mostly through admission and guiding fees, but can also come through other channels – Velondriake's members, for example, make an extra income from seaweed and sea-cucumber farming in their LMMA.

An Integrated Approach

Madagascar's efforts to set aside so much of its land for protection deserves plaudits. Protected status doesn't necessarily mean sustained success – in 2010, Unesco placed the Rainforests of the Atsinanana onto its List of World Heritage in Danger due to illegal logging and wildlife poaching in the parks, where they still remain as of 2023 – but research shows that it is the single most important factor in reducing deforestation. Conservation efforts can only then succeed if they address the needs of local communities, but this should be a holistic approach that tackles wider regional issues as well. Projects like Tatirano Social Enterprise, which harvests rainwater and delivers it as clean drinking water across the far south (including the drought-affected Androy region), could, for example, help alleviate the pressure to migrate to areas like Menabe Antimena.

If the future of conservation in Madagascar consists of new and enlarged protected areas, more community involvement, and sustainable approaches that enable the wilderness to thrive and the people to survive, then it may just be a bright one after all.

> SINCE 2009, THE MARAT KARPEKA LEMUR FOUNDATION HAS PLANTED 3 MILLION TREES IN KIANJAVATO, AN AREA EAST OF PARC NATIONAL RANOMAFANA THAT HARBOURS THE ELUSIVE AYE-AYE

AN ISLAND
BUILT ON SPICES

By Joe Bindloss

MEDIEVAL SAILORS DUBBED Madagascar the 'Great Red Island' in tribute to its fertile, iron-rich volcanic soils, which nourished dense stands of ebony, rosewood and other precious hardwoods, as well as the eatables that kept maritime trade afloat on the Indian Ocean.

But as ocean-going empires established permanent settlements on Madagascar, they found new uses for this mineral-rich dirt, filling the countryside with coiling vanilla vines, groves of fragrant ylang-ylang and clove trees, and plantations of valuable cash crops such as cocoa, cashew nuts and coffee.

Vanilla: The Precious Spice

The crops raised in Madagascar today serve as a living map of Madagascar's colonial influences. Take vanilla, originally from Mexico, but imported into Madagascar by the French via Île Bourbon (modern-day Réunion) in the 1880s. Today, Madagascar produces nearly 80% of the world's vanilla, adding scent and flavour to everything from sponge cakes to Yves Saint Laurent's Black Opium perfume.

This vine-like orchid made fortunes for traders along Madagascar's Vanilla Coast, flanking the humid jungles of Sava in the

Clockwise from top left: Woman carrying ylang-ylang; cocoa pods, Ambanja; woman pollinating vanilla flower; pink pepper

247

far northeast. A trip to Sambava – the island's vanilla capital – will take you through villages of humble, palm-thatched huts to a bustling city with drive-in supermarkets and gleaming, air-conditioned vanilla company offices.

Conversely, fluctuations in the global price of vanilla have plunged the Madagascan economy into crisis. In 2020, the government set an elevated price for vanilla to protect local growers (and the 25% of export earnings accounted for by vanilla production) leading to a global collapse of the vanilla market as food producers shifted to cheaper, artificially produced vanillin.

Natural disasters have also had a catastrophic impact. When Cyclone Hudah struck the vanilla plantations near Antalaha in 2000, it caused global vanilla shortages, as did Cyclone Enawo in 2017, which pushed vanilla prices above US$500 per kilo – more than double the normal price.

Unleashing the Power of Vanilla

The economic power of vanilla is all the more remarkable considering that the vanilla orchid has no natural pollinators in Madagascar. To coax vanilla vines to produce the seeded fruit containing the vanilla flavour, individual flowers have to be painstakingly pollinated by hand – a technique discovered by an enslaved 12-year-old from Réunionnais named Edmond Albius in 1841 (cruelly, he received no reward or recognition for his discovery).

The Albius technique allowed the French to establish profitable vanilla plantations on Nosy Be, and later along the east coast between Vohémar and Antalaha. However, vanilla originally reached the Indian Ocean via the Jardin des Plantes in Paris – where vines sneaked in from Spanish-controlled Mexico were carefully cultivated as part of a colonial-era campaign of horticultural espionage.

The French were prolific spice-pilferers, using their African, Caribbean and Indian Ocean colonies to propagate everything from Indian pepper to Indonesian cloves, in a concerted attempt to break the global spice monopolies of rival empires. The production of vanilla in the Indian Ocean sent the Mexican trade into a death spiral – today, Mexico produces just 1% of the world's vanilla, despite being home to the only natural pollinators of the vanilla plant.

A Cornucopia of Crops

The French were not the only seafarers to bring new crops to Madagascar. Turmeric arrived with the Bornean ancestors of the Merina people around the 9th centu-

Sugarcane being turned into alcohol, Canal des Pangalanes

ry, along with the popular greater yam, while cinnamon came from Sri Lanka in the 17th century, following trade routes between India's Mughal Empire and the Swahili kingdoms of East Africa.

Swahili ships were also responsible for bringing sorghum, maize, cowpeas and Bambara groundnuts to Madagascar from the coast of East Africa, while cassava and sweet potatoes – originally imported to Madagascar by the Portuguese – travelled in the opposite direction. Scientists are still undecided as to whether bananas reached Africa from Madagascar or the other way around!

Later, the French introduced pepper from India and cloves from Dutch-controlled Indonesia, aided by the horticultural experiments of Pierre Poivre, the state botanist of Réunion and Mauritius. Today, Madagascar is the world's largest producer of cloves, and the area around Tamatave (Toamasina) is known to Malagasies as Analanjirofo, meaning 'clove forest'.

Sweets & Treats

Ocean-going traders were responsible for giving Madagascar its sweet tooth. Sugarcane travelled to Madagascar from New Guinea, carried in by the Bornean ancestors of the Merina tribe.

Ylang-ylang extract

GUDKOV ANDREY/SHUTTERSTOCK ©. FAR LEFT: PIERRE-YVES BABELON/SHUTTERSTOCK ©

The premium-quality cocoa raised around Ambanja, Nosy Be and Sambava came to Madagascar with the French in the 1800s. Although only 1% of the world's cocoa is grown in Madagascar today, the local microclimate allows growers to harvest cocoa beans year-round, and Madagascan cocoa is highly sought-after by premium chocolatiers.

Cashew nuts and peanuts – a key ingredient in Madagascar's popular koba cake – arrived via European trade routes from South America. Unsurprisingly, it was the French who introduced coffee, imported from Mocha in Yemen via Réunion in the 18th century on the orders of the king of France.

Distilling Essential Oils

Madagascar has a long history of distilling essential oils, used in the manufacture of beauty products, health treatments and perfumes. The fragrant ylang-ylang tree evolved in the jungles of Indonesia and the Philippines, but German entrepreneurs pioneered the distillation of ylang-ylang oil in the 1860s, and the first trees were planted in Madagascar by the French in the 1890s.

Ylang-ylang oil became a sought-after ingredient for French perfumes – including, famously, Chanel No 5 – and expansive plantations were established on Nosy Be in the 1920s. Today, Madagascar produces a quarter of the world's supply and groves of ylang-ylang trees blanket Nosy Be's tumbling hills.

Another fragrant ingredient produced in Madagascar is eucalyptus oil, harvested from trees originally introduced from Australia. In the 1890s, the island's French administrators cleared vast stands of native forest to make space for eucalyptus plantations to supply the French empire with medicinal eucalyptus oil.

The plantations were a mixed success – eucalyptus oil was added to the list of colonial exports, but the trees had a devastating effect on the local water table, accelerating the loss of native tree species. Today, as well as providing essential oils, fast-growing eucalyptus trees are harvested to produce cooking charcoal, reducing the pressure on the remaining stands of native forest.

LIFE & DEATH
IN MADAGASCAR

By Joe Bindloss

MODERN MADAGASCAR TAKES many of its cultural cues from Europe, but Malagasy culture has hidden layers of complexity. In particular, Malagasies follow a complicated system of social and moral codes that travellers are often unaware of.

To say there is a single Malagasy culture would be an oversimplification. All of Madagascar's tribes have been influenced by the dominant Merina people of the central highlands, but each region has its own beliefs, particularly on the coast, where traditions imported from Asia and other parts of Africa still hold sway.

Shared Words

One thing that brings all the island's inhabitants together is the Malagasy language, originally the language of the Merina. However, even this is an ancient import – languages that resemble Malagasy are found not in Africa but in Southeast Asia and the South Pacific.

The ancestors of the Merina are thought to have reached Madagascar from Borneo, and Malagasy is the westernmost of the Malayo-Polynesian languages, which include Bahasa Indonesia, Tagalog and Hawaiian. French became the official language of business and government in the colonial period, and many locals can switch effortlessly between Malagasy and French without missing a beat.

Other languages are spoken only by minorities. Many Muslim Malagasies know basic Arabic from studying the Quran and a few small coastal communities speak Maore Comorian – an African language imported to the Comoros from East Africa by Swahili slave traders.

Beloved Ancestors

Malagasies are also bound together by respect for the ancestors, or *razana*, which is enshrined in a complex system of rituals and taboos. While many Malagasies describe themselves as Christian, locals think nothing of going to a Sunday church service and then making offerings to the spirits of the ancestors at a sacred lake or tree.

According to traditional Malagasy beliefs known as *fomba gasy*, the human body was formed by the earth deity Ratovantany (or Andriantompo), while life was gifted by the heavenly deity Zanahary. At the point of death, a spiritual presence known as *ambiroa*, akin to the immortal soul, lingers in or close to the body, eventually becoming one with the spirits of the ancestors.

Malagasies invoke the *razana* for protection, fertility or good health at sacred sites, easily recognised by the offerings left by devotees, which may include zebu horns, *lamba* (white cotton or silk scarves), coins and banknotes, glasses of alcohol, sacrificial blood, honey, sweets, and other symbols of respect.

Important ceremonies in Malagasy communities are often marked by the slaughter of a zebu. The blood and horns are valuable offerings for the ancestors, and the meat is shared by those attending, with the brown fat from the hump being highly sought after.

Many Malagasay believe in *hasina*, a concept of innate authority within the individual, which can be increased or decreased by human action. The royal families of powerful Malagasy tribes are believed to be the ultimate embodiment of *hasina*, and many people attribute magical powers to sites associated with royalty.

Members of the Sakalava tribe believe that the souls of royal ancestors known as *tromba* can possess the living, particularly in the region around Ambanja. During musical processions, young women allow themselves to be taken over by the spirits, entering a trance-like state and opening a channel of communication with the ancestors.

Turning the Bones

In many Malagasy communities, the dead play an ongoing role in the lives of the living. The area of land bearing the family tomb – known locally as *tanindrazana* – is the place where the nuturing spirits of the ancestors are most potent, tying people strongly to the place where they were born. The Merina and Betsileo people of the highlands take this idea to extremes with the ritual of *famadihana*, during which the bones of the dead are exhumed, paraded and reburied, bringing the living world and spirit world together.

At the heart of *famadihana* is the belief that the souls of the dead can only join the ancestors when the body is fully decomposed. Accordingly, the body is treated as part of the living world until decay is complete – a tradition shared with tribal communities in parts of Indonesia.

Famadihana ceremonies are a remarkable spectacle. Every five to seven years, families come together to open the tombs of their relatives, accompanied by feasting, drinking and dancing. Corpses are rewrapped in pristine white burial *lambas* (scarves), sprayed with perfume, meticulously labelled with felt-tip pens and paraded by relatives. A period of quiet follows, as family members commune with the souls of their ancestors.

July to September is the peak time for *famadihana* ceremonies in the highlands between Antananarivo and Ambositra, and respectful onlookers may be able to attend with permission from the family (best arranged through a hotel or tour agency). Only take photos if this has expressly been approved, and never intrude on a *famadihana* ceremony without an invitation.

The Right Thing at the Right Time

Many Malagasies also place a strong importance on auspicious timing – a tradition with origins in Islamic cosmology. The Malagasy concept of *vintana* (destiny) determines the most auspicious date for such activities as building a house or planting a new crop, and for important life events such as circumcisions, weddings and funerals.

According to Malagasy custom, *vintana* is created by god and is immutable, so locals pay close attention to the cosmic calendar. The months and weeks of the calendar year have inherent destinies known as *tonom'bintana*, and each day has a specific character – Wednesdays and Fridays are appropriate days for funerals, while Saturdays, associated with nobility, are an auspicious time for celebrations.

To help identify favourable dates, Malagasies consult astrologers known as *mpanandro* or *ombiasy*. During divinations known as *sikidy*, dried seeds are poured into four random piles and removed in twos until only one or two seeds are left in each pile, generating a sequence of numbers that can be used to determine whether an event is favourable or inauspicious.

Traditional Mahafaly tomb

Sacred Architecture

Vintana also contains concepts of sacred geometry, leading many Malagasies to orient their homes on a north-south axis, with the entrance to the west, facing the sunset. The northern portion of the house is assigned to male residents and guests, while the south is reserved for women and children. The northeast corner is reserved for prayers and making offerings to the ancestors.

Vintana also guides the construction of Malagasy tombs, which are usually set on plots of ancestral land just outside village compounds. The Antandroy and Mahafaly of southern Madagascar are famous for their elaborate wood and stone tombs, decorated with murals of daily life, horns from sacrificed zebu and carved memorial posts known as *aloalo*.

The term *aloalo* comes from the word *alo*, meaning 'messenger' or 'intermediary' – another sign of the perceived continuum between life and death in Malagasy culture. The *aloalo* on older Sakalava tombs often feature risqué carvings of nude figures and sexual acts, symbolising fertility and the continuation of life.

A Polite Society

Fihavanana – the concept of shared kinship and goodwill between physical and spiritual beings – is a constant thread running through Malagasy culture. You'll see it manifested in the polite way people interact in Madagascar and in the conspicuous absence of public arguments.

Malagasies prefer compromise to conflict in all aspects of life and will go out of their way to avoid confrontation in social situations. It is considered unseemly to talk about difficult subjects such as personal problems, and intrusive or indiscreet questions are to be avoided at all costs.

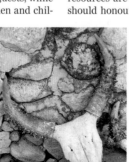

THE ANTANDROY AND MAHAFALY OF SOUTHERN MADAGASCAR ARE FAMOUS FOR THEIR ELABORATE WOOD AND STONE TOMBS, DECORATED WITH MURALS OF DAILY LIFE, HORNS FROM SACRIFICED ZEBU AND CARVED MEMORIAL POSTS KNOWN AS ALOALO

CRAIGI139/SHUTTERSTOCK ©

Politeness is important to the Malagasy, and impatience or pushy behaviour, such as queue jumping, is highly frowned upon. Welcoming strangers is another core value for Malagasies. It is considered a duty to offer food and water to a guest, even if these resources are scarce; in return, travellers should honour this hospitality by accepting what has been offered.

Many Malagasies also believe in a version of karma, known as *tody*, based on the concept of negative repercussions for harmful actions. People try to avoid behaviour that might attract *tsiny* (reproach or blame) from the community, as the accumulation of *tsiny* is believed to lead to unfavourable outcomes for individuals and their descendants.

Respecting the Spiritual Landscape

One tradition you'll quickly become aware of in Madagascar – not least because guides are quick to point it out to travellers – is the concept of *fady*, a complex system of ritual taboos based on respect for the ancestors.

Fady can take innumerable forms, and traditions vary from region to region, and even from village to village. It may be *fady* to whistle on a particular stretch of beach, to walk past a sacred tree, to eat certain foods in a certain location (p000), to urinate near a particular piece of forest, or to swim in a certain lake or river. Visiting some sites, such as the island of Nosy Lonja near Diego Suarez (Antsiranana), is completely *fady* for non-Malagasies.

Although foreigners are generally given some slack for inadvertently breaking *fady*, it's important to make an effort to respect these taboos. Ask locals for advice, and be particularly careful when visiting sacred sites, locations associated with royalty, and tombs or burial sites.

INDEX

'Madagascar catches the brunt of the Roaring Forties, powerful westerly winds that come barrelling around the Cape of Good Hope to hit the country's southern coastlines. The result is consistently good swell and some sizeable waves (p39).'

KEITH DREW

'Visible throughout the city, the Rova of Antananarivo (p49) was the seat of power of Merina kings and queens for nearly 300 years.'

KEITH DREW

Mapping data sources:
© Lonely Planet
© OpenStreetMap http://openstreetmap.org/copyright

THIS BOOK

Destination Editor
James Smart

Production Editor
Alison Killilea

Book Designer
Aomi Ito

Cartographer
Hunor Csutoros

Assisting Editors
Mani Ramaswamy

Cover Researcher
Gwen Cotter

Thanks Ronan Abayawickrema, Sofie Andersen, James Appleton

MIX
Paper from responsible sources
FSC™ C021741
www.fsc.org

Paper in this book is certified against the Forest Stewardship Council™ standards. FSC™ promotes environmentally responsible, socially beneficial and economically viable management of the world's forests.

Published by Lonely Planet Global Limited
CRN 554153
10th edition – Dec 2023
ISBN 978 1 78868 840 6
© Lonely Planet 2023 Photographs © as indicated 2023
10 9 8 7 6 5 4 3 2 1
Printed in China